WITHDRAWN

MOMENTS OF TRUTH

MOMENTS OF TRUTH

Unleashing God's Word One Day at a Time

John MacArthur

NASHVILLE DALLAS MEXICO CITY RIO DE JANEIRO

© 2012 by John MacArthur

All rights reserved. No portion of this book may be reproduced, stored in a retrieval system, or transmitted in any form or by any means—electronic, mechanical, photocopy, recording, scanning, or other—except for brief quotations in critical reviews or articles, without the prior written permission of the publisher.

Published in Nashville, Tennessee, by Thomas Nelson. Thomas Nelson is a trademark of Thomas Nelson, Inc.

Unleashing God's Truth, One Verse at a Time® is a trademark of Grace to You. All rights reserved.

Thomas Nelson, Inc., titles may be purchased in bulk for educational, business, fund-raising, or sales promotional use. For information, please e-mail SpecialMarkets@ThomasNelson.com.

Unless otherwise indicated, Scripture quotations are taken from THE NEW KING JAMES VERSION. © 1982 by Thomas Nelson, Inc. Used by permission. All rights reserved.

Scripture quotations marked NASB are taken from the NEW AMERICAN STANDARD BIBLE®, © The Lockman Foundation 1960, 1962, 1963, 1968, 1971, 1972, 1973, 1975, 1977, 1995. Used by permission.

Scripture quotations marked HCSB are taken from the HOLMAN CHRISTIAN STANDARD BIBLE. © 1999, 2000, 2002, 2003 by Broadman and Holman Publishers. All rights reserved.

Scripture quotations marked KJV are taken from the King James Version.

Library of Congress Cataloging-in-Publication Data

MacArthur, John, 1939-
Moments of truth : unleashing God's word one day at a time / John MacArthur.
p. cm.
ISBN 978-1-4002-0371-0 (alk. paper)
1. Bible–Meditations. 2. Devotional calendars. I. Title.
BS491.5.M3 2012
242'.2–dc23 2011026715

Printed in the United States of America

12 13 14 15 16 QG 6 5 4 3 2 1

42.2 MAC 1 CP.

Contents

PUBLIC LIBRARY
DANVILLE, ILLINOIS

Introduction

Truth seems to be elusive these days. Some don't want to acknowledge what they know to be true about God, life, the world, and themselves; some are afraid of the facts; some refuse to face the truth. And the prevailing mood seems to be that truth is either elusive or relative. This isn't a new problem, of course. Pilate stood before the One who claimed to be the Truth (John 14:6) and asked, "What is truth? (John 18:38) and then washed his hands and turned away from the Truth.

But truth matters, with absolute truth mattering absolutely—and we ignore it to our peril.

John MacArthur has been and continues to be a champion for truth—God's absolute truth as revealed in His Word. And during the course of his life and ministry, John has written a virtual library of resources for finding and applying God's truth.

This book features excerpts from many of those books, giving you a daily "moment of truth." As you read, may you gain a deeper appreciation for and understanding of God's truth, every day.

April 28 conscience read
May 28 adopted forever
May 31 repentance
June 1
June 26 cleansed conscience
June 27 true cleansing
July 1 War with the flesh
July 2 How to be free
July 3 How to free sinners
July 9 pray for our leaders
July 22 sinners to be disciples
July 31 The real battle
Aug 13 All Christians sin
Aug 20 Sanctification
Aug 31 True faith seeks God
Aug 27 What is repentance
Sept 3 4 5 Prayer
Sept 7 True confession
Sept 20 Why we obey

JANUARY

BEGINNINGS

The Importance of Truth

And you shall know the truth, and the truth shall make you free.

JOHN 8:32

Every true Christian should know and love the truth. Scripture says one of the key characteristics of "those who perish" (people who are damned by their unbelief) is that they "did not receive the love of the truth, that they might be saved" (2 Thess. 2:10). The clear implication is that a genuine love for the truth is built into saving faith. It is therefore one of the distinguishing qualities of every true believer. In Jesus' words, they have known the truth, and the truth has set them free (John 8:32).

In an age when the very idea of truth is being scorned and attacked (even within the church, where people *ought* to revere the truth most highly), Solomon's wise advice has never been more timely: "Buy the truth, and do not sell it" (Prov. 23:23).

Nothing in all the world is more important or more valuable than the truth. And the church is supposed to be "the pillar and ground of the truth" (1 Tim. 3:15).

Not knowing what you believe is by definition a kind of unbelief. Refusing to acknowledge and defend the revealed truth of God is a particularly stubborn and pernicious kind of unbelief. Advocating ambiguity, exalting uncertainty, or otherwise deliberately clouding the truth is a sinful way of nurturing unbelief.

Where are you unclear in your beliefs?

The Truth War, xi–xii

The Definition of Truth

Jesus said to him, "I am the way, the truth, and the life. No one comes to the Father except through Me."

JOHN 14:6

So what is truth?

Here is a simple definition drawn from what the Bible teaches: *truth is that which is consistent with the mind, will, character, glory, and being of God*. Even more to the point: *truth is the self-expression of God*. That is the biblical meaning of truth. Because the definition of truth flows from God, truth is *theological*.

Truth is also *ontological*—which is a fancy way of saying it is the way things really are. Reality is what it is because God declared it so and made it so. Therefore God is the author, source, determiner, governor, arbiter, ultimate standard, and final judge of all truth.

The Old Testament refers to the Almighty as the "God of truth" (Deut. 32:4; Ps. 31:5; Isa. 65:16). When Jesus said of Himself "I *am* . . . the truth" (John 14:6, emphasis added), He was thereby making a profound claim about His own deity. He was also making it clear that *all* truth must ultimately be defined in terms of God and His eternal glory. After all, Jesus is "the brightness of [God's] glory and the express image of His person" (Heb. 1:3). *He is truth incarnate*—the perfect expression of God and therefore the absolute embodiment of all that is true.

Jesus also said that the written Word of God is truth. It does not merely contain nuggets of truth; it *is* pure, unchangeable, and inviolable truth that (according to Jesus) "cannot be broken" (John 10:35).

God has revealed Himself to humanity through Scripture and through His Son. Both perfectly embody the essence of what truth is.

In what ways do you need to submit to the truth God has revealed in His Word?

The Truth War, 2–3

The True Beginning

In the beginning God created the heavens and the earth.

Genesis 1:1

God *did* create the heavens and the earth. And there is only one document that credibly claims to be a divinely revealed record of that creation, the book of Genesis. Unless we have a creator who left us with no information about where we came from or what our purpose is, the text of Genesis 1–2 stands for all practical purposes unchallenged as the only divinely revealed description of creation. In other words, if there is a God who created the heavens and the earth, and if He revealed to humanity any record of that creation, Genesis is that record. If the God of Scripture did not create the heavens and the earth, then we have no real answers to anything that is truly important. Everything boils down to those two simple options.

So whether we believe the Genesis record or not makes all the difference in the world.

We can either believe what Genesis says, or not. If Genesis 1:1 is true, then the universe and everything in it was created by a loving and personal God and His purposes are clearly revealed to us in Scripture. Further, if the Genesis account is true, then we bear the stamp of God and are loved by Him—and *because* we are made in His image, human beings have a dignity, value, and obligation that transcends that of all other creatures. Moreover, if Genesis is true, then we not only have God's own answers to the questions of what we are here for and how we got where we are, but we also have the promise of salvation from our sin.

How does the fact that God created the world affect the way you view life?

The Battle for the Beginning, 42–43

Don't Give Up the True Beginning

We should no longer be children, tossed to and fro and carried about with every wind of doctrine.

EPHESIANS 4:14

Many who should know better—pastors and Christian leaders who defend the faith against false teachings regularly—have been tempted to give up the battle for the opening chapters of Genesis. An evangelical pastor recently approached me after I preached. He was confused and intimidated by several books he had read—all written by ostensibly evangelical authors—yet all arguing that the earth is billions of years old. These authors treat most of the evolutionists' theories as indisputable scientific fact. And in some cases they wield scientific or academic credentials that intimidate readers into thinking their views are the result of superior expertise, rather than naturalistic presuppositions they have brought to the biblical text. This pastor asked if I believed it possible that the first three chapters of Genesis might really be just a series of literary devices—a poetic saga giving the "spiritual" meaning of what actually occurred through billions of years of evolution.

I answered unapologetically, *No, I do not*. I am convinced that Genesis 1–3 ought to be taken at face value—as the divinely revealed history of creation. Nothing about the Genesis text itself suggests that the biblical creation account is merely symbolic, poetic, allegorical, or mythical. The main thrust of the passage simply cannot be reconciled with the notion that creation occurred via natural evolutionary processes over long periods of time. And I don't believe a faithful handling of the biblical text, by any acceptable principles of hermeneutics, can possibly reconcile these chapters with the theory of evolution or any of the other allegedly scientific theories about the origin of the universe.

How have you been tempted to give in to the world's idea of the truth?

The Battle for the Beginning, 18–19

Rejecting the Beginning Rejects the Truth

For do I now persuade men, or God? Or do I seek to please men? For if I still pleased men, I would not be a bondservant of Christ.

GALATIANS 1:10

The starting point for Christianity is not Matthew 1:1, but Genesis 1:1. Tamper with the book of Genesis and you undermine the very foundation of Christianity. You cannot treat Genesis 1 as a fable or a mere poetic saga without severe implications to the rest of Scripture. The creation account is where God starts His account of history. It is impossible to alter the beginning without impacting the rest of the story—not to mention the ending. If Genesis 1 is not accurate, then there's no way to be certain that the rest of Scripture tells the truth. If the starting point is wrong, then the Bible itself is built on a foundation of falsehood.

In other words, if you reject the creation account in Genesis, you have no basis for believing the Bible at all. If you doubt or explain away the Bible's account of the six days of creation, where do you put the reins on your skepticism? Do you start with Genesis 3, which explains the origin of sin, and believe everything from chapter 3 on? Or maybe you don't sign on until sometime after chapter 6, because the Flood is invariably questioned by scientists too. Or perhaps you find the Tower of Babel too hard to reconcile with the linguists' theories about how language originated and evolved. If we're worried about appearing "unscientific" in the eyes of naturalists, we're going to have to reject a lot more than Genesis 1–3.

What beliefs have you been tempted to give up because of how you would appear to others?

The Battle for the Beginning, 44

Scripture, Not Science, Interprets Scripture

And who can proclaim as I do? Then let him declare it and set it in order for Me, since I appointed the ancient people. And the things that are coming and shall come, let them show these to them.

ISAIAH 44:7

Modern scientific opinion is not a valid hermeneutic for interpreting Genesis (or any other portion of Scripture, for that matter). Scripture is God-breathed (2 Tim. 3:16)—inspired truth from God. Scripture "never came by the will of man, but holy men of God spoke as they were moved by the Holy Spirit" (2 Peter 1:21). Jesus summed the point up perfectly when He said, "Thy word is truth" (John 17:17 KJV). The Bible is supreme truth, and therefore it is the standard by which scientific theory should be evaluated, not vice versa.

And Scripture always speaks with absolute authority. It is as authoritative when it instructs us as it is when it commands us. It is as true when it tells the future as it is when it records the past. Although it is not a textbook on science, wherever it intersects with scientific data, it speaks with the same authority as when it gives us moral precepts.

It is therefore a serious mistake to imagine that modern scientists can speak more authoritatively than Scripture on the subject of origins. Scripture is God's own eyewitness account of what happened in the beginning.

A clear pattern for interpreting Genesis is given to us in the New Testament. In every New Testament reference to Genesis, the events recorded by Moses are treated as historical events. And in particular, the first three chapters of Genesis are consistently treated as a literal record of historical events.

When have you felt that your opinion is more reliable than something God has said?

The Battle for the Beginning, 22–23

The Truth About Science

Beware lest anyone cheat you through philosophy and empty deceit, according to the tradition of men, according to the basic principles of the world, and not according to Christ.

COLOSSIANS 2:8

Although the biblical account clashes at many points with naturalistic and evolutionary hypotheses, it is not in conflict with a single scientific fact. Indeed, all the geological, astronomical, and scientific data can be easily reconciled with the biblical account. The conflict is not between science and Scripture, but between the biblicist's confident faith and the naturalist's willful skepticism.

Science has never disproved one word of Scripture, and it never will. On the other hand, evolutionary theory has always been in conflict with Scripture and always will be. But the notion that the universe evolved through a series of natural processes remains an unproven and untestable hypothesis, and therefore it is not "science." There is no proof whatsoever that the universe evolved naturally. Evolution is a mere theory—and a questionable, constantly changing one at that. Ultimately, if accepted at all, the theory of evolution must be taken by sheer faith.

How much better to base our faith on the sure foundation of God's Word! There is no ground of knowledge equal to or superior to Scripture. Unlike scientific theory, God's Word is eternally unchanging. Unlike the opinions of man, its truth is revealed by the Creator Himself! It is not, as many suppose, at odds with science. True science has always affirmed the teaching of Scripture. Archaeology, for instance, has demonstrated the truthfulness of the biblical record time and time again. Wherever Scripture's record of history may be examined and either proved or disproved by archaeological evidence or reliable, independent documentary evidence, the biblical record has always been verified.

Where have you seen people take views that clearly conflict with God's Word?

The Battle for the Beginning, 28

The Invention of Lies

For everyone practicing evil hates the light and does not come to the light, lest his deeds should be exposed.

JOHN 3:20

Evolution was introduced as an atheistic alternative to the biblical view of creation. According to evolution, man created God rather than vice versa. And as we have seen, the evolutionists' ultimate agenda is to eliminate faith in God altogether and thereby do away with moral accountability.

Intuition suggests a series of questions to the human mind when we contemplate our origin: Who is in control of the universe? Is there Someone who is sovereign—a Lawgiver? Is there a universal Judge? Is there a transcendent moral standard to live by? Is there Someone to whom we will be accountable? Will there be a final assessment of how we live our lives? Will there be any final judgment?

Those are the very questions evolution was invented to avoid.

Evolution was devised to explain away the God of the Bible—not because evolutionists really believed a Creator was unnecessary to explain how things began, but because they did not want the God of Scripture as their Judge.

To put it simply, evolution was invented in order to eliminate the God of Genesis and thereby to oust the Lawgiver and obliterate the inviolability of His law. Evolution is simply the latest means our fallen race has devised in order to suppress our innate knowledge and the biblical testimony that there is a God and that we are accountable to Him (cf. Rom. 1:28). By embracing evolution, modern society aims to do away with morality, responsibility, and guilt. Society has embraced evolution with such enthusiasm because people imagine that it eliminates the Judge and leaves them free to do whatever they want without guilt and without consequences.

Which of the questions above challenges you the most?

The Battle for the Beginning, 24–25

The Clear Truth of Creationism

For the wrath of God is revealed from heaven against all ungodliness and unrighteousness of men, who suppress the truth in unrighteousness, because what may be known of God is manifest in them, for God has shown it to them.

ROMANS 1:18–19

The Bible says here that there is evidence about God (Rom. 1:19). What is known about God is evident through reason. Reason looks at creation (v. 20) and says, "There must be a Creator." Reason looks at the diversity and says, "He must have an immense mind." It looks at the design and says, "He's a God of order." It looks at the beauty and says, "He's a God of beauty and harmony." It looks at vast variety and says, "He's a God of incredible power and complexity."

Yes, that's all true. So true, in fact, that God's eternal power and divine nature are visible through reason looking at creation. You simply can't look at the results of creation and doubt there's a Creator. You'd have to commit intellectual suicide to deny there is a cause for the effect of the universe, that there is a supreme Maker. The end of verse 20—"His invisible attributes are clearly seen, being understood by the things that are made, even His eternal power and Godhead, so that they are without excuse"—makes this so clear that people have absolutely no excuse for being evolutionists. None. It is absolute idiocy. Paul used *moria*, the Greek term for "moron," translated "fool" or "foolish." Any rational, thinking person, who sees anything that exists, assumes somebody made it. And the universe certainly demands a Creator.

The problem is that men "suppress the truth in unrighteousness." People dishonor the Creator even though the knowledge of God as Creator is obvious around them.

How have you seen God's attributes in creation?

Hard to Believe, 196–197

Truth in Nature

The law of the LORD is perfect, converting the soul; the testimony of the LORD is sure, making wise the simple.

PSALM 19:7

Nothing in Scripture suggests that *everything* we need to know about God is revealed to us in nature. On the contrary, the whole point of Psalm 19 is to underscore the necessity, the absolute sufficiency, and the preeminence of *special* revelation—Scripture. Nature simply puts God's glory on display in a mute testimony that declares His majesty, power, divinity, and existence to all—and leaves people without excuse if they ignore or reject the God of the Bible. In other words, natural revelation is sufficient to condemn sinners, but not to save them. Scripture, on the other hand, is perfect, sure, right, pure, clean, and altogether true (vv. 7–9). Unlike the general revelation available to us in nature, the truth of Scripture converts the soul, makes wise the simple, enlightens the eyes, and endures forever (vv. 7–9). So the psalm plainly underscores the *superiority* of Scripture. Its whole point is that the revelation of God in nature is not as powerful, as enduring, as reliable, as clear, or as authoritative as Scripture. Scripture is *sufficient* revelation; nature is not. Scripture is clear and complete; nature is not. Scripture therefore speaks with more authority than nature and should be used to assess scientific opinion, not vice versa.

Unlike nature, Scripture is *perspicuous;* its meaning is clear and easy to understand. Not all Scripture is *equally* perspicuous, of course. Some portions are notoriously hard to understand (2 Peter 3:16), and even the simplest passage of Scripture must be correctly interpreted in order to yield its true meaning. But the perspicuity and the comprehensiveness of Scripture are vastly superior to that of nature. And therefore Scripture should be the rule by which we measure science, rather than the reverse approach.

How has Scripture clarified something you have experienced?

The Battle for the Beginning, 61

The Testimony of Creatures

I will praise You, for I am fearfully and wonderfully made;
marvelous are Your works, and that my soul knows very well.

PSALM 139:14

All living organisms have three amazing properties. First, they are *self-sustaining*, meaning that they have means by which they sustain their own life—getting nourishment, breathing their atmosphere (even fish in the water), and defending themselves from predators or other threats in their habitat. All of them have unique ways of doing this that are perfectly suited to their environment. Second, they are *self-repairing*. If injured, they have means to heal. If fatigued, they can recoup strength by rest. Third, they are *self-reproducing*. They have built into them some means by which they can propagate and thereby produce more organisms of their own species. All three of those capabilities are inherent features of life itself.

And that fact argues powerfully for an intelligent Designer. Consider the difficulty in creating a machine that is self-sustaining, self-repairing, and self-reproducing. Such machines currently exist only in theory. They are called "Von Neumann machines" after a Hungarian scientist and mathematician named John Von Neumann, who lived in the first half of the twentieth century. Von Neumann hypothesized that it should be possible to create a machine that would sustain itself, repair itself, and reproduce itself. Modern research into artificial intelligence still draws heavily on Von Neumann's work, and modern computers are based on his groundbreaking ideas. But science has not yet been able to develop a truly self-sustaining, self-repairing, and self-replicating machine. The difficulty and complexity of creating something with all those capabilities is still out of reach for modern science. Yet remarkably, every single living cell has all those capabilities. If this isn't convincing proof of an intelligent Designer, what is?

Where have you seen evidence of God's design in creation?

The Battle for the Beginning, 132–133

The Triune God Was in the Beginning

In the beginning was the Word, and the Word was with God, and the Word was God. . . . All things were made through Him, and without Him nothing was made that was made.

JOHN 1:1, 3

In Genesis 1:26 God introduces Himself with personal pronouns. Significantly, they are plural pronouns. Not, "Let *Me* . . ."; but, "Let *Us* make man in Our image," and thus we are introduced to a plurality of relationships in the Godhead. Here is the first major, unmistakable evidence of the Trinity. It is by no means a full revelation of the doctrine of the Trinity, but it is an unmistakable reference to plurality within the Godhead, and it begins to lay the groundwork for what we later learn of the Trinity from the New Testament.

There was at least one other earlier hint of the Trinity in verse 2, where we were told that the Spirit of God hovered above the face of the waters. But now we see even more clearly that there is a sort of divine executive committee—a council in the Godhead.

The same truth is unfolded with even more clarity in John 1:1–3, which begins with an echo of Genesis 1:1. "The Word" refers to the Second Member of the Trinity, Jesus Christ (cf. v. 14)—who was with God at creation and is Himself God.

By putting all those passages together, we see that all three Members of the Trinity were active in creation. The Father was overseeing and decreeing the work. The eternal Word was "with God" and involved in every aspect of the creative process. And the Spirit was brooding over the waters, which also suggests the most intimate kind of hands-on involvement in the process.

How does it change your perspective to know that God was wholly involved in creating the world?

The Battle for the Beginning, 160

The Greatness of God and His Concern for Humans

For thus says the LORD, who created the heavens, who is God, who formed the earth and made it, who has established it, who did not create it in vain, who formed it to be inhabited: I am the LORD, and there is no other.

ISAIAH 45:18

Naturalistic science has always struggled to explain all the stars and planets that exist in the universe. How could so much have evolved out of nothing? What set the stars ablaze, and where did the planets come from?

Genesis 1 gives a simple answer: God made them all. He spoke them into existence. Their vastness, their complexity, their beauty, and their sheer number all reveal the glory and wisdom of an all-powerful Creator. And they remind us how amazing it is that such a great Creator would lavish His grace and favor on the human race.

David celebrated this fact in Psalm 8:3–4:

> *When I consider Your heavens, the work of Your fingers,*
> *The moon and the stars, which You have ordained,*
> *What is man that You are mindful of him,*
> *And the son of man that You visit him?*

As David gazed into an unfathomably large universe, he realized it was just finger work for God. As great as the universe is, God is infinitely greater. And the human race is nothing by comparison.

Yet God's creative purpose has always had the human race as its center. We alone of all His creatures are made in His image. The entire creation account in Genesis is told from an earthly perspective, underscoring the centrality of this tiny planet in the creative purpose of God.

How does it affect your view of life to see humans as the center of God's creation?

The Battle for the Beginning, 105–106

The Importance of the Human Race

Bring My sons from afar, and My daughters from the ends of the earth—everyone who is called by My name, whom I have created for My glory; I have formed him, yes, I have made him.

Isaiah 43:6–7

The creation of the human race was the central object of God's creative purpose from the beginning. In an important sense, everything else was created *for* humanity, and every step of creation up to this point had one main purpose: to prepare a perfect environment for Adam.

The human race is *still* at the center of God's purpose for the entire material universe. We know this because Scripture says everything else will eventually perish. It will all go out of existence. According to Jesus, there is coming a time when even "the sun will be darkened, and the moon will not give its light; the stars of heaven will fall, and the powers in the heavens will be shaken" (Mark 13:24–25). Ultimately, even the heavens will roll up like a scroll (Rev. 6:13–14). "The heavens will pass away with a great noise, and the elements will melt with fervent heat; both the earth and the works that are in it will be burned up" (2 Peter 3:10). In effect, everything that was created will be uncreated. Everything in this universe will cease to exist.

Except humanity. God created man to glorify Him and to enjoy Him *forever*. And when every other element of this universe is long gone, a vast multitude of the redeemed human race will dwell in the presence of the Lord forever.

This is the purpose for which the entire universe was created; so that God's grace, mercy, and compassion could be lavished on this creature whom God created in His own image.

What does it look like to glorify and enjoy God?

The Battle for the Beginning, 157

The Image of God

Then God said, "Let Us make man in Our image, according to Our likeness; let them have dominion over the fish of the sea, over the birds of the air, and over the cattle, over all the earth and over every creeping thing that creeps on the earth."

GENESIS 1:26

What is the image of God? The Hebrew word for "image," *tselem*, comes from a root that speaks of carving. It is the same word used to speak of graven images (Ex. 20:4). It almost seems to convey the idea that man was carved into the shape of God. It suggests that God was, in essence, the pattern for the personhood of man. That is not true of anything else in the space-time universe.

Clearly, because the image of God is unique to humanity, it must describe some aspect of human nature that is not shared by animals.

It isn't talking about biology or physiology. It certainly isn't a reference to the way that we look as creatures made of flesh and bone. After all, "God is Spirit" (John 4:24). And "a spirit does not have flesh and bones" (Luke 24:39).

Clearly this deals primarily with man's spiritual attributes—our self-consciousness, our moral consciousness, and our consciousness of others—especially our consciousness of God Himself. (Animals are conscious, but they are not self-conscious, morally aware, or able to have a truly personal relationship.)

But above all, the image of God can be summed up by the word *personhood*. We are *persons*. Our lives involve relationships. We are capable of fellowship. We are able to love other persons in a Godlike sense. We understand communion. We have an amazing capacity for language.

The image of God is personhood, and personhood can function only in the context of relationships.

How can you reflect God's qualities today in your relationships?

The Battle for the Beginning, 163–164

Our Bodies Even Point to God

Or do you not know that your body is the temple of the Holy Spirit who is in you, whom you have from God, and you are not your own? For you were bought at a price; therefore glorify God in your body and in your spirit, which are God's.

1 Corinthians 6:19–20

Physically, we are made of earthly elements—the dust of the earth. And our bodies will eventually return to dust. That is not like God. The seat of God's image is therefore found in our immaterial beings.

That is not to suggest that our bodily form is utterly devoid of anything relevant to the divine image. As John Calvin said, "The image of God extends to everything in which the nature of man surpasses that of all other species of animals. And though the primary seat of the divine image was in the mind and the heart, or in the soul and its powers, there was no part even of the body in which some rays of glory did not shine."

Man's very posture, standing upright, distinguishes him from four-footed beasts and creeping things. The animals' natural posture directs their gaze downward, toward the earth. Man, on the other hand, is naturally positioned to look upward, toward the heavens, where he can contemplate the glory of God displayed there. This is one of many ways the glory of God is displayed even in the physical makeup of our race.

Our tongues, with their ability to form words and speak meaningful language, also reflect our likeness to God.

Even our faces, with their naturally expressive eyes and a host of meaningful expressions, are especially suited for relationships. So while the human body itself is neither the seat nor the primary expression of the image of God in man, even the body is specially made so that it can serve as a vehicle through which that image is manifest.

How can you act bodily to glorify God this week?

The Battle for the Beginning, 165–166

Tasks for Humans

Then the L*ORD God took the man and put him in the garden of Eden to tend and keep it.*

GENESIS 2:15

The human race was designed for and given a mandate to exercise dominion over the rest of creation. Immediately after saying, "Let Us make man in Our image, according to Our likeness," God said, "let them have dominion over the fish of the sea, over the birds of the air, and over the cattle, over all the earth and over every creeping thing that creeps on the earth" (Gen. 1:26). In verse 28, God reiterates this purpose in His instructions to Adam: "Fill the earth and subdue it; have dominion over the fish of the sea, over the birds of the air, and over every living thing that moves on the earth." Man was intended by God to be the sovereign of the planet. He was literally instructed to subdue the planet, take dominion, and rule over everything God had placed on earth. Of course this speaks collectively of the whole human race—not just Adam.

And the scope of humanity's dominion over the earth was very broad too. It was to include every living creature. God's mandate to Adam expressly listed the creatures in the order of their creation: "the fish of the sea . . . the birds of the air . . . the cattle . . . [and] every creeping thing" (v. 26).

The first step of this dominion involved something very practical. He had to look at the characteristics of each creature and give it a fitting name.

Another responsibility was assigned to Adam. He was made the gardener in Eden.

What can you do to take better care of creation?

The Battle for the Beginning, 141–142

The Creation of the First Woman

Then the rib which the LORD God had taken from man He made into a woman, and He brought her to the man. And Adam said: "This is now bone of my bones and flesh of my flesh; she shall be called Woman, because she was taken out of Man."

GENESIS 2:22–23

The unique method of Eve's creation reminds us of several crucial truths about womanhood in general.

First, it speaks of Eve's fundamental equality with Adam. They shared the same essential nature. She was in no way an inferior character made merely to serve him, but she was his spiritual counterpart, his intellectual coequal, and in every sense his perfect mate and companion.

Second, the way Eve was created reminds us of the essential unity that is the ideal in every marriage relationship. Jesus referred to Eve's creation in Matthew 19:4–6 to prove that God's plan for marriage was established at the very beginning of human history and was based on the principles of monogamy, solidarity, and inviolability.

Third, the circumstances of Eve's creation illustrate how deep and meaningful the marriage of husband and wife is designed to be. It is not *merely* a physical union, but a union of heart and soul as well. Eve was Adam's complement in every sense, designed by God to be the ideal soul-companion for him.

Fourth, Eve's creation contains some important biblical lessons about the divinely designed role of women. Although Eve was spiritually and intellectually Adam's peer; although they were both of one essence and therefore equals in their standing before God and in their rank above the other creatures; there was nonetheless a clear distinction in their earthly roles. Adam was the head; Eve was his helper. Adam was designed to be a father, provider, protector, and leader. Eve was designed to be a mother, comforter, nurturer, and helper.

Where can you better fulfill your role as a man or woman?

Twelve Extraordinary Women, 5–6

Adam's Sin as Our Representative

Therefore, as through one man's offense judgment came to all men, resulting in condemnation, even so through one Man's righteous act the free gift came to all men, resulting in justification of life.

Romans 5:18

People sometimes ask why it was *Adam's* failure that was so decisive for humanity and why Scripture treats Adam's disobedience as the means by which sin entered the world. After all, Eve actually ate the forbidden fruit first. She was the one who succumbed to the original temptation, allowed herself to be drawn away by an appeal to lust, and disobeyed God's command. Why is Adam's transgression deemed the original sin?

Remember, first of all, that 1 Timothy 2:14 says, "Adam was not deceived, but the woman being deceived, fell into transgression." Adam's sin was deliberate and willful in a way Eve's was not. Eve was deceived. But Adam chose to partake of the fruit Eve offered him with full knowledge that he was engaging in deliberate rebellion against God.

There is, however, an even more important reason why Adam's sin, rather than Eve's, led to the fall of all humanity. Because of Adam's unique position as head of the original family and therefore captain of the whole human race, Adam's headship had particular significance for all of humanity. God dealt with him as a kind of legal delegate for himself, his wife, and all their offspring. When Adam sinned, he sinned as our representative before God. When he fell, we fell with him. That is precisely why Scripture teaches that we are *born* sinful (see Gen. 8:21; Ps. 51:5; 58:3) and that we all share in *Adam's* guilt and condemnation (Rom. 5:18).

Adam, who in effect was acting as an agent and proxy for the entire human race, plunged *all of humanity at once* into sin.

In what ways are you responsible for the well-being of others?

Twelve Extraordinary Women, 13–14

The Reason for a Week

Then God blessed the seventh day and sanctified it, because in it He rested from all His work which God had created and made.

GENESIS 2:3

There is no rational reason, no cosmic reason, no philosophical reason, no mathematical reason, and no scientific reason for seven-day weeks. There is frankly no other explanation for why the 365 days of our solar years were divided into sevens. The year doesn't even divide neatly that way. So why are our calendars ordered by week? There is only one reason: God Himself established that order in the pattern of His creation. Every week of our lives we go through a cycle that is intended by God to remind us that He created the world in six days and rested on the seventh.

Every seventh day is a memorial and a reminder that God created the entire universe in one week. And for that glorious accomplishment He deserves our praise.

What does this mean in practical terms? It suggests that Saturday should be identified in our minds with the completion of creation. Just as Sunday is set aside for celebrating the finished work of the Savior, Saturday ought to be a remembrance of the finished work of the Creator.

This is not to suggest that we are bound by the ceremonial requirements of the Mosaic law with regard to the Sabbath. Again, nothing in Genesis suggests that Adam—or anyone else from Adam to Moses—was given any ceremonial restrictions that forbade any kind of activity on Saturday. But the text simply says that God hallowed the day. He set it apart as a memorial. And the seventh day is still a reminder and perpetual witness that God finished the work of creation.

What can you do on the Sabbath to honor God's finished work?

The Battle for the Beginning, 188–189

Our True Problem

Therefore, just as through one man sin entered the world, and death through sin, and thus death spread to all men, because all sinned . . . so also by one Man's obedience many will be made righteous.

ROMANS 5:12, 19

Genesis 3 is one of the most vitally important chapters in all the Bible. It is the foundation of everything that comes after it. Without it, little else in Scripture or in life itself would make sense. Genesis 3 explains the condition of the universe and the state of humanity. It explains why the world has so many problems. It explains the human dilemma. It explains why we need a Savior. And it explains what God is doing in history.

In other words, the truth revealed in Genesis 3 is the necessary foundation for a true and accurate worldview. Every worldview that lacks this foundation is utterly and hopelessly wrong.

When God completed His perfect creation, there was no disorder, no chaos, no conflict, no struggle, no pain, no discord, no deterioration, and no death. Yet our lives today are filled with these things all the time. Frankly, we find it hard to imagine what a perfect world would have been like. Genesis 3 explains how we got from that paradise of unimaginable perfection to where we are today.

How did we get in this state? Genesis 3 answers that question with clarity and simplicity. Our first ancestor, Adam, deliberately disobeyed God. Somehow his sin defiled the whole race, and now every one of his natural offspring has inherited a love for sin and a contempt for true righteousness. And this manifests itself in our behavior.

Every one of us inherits sin and guilt from Adam. And that is what is wrong with us.

Where have you seen a love for sin in your own life?

The Battle for the Beginning, 195–197

The Curse of Sin

For the creation was subjected to futility.

ROMANS 8:20

The curse (Gen. 3:14–19) has a number of significant features. The serpent was condemned to crawl on his belly in the dust. All his offspring would be slithering creatures, symbolic of all that is loathsome, feared, and avoided by humans, "cursed more than all cattle, and more than every beast of the field."

Notice the subtle implication: cattle and other beasts of the field were cursed too. In fact, all creation was affected by Adam's sin—"subjected to futility" (Rom. 8:20). Weeds and thorns would henceforth infest the ground. Pain, weariness, and sweat would make life difficult. In addition to the troubles expressly named in Genesis 3, a number of other woes have made human life difficult from that point on. For example, harmful germs and viruses, disease, disaster, and decay of all kinds also stem from the divine curse. Insects and other creatures have overstepped their original beneficial purposes and become annoying pests. Nature itself often becomes destructive, with floods, earthquakes, droughts, famines, and other natural disasters. That is why all creation "groans and labors with birth pangs" (Rom. 8:22), waiting for the consummation of God's redemptive work.

The woman would be afflicted with pain in childbirth. That pain would be a perpetual reminder that the woman helped conceive sin in the human race and passes it on to her children. The Lord also told her that she would from now on chafe under her husband's authority.

And then the Lord told Adam he was condemned to a life of labor and sweat, tilling the cursed earth, to which he would one day return in death.

What consequences has sin had in your life?

The Battle for the Beginning, 216

The Beginning of a Promise

And I will put enmity between you and the woman, and between your seed and her Seed; He shall bruise your head, and you shall bruise His heel.

Genesis 3:15

Within the curse upon sin is the first promise of the Redeemer, Christ, in Genesis 3:15. Consider what is revealed about Him here.

First, He would be the Seed of *the woman*. This is significant language, because normally offspring are spoken of as the seed of their fathers. This seems to be a subtle reference to Christ's virgin birth.

Second, there would be enmity between Him and the serpent. This signifies the continuous conflict between Satan and Christ. Satan, the destroyer of men's souls, opposes Christ, the Savior of the world. The evil one hates the Holy One and has therefore set himself and "his seed"—all those who belong to his kingdom (both demons and humans)—against the Seed of the woman.

Third, the Seed of the woman would suffer. Satan would bruise His heel. This speaks of Christ's suffering on the cross (see Isa. 53:5).

Fourth, the Savior would triumph. He would end the enmity forever by crushing the serpent's head. Satan, the serpent, did his best to destroy Christ, but in the end it left only a bruise that would heal. Christ rose from the dead in triumph, gaining redemption for Adam's fallen race, while destroying the works of the devil. And in that act he sealed Satan's final defeat, crushing the serpent's head as promised.

Remember, the first glimmer of hope that all this would occur shone forth, of all places, in the curse God pronounced after Adam sinned! And the rest of Scripture, from this point on, merely fills in the gaps in the drama of redemption.

How does it change your outlook to know that God promised a Redeemer from the beginning?

The Battle for the Beginning, 218–219

Moralism Is Not the True Gospel

These things indeed have an appearance of wisdom in self-imposed religion, false humility, and neglect of the body, but are of no value against the indulgence of the flesh.

COLOSSIANS 2:23

In Matthew 23:13–39, Jesus pronounced a series of woes on the religious leaders of His time. Again, these were the *most* moral people of His society, people who were obsessive about keeping the smallest of Old Testament laws and Jewish traditions. They even gave a tithe of the little seeds in their spice cabinets (v. 23). Yet Jesus' discourse against them was the harshest sermon He ever gave. He condemned their moralism as mere hypocrisy: "Woe to you, scribes and Pharisees, hypocrites! For you are like whitewashed tombs which indeed appear beautiful outwardly, but inside are full of dead men's bones and all uncleanness. Even so you also outwardly appear righteous to men, but inside you are full of hypocrisy and lawlessness" (vv. 27–28). Jesus never used harsh words like that against the outcasts, the prostitutes, the tax collectors, or the criminals of His day. In fact, He spent His time ministering graciously to such people—so much so that the Pharisees accused Him of being "a glutton and a winebibber, a friend of tax collectors and sinners!" (Luke 7:34).

Moralism was never the message of the Old Testament prophets. It was never the message of the Messiah. It was never the message of the apostles. It is not the message of the New Testament. It has never been God's message to the world. In fact, God's assessment of moralism is given in Isaiah 57:12: "I will declare your righteousness and your works, for *they will not profit you*" (emphasis added).

Where has moralism crept into your spiritual life?

Can God Bless America? 70–72

What Does It Mean to Be a Christian?

For in Christ Jesus neither circumcision nor uncircumcision avails anything, but faith working through love.

Galatians 5:6

For some, being "Christian" is primarily cultural and traditional, a nominal title inherited from a previous generation, the net effect of which involves avoiding certain behaviors and occasionally attending church. For others, being a Christian is largely political, a quest to defend moral values in the public square or perhaps to preserve those values by withdrawing from the public square altogether. Still more define Christianity in terms of a past religious experience, a general belief in Jesus, or a desire to be a good person. Yet all of these fall woefully short of what it truly means to be a Christian from a biblical perspective.

Interestingly, the followers of Jesus Christ were not called "Christians" until ten to fifteen years after the church began. Before that time, they were known simply as disciples, brothers, believers, saints, and followers of the Way.

The name was initially coined by unbelievers as an attempt to deride those who followed a crucified Christ. But what began as ridicule soon became a badge of honor. To be called Christians (in Greek, *Christianoi*) was to be identified as Jesus' disciples and to be associated with Him as loyal followers. In a similar fashion, those in Caesar's household would refer to themselves as *Kaisarianoi* ("those of Caesar") in order to show their deep allegiance to the Roman emperor.

Thus, to be a *Christian*, in the true sense of the term, is to be a wholehearted follower of Jesus Christ.

How well does this definition match the way you have defined being a Christian?

Slave, 10–11

Faith Has Substance

But without faith it is impossible to please Him, for he who comes to God must believe that He is, and that He is a rewarder of those who diligently seek Him.

HEBREWS 11:6

Absolutely nothing we do can please God apart from this kind of faith. Without faith, pleasing God is *impossible*. Religion, racial heritage, meritorious works—everything the Hebrews regarded as pleasing to God—is utterly futile apart from faith.

The beginning of faith is simply believing that God *is*. This certainly means far more than believing in an unnamed and unknown supreme being. The Hebrews knew God's name as I AM (Ex. 3:14). The phrase "he who comes to God must believe that He is" is a call for faith in the one God who had revealed Himself in Scripture. This verse does not ratify belief in some abstract deity—the "ground of being," the "man upstairs," Allah, the "Unknown god" of the Greek philosophers (Acts 17:23), or any of the other manmade gods. It is speaking of faith in the one God of the Bible, whose highest revelation of Himself is in the Person of His Son, the Lord Jesus Christ.

Clearly, true faith has objective substance. There *is* an intellectual content to our faith. Believing is not a mindless leap in the dark or some ethereal kind of trust apart from knowledge. There is a factual, historical, intellectual basis for our faith. Faith that is not grounded in this objective truth is no faith at all.

What have you relied on to please God apart from faith?

The Gospel According to the Apostles, 29–30

What Makes Christianity Different

For if Abraham was justified by works, he has something to boast about, but not before God. For what does the Scripture say? "Abraham believed God, and it was accounted to him for righteousness."

ROMANS 4:2–3

There are, after all, only two kinds of religion in all the world. Every false religion ever devised by mankind or by Satan is a *religion of human merit*. Pagan religion, humanism, animism, and even false Christianity all fall into this category. They focus on what people must *do* to attain righteousness or please the deity.

Biblical Christianity alone is the *religion of divine accomplishment*. Other religions say, "Do this." Christianity says, "It is done" (cf. John 19:30). Other religions require that the devout person supply some kind of merit to atone for sin, appease deity, or otherwise attain the goal of acceptability. Scripture says Christ's merit is supplied on behalf of the believing sinner.

The Pharisees in Paul's day had turned Judaism into a religion of human achievements. Paul's own life before salvation was one long and futile effort to please God through personal merit. He had been steeped in the Pharisaic tradition, "a Pharisee, the son of a Pharisee" (Acts 23:6; see also Phil. 3:5–6). Paul understood the religious culture of his day as well as anyone. He knew that the Pharisees revered Abraham as the father of their religion (John 8:39). So he singled him out to prove that justification before God is by faith in what God has accomplished.

By appealing to the Old Testament Scriptures, Paul was showing that Judaism had moved away from the most basic truths affirmed by all believing Jews since Abraham himself. Abraham did not practice the Pharisees' religion of merit.

How does it change your perspective to know that salvation depends on God's actions rather than yours?

The Gospel According to the Apostles, 99–100

An Unpopular Truth

Nor is there salvation in any other, for there is no other name under heaven given among men by which we must be saved.

ACTS 4:12

Plenty of tolerant people out there say, "Okay, you're into this cross thing, and Jesus being crucified, and that's your truth. Good for you—we are an inclusive people. That's fine if that's your truth. But that's not our truth."

Well, here's the rub: It *is* your truth. It's *everybody's* truth. It's the *only* truth. The power of the crucified Christ is the only power of God by which He saves. Salvation comes only through a belief in that gospel, the gospel of Jesus. No gospel, no salvation. The absolute exclusivity of it has always been a shameful, embarrassing, inconvenient message to worldly wise sinners, but the truth is nonnegotiable. Other religions are not truth and lead only to eternal damnation. Islam is a damning system. Buddhism is a damning system. Hinduism is a damning system. Simply not believing the gospel is itself enough to damn a person.

People in false religions do not worship the true God by another name, as some suggest. They unwittingly worship Satan's demons. Here is what the Bible says: "The things which the Gentiles sacrifice they sacrifice to demons and not to God" (1 Cor. 10:20). Even so, a book called *The Christ of Hinduism* actually exists, and it argues that Hinduism's symbols and doctrines contain the Christian message. But there is no Christ of Hinduism, nor has the true God any part in Hinduism. Christ is the only way to the one true God, and biblical Christianity is the only way to the one true Christ. I didn't make this up. This isn't my theology. This is Christianity 101.

How can you respond to people who want salvation to include people outside of Christ?

Hard to Believe, 37–38

PUBLIC LIBRARY
DANVILLE, ILLINOIS

The Good News Begins with Bad News

My dishonor is continually before me, and the shame of my face has covered me.

Psalm 44:15

Romans 1:16 begins an extended, systematic treatment of the gospel that continues throughout the epistle. Paul crowned his introduction and greeting to the Roman believers with these words: "I am not ashamed of the gospel, for it is the power of God for salvation to everyone who believes, to the Jew first and also to the Greek. For in it the righteousness of God is revealed from faith to faith; as it is written, 'But the righteous man shall live by faith'" (Rom. 1:16–17 NASB).

Right there, just when it seemed Paul was going to begin talking about the *good news* and the power of God unto salvation, he unleashed this thunderbolt: "For the wrath of God is revealed from heaven against all ungodliness and unrighteousness of men who suppress the truth in unrighteousness" (v. 18 NASB).

It turns out that the good news about salvation starts with the bad news about sin. As Jesus said, "It is not those who are healthy who need a physician, but those who are sick; I did not come to call the righteous, but sinners" (Mark 2:17 NASB). Paul knew that those who underestimate the enormity and gravity of human sinfulness—especially those who do not see their own depravity—cannot apply the only effective remedy to their problems.

There can be no salvation for those who aren't convinced of the seriousness of their sin. There can be no word of reconciliation for sinners who remain oblivious to their estrangement from God. True fear of God cannot grip those who are blind to the depth of their sinfulness. And no mercy is available for those who do not tremble at God's holy threats.

How have you felt the weight of your own sin before God?

The Vanishing Conscience, 59–60

The Two Essential Truths

For I determined not to know anything among you except Jesus Christ and Him crucified.

1 Corinthians 2:2

When I'm interviewed by a TV network, or in any fast-paced situation where I've got to make my point in a fifteen-second sound bite, I want to say two black-and-white things: I want to proclaim the absolute and single authority of Scripture, and the absolute exclusivity of Jesus Christ. It's kind of a response to the electronic version of Broadway producer David Belasco's challenge: "If you can't write your idea on the back of my business card, you don't have an idea."

There I am, with monitors flashing and technicians moving around just off camera; the host is listening to me with one ear, and to his producer through an earpiece in the other; we're jammed together on this tiny set with our knees bumping; and when the host levels his laser-beam gaze at me and says, "Before we go to a commercial, what do you think about that, John?" I'd better know what I think. I think the world needs to know the Bible is the only truth of God, and Jesus Christ the only Savior.

Every argument eventually works its way around to those two unflinching, unbreachable truths of the genuine gospel. They reveal that there is only one true religion and the rest is false, and that there is the right and all else is wrong. All the way through the Sermon on the Mount, Jesus contrasted the true religion of Christ with the false Judaism of the scribes and Pharisees and their followers. He offered not a lot of choices, only two. The gospel saves; anything else condemns.

How would you express these two truths?

Hard to Believe, 76–77

Where Repentance Begins

But when he came to himself, he said, "How many of my father's hired servants have bread enough and to spare, and I perish with hunger! I will arise and go to my father, and will say to him, 'Father, I have sinned against heaven and before you.'"

LUKE 15:17–18

Here, I am convinced, is where true repentance always begins: with an accurate assessment of one's own condition. Everyone—from the profligate sinner who is a complete wastrel (such as the prodigal son) to the most fastidious, patronizing Pharisee—needs to face the reality that the sinfulness we have inherited from Adam has made us spiritual paupers. No sinner has the means to atone for his or her own sin or the ability to overcome the power of sin that holds us. Our sin has put us in a desperate situation.

Of course, that is much harder for a pompous, respectable sinner to acknowledge than it is for a wretched swineherd. "Those who are well have no need of a physician, but those who are sick" (Matt. 9:12). Multitudes are kept in spiritual darkness and under the condemnation of heaven because they simply refuse to confess how needy they are. That was precisely the situation the Pharisees were in.

The prodigal, on the other hand, had already lost whatever pretense of dignity and self-confidence he once might have maintained. He no longer had any resources of his own, no one else gave him anything, and he couldn't even scavenge sufficient nourishment from the pigs' food. It was absolutely the end of the road for him, and he confessed that.

Simply and honestly facing the reality of his own circumstances is what caused such a monumental change in the prodigal's attitude toward his father.

How are the circumstances in your life driving you to repentance?

A Tale of Two Sons, 89–90

February

LOVE

The Truth to Fight For

But even if we, or an angel from heaven, preach any other gospel to you than what we have preached to you, let him be accursed.

GALATIANS 1:8

It may not always be easy to determine whether a disagreement is merely petty or truly weighty, but a careful, thoughtful application of biblical wisdom will usually settle whatever questions we may have about the relative importance of any given truth. Scripture makes clear, for example, that we must take a zero-tolerance stance toward anyone who would tamper with or alter the gospel message (Gal. 1:8–9). And anyone who denies the deity of Christ or substantially departs from His teaching is not to be welcomed into our fellowship or given any kind of blessing (2 John 7–11).

The principle is clear: the closer any given doctrine is to the heart of the gospel, the core of sound Christology, or the fundamental teachings of Christ, the more diligently we ought to be on guard against perversions of the truth—and the more aggressively we need to fight the error and defend sound doctrine.

Differentiating between truly essential and merely peripheral spiritual truths does require great care and discernment. The distinction is not always immediately obvious. But it is not nearly as difficult to draw that line as some people today pretend it is.

Scripture suggests that the gospel is the best gauge for determining the true essentials of Christianity. Misconstrue the gospel or adapt it to suit a particular subculture's preferences and the inevitable result will be a religion of works and a system that breeds self-righteousness.

That is exactly what Jesus' conflict with the Pharisees was all about.

Where in your life can you defend the gospel against claims that compete with it?

The Jesus You Can't Ignore, xii–xiv

In Christ

Therefore we were buried with Him through baptism into death, that just as Christ was raised from the dead by the glory of the Father, even so we also should walk in newness of life.

ROMANS 6:4

In Christ" is one of Paul's favorite phrases (cf. Rom. 8:1; 12:5; 16:7; 1 Cor. 1:2; Col. 1:28). Because we are "in Christ Jesus" He has become to us "wisdom from God—and righteousness and sanctification and redemption" (1 Cor. 1:30). Our life is hidden with Christ in God (Col. 3:3). We are buried with Him by baptism into death (Rom. 6:4; Col. 2:12). We are one body in Him (Rom. 12:5). Christ is our life (Col. 3:4). Christ is in us, the hope of glory (Col. 1:27). Those verses describe the absolute identification with Christ that is the essential characteristic of the elect. We are indivisibly linked in a spiritual sphere of new life.

To be "in Christ" is not only to believe some truths *about* Him, but rather to be united *to* Him inseparably as the source of our eternal life, as both the "author *and perfecter* of faith" (Heb. 12:2 NASB, emphasis added).

We are united with Christ specifically in His death and resurrection (Rom. 6:3–10). This truth is far too wonderful for us to comprehend fully, but the main idea Paul wants to convey here is that we died with Christ so that we might have life through Him and live like Him. The whole purpose of our union in Christ's death and resurrection with Christ is so that "we also should walk in newness of life" (v. 4). How could we continue in the realm of sin?

The certain consequence of our union in Christ's death to sin and His resurrection to life is that we will share in His holy walk.

How does being "in Christ" change your perspective on your everyday life?

The Gospel According to the Apostles, 115–116

Preaching the Truth

Therefore many of His disciples, when they heard this, said, "This is a hard saying; who can understand it?" . . . From that time many of His disciples went back and walked with Him no more.

JOHN 6:60, 66

Sermons featuring straight biblical exposition, precise doctrine, difficult truths, or negative-sounding topics are strongly discouraged by virtually all the leading gurus of cultural relevance. Teaching, reproof, correction, and training in righteousness (cf. 2 Tim. 3:16) are out. Catering to itchy ears is in (cf. 4:3). No truly clued-in preacher nowadays would think to fill his message with reproof, rebuke, or exhortation (cf. 4:2). Instead, he does his best to suit the felt needs, preoccupations, and passions of the audience.

The contemporary craving for shallow sermons that please and entertain is at least partly rooted in the popular myth that Jesus Himself was always likable, agreeable, winsome, and at the cutting edge of His culture's fashions.

Even a cursory look at Jesus' preaching ministry reveals a totally different picture. Jesus' sermons *usually* featured hard truths, harsh words, and high-octane controversy. His own disciples complained that His preaching was too hard to hear!

That's why Jesus' preaching heads the list of things that make Him impossible to ignore. No preacher has ever been more bold, prophetic, or provocative. Jesus made it impossible for any hearer to walk away indifferent. Some left angry; some were deeply troubled by what He had to say; many had their eyes opened; and many more hardened their hearts against His message. Some became His disciples, and others became His adversaries. But no one who listened to Him preach for very long could possibly remain unchanged or apathetic.

How are you responding to Jesus' hard truths?

The Jesus You Can't Ignore, 161–162

How We Come to Faith

No one can come to Me unless the Father who sent Me draws him . . . no one can come to Me unless it has been granted to him by My Father.

John 6:44, 65

The manner of Lydia's conversion is a fine illustration of how God always redeems lost souls. From our human perspective, we may think that we are seeking Him, that trusting Christ is merely a "decision" that lies within the power of our own will to choose, or that we are sovereign over our own hearts and affections. In reality, wherever you see a soul like Lydia's truly seeking God, you can be certain God is drawing her. Whenever someone trusts Christ, it is God who opens the heart to believe. If God Himself did not draw us to Christ, we would never come at all. Jesus was quite clear about this (John 6:44–65).

Acts 16:14 describes Lydia as a woman "who worshiped God." Intellectually, at least, she already knew that YHWH was the one true God. She apparently met regularly with the Jewish women who gathered to pray on the Sabbath, but she had not yet become a convert to Judaism.

Her heart was truly open. She was a genuine seeker of God. But notice Luke's whole point: it was not that Lydia opened her own heart and ears to the truth. Yes, she was seeking, but even that was because God was drawing her. She was listening, but it was God who gave her ears to hear. She had an open heart, but it was God who opened her heart. Luke expressly affirms the sovereignty of God in Lydia's salvation: "The Lord opened her heart to heed the things spoken by Paul" (16:14).

How have you sensed God drawing you?

Twelve Extraordinary Women, 192–193

Enter In!

Then Jesus said to them again, "Most assuredly, I say to you, I am the door of the sheep. . . . If anyone enters by Me, he will be saved, and will go in and out and find pasture."

John 10:7, 9

It is not enough to listen to preaching about the gate; it is not enough to respect the ethics; you've got to walk through the gate. And you can't come unless you abandon your self-righteousness, see yourself as a beggar in spirit, mourning over sin, meek before a holy God, not proud and boastful, hungering and thirsting for righteousness, and not believing you have it. Hell will be full of people who thought highly of the Sermon on the Mount. You must do more than that. You must obey it and take action.

You can't stand outside and admire the narrow gate; you've got to drop everything and walk through it. There's that self-denial again. You come through, stripped of everything. But isn't that narrow-minded? Does that mean Christianity doesn't allow room for opposing viewpoints? No compassionate tolerance? No diversity?

That's exactly right. We don't do it that way because we're selfish or prideful or egotistical; we do it that way because that's what God said to do. If God said there were forty-eight ways to salvation, I'd preach and write about all forty-eight of them. But there aren't: "Nor is there salvation in any other, for there is no other name under heaven given among men by which we must be saved," Acts 4:12 reminds us, no other name but Jesus.

That's a narrow viewpoint. But that is Christianity. And it is the truth. You have to enter on God's terms, through God's prescribed gate. Christ is that gate. Holy God has the right to determine the basis of salvation, and He has determined that it is Jesus Christ and Him alone.

What other gates have you been tempted to enter to find righteousness, peace, or joy?

Hard to Believe, 81–82

God So Loved the World

For scarcely for a righteous man will one die; yet perhaps for a good man someone would even dare to die. But God demonstrates His own love toward us, in that while we were still sinners, Christ died for us.

Romans 5:7–8

As much as God hates sin, He loves sinners. Set against the dark background of our sin, the grace of God becomes all the more wondrous. The most familiar passage in all Scripture is John 3:16. Without an understanding of the wickedness of sin, however, we cannot grasp the tremendous significance of this verse.

"God so loved . . ." Why would God love me despite my sin?

"God so loved the world . . ." Why would God love a whole world of sinners?

"God so loved the world, that He gave His only begotten Son . . ." Why would God's love for sinners be so compelling as to make Him sacrifice His beloved Son in such agony and humiliation?

"God so loved the world that He gave His only begotten Son, that whoever believes in Him . . ." Why would God make salvation so simple for sinners, requiring only faith of us, and having done all the necessary expiatory work Himself?

"God so loved the world that He gave His only begotten Son, that whoever believes in Him should not perish . . ." Why would God want to exempt sinners from the judgment they themselves deserve, even to the point of allowing His only begotten Son to accept that judgment on behalf of those who do not deserve His mercy?

"God so loved the world that He gave His only begotten Son, that whoever believes in Him should not perish but have everlasting life." Why would God want to give everlasting life in His presence to sinners who have done nothing but oppose Him and hate Him?

The answer is found in *God's grace* (Eph. 2:4–5).

How do you react to God's free offer of salvation?

The Vanishing Conscience, 118–119

True Love

Love suffers long and is kind; love does not envy; love does not parade itself, is not puffed up; does not behave rudely, does not seek its own, is not provoked, thinks no evil; does not rejoice in iniquity, but rejoices in the truth; bears all things, believes all things, hopes all things, endures all things.

1 CORINTHIANS 13:4–7

The love that we hear about in popular songs is almost always portrayed as a *feeling*—usually involving unfulfilled desire. Most love songs describe love as a longing, a passion, a craving that is never quite satisfied, a set of expectations that are never met.

Most love songs not only reduce love to an emotion, but also make it an involuntary one. People "fall" in love. They get swept off their feet by love. They can't help themselves.

It may seem a nice romantic sentiment to characterize love as uncontrollable passion, but those who think carefully about it will realize that such "love" is both selfish and irrational. It is far from the biblical concept of love. Love, according to Scripture, is not a helpless sensation of desire. Rather, it is a purposeful act of self-giving. The one who genuinely loves is deliberately devoted to the one loved. True love arises from the will—not from blind emotion. Consider, for example, this description of love from the pen of the apostle Paul (1 Cor. 13:4–7). That kind of love cannot possibly be an emotion that ebbs and flows involuntarily. It is not a mere feeling. All the attributes that Paul lists involve the mind and the volition. In other words, the love he describes is a thoughtful, willing commitment.

If love is a giving of oneself, then the greatest love is shown by laying down one's very life. And of course, such love is perfectly modeled by Christ.

What quality of love do you need to grow in most?

The God Who Loves, 25–26

God Is Love

And we have known and believed the love that God has for us. God is love, and he who abides in love abides in God, and God in him.

1 John 4:16

By saying "God is love," the apostle is making a very strong statement about the character and the essence of God. It is God's very nature to love—love permeates who He is.

This statement, "God is love," is so profound that no less than Augustine saw it as an important evidence for the doctrine of the Trinity. If God is love—that is, if love is intrinsic to His very nature—then He has always loved, even from eternity past, before there was any created object for His love. Augustine suggested that this love must have existed between the Persons of the Trinity, with the Father loving the Son, and so on. So according to Augustine, the very fact that God is love corroborates the doctrine of the Trinity.

Clearly the love this text describes is an eternal reality. It flows from the very nature of God and is not a response to anything outside of God. The apostle does not say, "God is *loving*," as if he were speaking of one of many divine attributes, but "God is *love*"—as if to say that love pervades and influences all His attributes.

Love surely tempers even God's judgments. What a wonder it is that He who is a consuming fire, He who is unapproachable light, is also the personification of love! He postpones His judgments against sin while pleading with sinners to repent. Divine love not only keeps divine wrath in check while God appeals to the sinner—but it also proves that God is just when He finally condemns.

How can you grow in your awareness of God's love?

The God Who Loves, 29–30

Love and Wrath Not at Odds

Mercy and truth have met together; righteousness and peace have kissed.

Psalm 85:10

God's love cannot be isolated from His wrath and vice versa. Nor are His love and wrath in opposition to each other like some mystical yin-yang principle. Both attributes are constant, perfect, without ebb or flow. God Himself is immutable—unchanging. He is not loving one moment and wrathful the next. His wrath coexists with His love; therefore, the two never contradict. Such are the perfections of God that we can never begin to comprehend these things. Above all, we must not set them against one another, as if there were somehow a discrepancy in God. God is always true to Himself and true to His Word (Rom. 3:4; 2 Tim. 2:13).

Both God's wrath and His love work to the same ultimate end—His glory. God is glorified in the condemnation of the wicked, and He is glorified in the salvation of His people. The expression of His wrath and the expression of His love are both necessary to display His full glory. Since His glory is the great design of His eternal plan, and since all that He has revealed about Himself is essential to His glory, we must not ignore any aspect of His character. We cannot magnify His love to the exclusion of His other attributes.

How have you been tempted to ignore God's love or His wrath?

The God Who Loves, 18–19

The Truth of Love Needs the Truth of Wrath

My flesh trembles for fear of You, and I am afraid of Your judgments.

Psalm 119:120

Scripture tells us repeatedly that *fear* of God is the very foundation of true wisdom (Job 28:28; Ps. 111:10; Prov. 1:7; 9:10; 15:33). People often try to explain the sense of these verses away by saying that the "fear" called for is a devout sense of awe and reverence. Certainly the fear of God includes awe and reverence, but it does not *exclude* literal holy terror. "It is the Lord of hosts whom you should regard as holy. And He shall be your fear, and He shall be your dread" (Isa. 8:13 NASB).

We must recapture some of the holy terror that comes with a right understanding of God's righteous anger. We need to remember that God's wrath *does* burn against impenitent sinners (Ps. 38:1–3). That reality is the very thing that makes His love so amazing. We must therefore proclaim these truths with the same sense of conviction and fervency we employ when we declare the love of God. It is only against the backdrop of divine wrath that the full significance of God's love can be truly understood. That is precisely the message of the cross of Jesus Christ. After all, it was on the cross that God's love and wrath converged in all their majestic fullness.

Only those who see themselves as sinners in the hands of an angry God can fully appreciate the magnitude and wonder of His love.

How can you grow in your fear of God?

The God Who Loves, 11

God's Love for the Unbelieving World

"Do I have any pleasure at all that the wicked should die?" says the Lord GOD, *"and not that he should turn from his ways and live?"*

EZEKIEL 18:23

We know from human experience that love and hate are not mutually exclusive. It is not the least bit unusual to have concurrent feelings of love and hatred directed at the same person. There is no reason to deny that in an infinitely purer and more noble sense, God's hatred toward the wicked is accompanied by a sincere, compassionate love for them as well.

The fact that God will send to eternal hell all sinners who persist in sin and unbelief proves His hatred toward them. On the other hand, the fact that God promises to forgive and bring into His eternal glory all who trust Christ as Savior—and even pleads with sinners to repent—proves His love toward them.

We must understand that it is God's very nature to love. The reason our Lord commanded us to love our enemies is "so that you may be sons of your Father who is in heaven; for He causes His sun to rise on the evil and the good, and sends rain on the righteous and the unrighteous" (Matt. 5:45 NASB). Here Jesus clearly characterized His Father as One who loves even those who purposefully set themselves at enmity against Him.

While we are all eager to ask why a loving God lets bad things happen to His children, surely we should also ask why a holy God lets good things happen to bad people. The answer is that God is merciful even to those who are not His own.

Where have you felt this mixture of love and hatred?

The God Who Loves, 15–16

The Source of True Love

We love Him because He first loved us.

1 JOHN 4:19

From the truth that God is love, the apostle John draws this corollary: "Love is of God" (1 John 4:7). God is the source of all true love. Love is therefore the best evidence that a person truly knows God: "Everyone who loves is born of God and knows God. He who does not love does not know God" (vv. 7–8). In other words, love is the proof of a regenerate heart. Only true Christians are capable of genuine love.

Clearly, the kind of love the apostle is speaking of is a higher, purer form of love than we commonly know from human experience. The love of which he speaks does not flow naturally from the human heart. It is not a carnal love, a romantic love, or even a familial love. It is a supernatural love that is peculiar to those who know God. It is *godly* love.

In fact, the apostle employed a Greek word for "love" (*agape*) that was highly unusual in first-century culture. In the sense that John uses it here, *agape* is unique to God. He is the sole source of it.

His love is *perfect* love. It is that pure, holy, godly love that can be known only by those who are born of Him. It is the same unfathomable love that moved God to send "His only begotten Son into the world, that we might live through Him" (1 John 4:9).

All true believers have this love; and all who have it are true believers.

How has God's love for you flowed out as a love for others?

The God Who Loves, 30–32

Love as a Mark of a True Believer

*By this all will know that you are My disciples,
if you have love for one another.*

JOHN 13:35

If God lives in you, if you share His life, you will also love, because "God is love" (1 John 4:8). This is not just a responsibility; it is evidence of God's presence and your changed life. It is impossible for a true believer not to love other believers.

The apostle Peter added, "Since you have purified your souls in obeying the truth through the Spirit in sincere love of the brethren, love one another fervently with a pure heart" (1 Peter 1:22). That is characteristic of a true believer—it is who you are: you obeyed the truth, your soul was cleansed, and that produced a genuine love for the brethren.

If you don't have a love for God's people, for the members of your new family in Christ, that's clear evidence you're still a product of your sinful self, separated from the life and love of God. If you are a true Christian, the proof will be in your love. Though it will be an imperfect effort, you'll do everything in your power to exhibit a heart of love, not of hatred. Your desire will be to serve others, not make demands on them; to help others, not harm them; to encourage others, not tear them down; to love others as you love yourself and as God your Creator loves you—a love so total and complete that He sacrificed His only Son that you might live and love forever.

How have other believers shown God's love toward you?

Welcome to the Family, 64–65

The Witness of the Church

Let your light so shine before men, that they may see your good works and glorify your Father in heaven.

Matthew 5:16

The entire church is the temple of the Holy Spirit, just as the individual member is. The Spirit indwells the corporate body to witness to the world about the Father and the Son.

The body presents a single collective testimony in two ways. First, the body witnesses by its visible unity. Jesus prayed, "I do not pray for these alone, but also for those who will believe in Me through their word; that they all may be one, as You, Father, are in Me, and I in You; that they also may be one in Us, that the world may believe that You sent Me" (John 17:20–21).

The second way the body witnesses is by love. Jesus told the disciples that love is the mark of all genuine believers: "Little children, I shall be with you a little while longer. You will seek Me; and as I said to the Jews, 'Where I am going, you cannot come,' so now I say to you. A new commandment I give to you, that you love one another; as I have loved you, that you also love one another. By this all will know that you are My disciples, if you have love for one another" (John 13:33–35). The more consistently Christians show love for one another, the more powerful our impact on the world will be. Individual members of the body are the last link in the witness of the Father. The testimony of Christ must not break down with us.

How have you seen a witness for Christ break down because of disunity and conflict among believers?

Welcome to the Family, 96–97

Giving Is Loving

So let each one give as he purposes in his heart, not grudgingly or of necessity; for God loves a cheerful giver.

2 Corinthians 9:7

Biblical giving is not done in a vacuum or in isolation from other Christian virtues. For your giving to be biblical, it should occur in perfect harmony with all the other positive traits of your regenerate nature, "But just as you abound in everything, in faith and utterance and knowledge and in all earnestness and in the love we inspired in you, see that you abound in this gracious work also" (2 Cor. 8:7).

If your giving is operating right along with other Christian virtues, you're motivated by the greatest virtue of all, love (cf. 1 Cor. 13:3; 1 Peter 1:22; 1 John 3:17–18). More than anything else, it underscores that your giving is biblical. You can give without loving (that's merely legalistic, required giving), but you can't love without giving (true affection leads to generosity).

Biblical giving is perhaps the surest way to demonstrate genuine love for others. Paul asks us again to measure ourselves against the example of the Macedonians to verify the quality of our own love, "but as proving through the earnestness of others [the Macedonians] the sincerity of your love also" (2 Cor. 8:8 NASB). The true test of sincere love is not positive emotions and good intentions, but tangible actions (James 2:14–18), such as biblical giving. Such giving proves that you love the Lord, His church, and those in need. It is the path to God's abundant blessing, a path I trust you're eager to walk.

How can you use giving to express and grow your love for God and others?

Whose Money Is It Anyway? 92–93

Truth and Love

Now John answered Him, saying, "Teacher, we saw someone who does not follow us casting out demons in Your name, and we forbade him because he does not follow us."

MARK 9:38

The apostle John was always committed to truth, and there's certainly nothing wrong with that, but it is not enough. Zeal for the truth must be balanced by love for people. Truth without love has no decency; it's just *brutality*. On the other hand, love without truth has no character; it's just *hypocrisy*.

Many people are just as imbalanced as John was, only in the other direction. They place too much emphasis on the love side of the fulcrum. Some are merely ignorant; others are deceived; still others simply do not care about what is true. In each case, truth is missing, and all they are left with is error, clothed in a shallow, tolerant sentimentality. It is a poor substitute for genuine love. They talk a lot about love and tolerance, but they utterly lack any concern for the truth. Therefore even the "love" they speak of is a tainted love. Real love "does not rejoice in iniquity, but rejoices in the truth" (1 Cor. 13:6).

On the other hand, there are many who have all their theological ducks in a row and know their doctrine but are unloving and self-exalting. They are left with truth as cold facts, stifling and unattractive. Their lack of love cripples the power of the truth they profess to revere.

The truly godly person must cultivate both virtues in equal proportions. If you could wish for anything in your sanctification, wish for that. If you pursue anything in the spiritual realm, pursue a perfect balance of truth and love. Know the truth, and uphold it in love.

How is your balance of truth and love?

Twelve Ordinary Men, 106

Why We Fight for the Truth

For the weapons of our warfare are not carnal but mighty in God for pulling down strongholds, casting down arguments and every high thing that exalts itself against the knowledge of God, bringing every thought into captivity to the obedience of Christ.

2 CORINTHIANS 10:4–5

Spiritual warfare is necessary because of sin and the curse—not because there's anything inherently glorious or virtuous about fighting. Zeal without knowledge is spiritually deadly (Rom. 10:2), and even the most sincere passion for the truth needs to be always tempered with gentleness and grace (Eph. 4:29; Col. 4:6). Eager enthusiasm for calling down fire from heaven against blasphemers and heretics is far from the spirit of Christ (Luke 9:54–55).

I do agree that *usually* it is far better to be gentle than to be harsh. Peacefulness is a blessed quality (Matt. 5:9); pugnaciousness is a disqualifying character flaw (Titus 1:7). Patience is indeed a sweet virtue, even in the face of unbelief and persecution (Luke 21:19). We always ought to listen sufficiently before we react (Prov. 18:13). A kind word can usually do far more good than a curt reaction, because "a soft answer turns away wrath, but a harsh word stirs up anger" (Prov. 15:1)—and any person who delights to stir up strife is a fool (v. 18).

If those were the only verses in Scripture that told us how to deal with error, we might be justified in thinking those principles are absolute, inviolable, and applicable to every kind of opposition or unbelief we encounter.

But that's not the case. We're instructed to contend earnestly for the faith (Jude v. 3). Immediately after the apostle Paul urged Timothy to "pursue righteousness, godliness, faith, love, patience, gentleness" (1 Tim. 6:11), he exhorted him to "fight the good fight of faith" (v. 12).

Where do you need to speak the truth boldly?

The Jesus You Can't Ignore, xxix–xxx

Not Afraid to Say Someone Is Wrong

He who abides in the doctrine of Christ has both the Father and the Son. If anyone comes to you and does not bring this doctrine, do not receive him into your house nor greet him; for he who greets him shares in his evil deeds.

2 JOHN 9–11

Paul was certainly fair with his opponents in the sense that he never misrepresented what they taught or told lies about them. But Paul plainly recognized their errors for what they were and labeled them appropriately. He spoke the truth. In his everyday teaching style, Paul spoke the truth gently and with the patience of a tender father. But when circumstances warranted a stronger type of candor, Paul could speak very bluntly—sometimes even with raw sarcasm (1 Cor. 4:8–10). He could also employ derision effectively and appropriately, to highlight the ridiculousness of serious error (Gal. 5:12).

Paul didn't seem to suffer from the same overscrupulous angst that causes so many people today to whitewash every error as much as language permits; to grant even the grossest of false teachers the benefit of every doubt; and to impute the best possible intentions even to the rankest of heretics. The apostle's idea of "gentleness" was not the sort of faux benevolence and artificial politeness people today sometimes think is the true essence of charity. We never once see him inviting false teachers or casual dabblers in religious error to dialogue. Paul drew the boundaries of godly amiability and Christian hospitality pretty much where the apostle John did. When false teachers seek refuge under the umbrella of your fellowship, John said, don't give them the time of day.

When have you been tempted to sugarcoat spiritual error?

The Jesus You Can't Ignore, xxiii–xxxiv

Why Jesus Spoke Harshly

You search the Scriptures, for in them you think you have eternal life; and these are they which testify of Me. But you are not willing to come to Me that you may have life.

John 5:39–40

John 5 is an example of Jesus' candid straightforwardness.

Jesus is not doing any bridge building with the religious establishment here; He is upbraiding them, and none too gently. Rather than tiptoeing around their well-known religious sensibilities and trying to avoid offense, He portrays them as utterly unregenerate, spiritually lifeless men (v. 40). And He drives His point home repeatedly, with some of the sharpest words possible: "You do not have His word abiding in you" (v. 38); "You do not have the love of God in you" (v. 42); "You do not believe" (vv. 38, 47).

On the other hand, Jesus is not trying to provoke them merely for sport. He had a gracious reason for using the kind of harsh speech many today would unthinkingly label ungracious: "I say these things that you may be saved," He told them (v. 34). The religious leaders of Israel were lost and progressively hardening their hearts against Jesus. They *needed* some harsh words. He would not permit them to ignore Him, or to ignore His truth, under the guise of showing them the kind of deference and public honor they craved from Him.

Might Jesus have averted all further conflict with the Sanhedrin simply by toning down His message a little and holding a cordial colloquy with the Jewish council right here?

Perhaps.

But the cause of truth would not have been served by that, and the price of compromise with Israel's religious elite would have been the loss of redemption for all sinners. So Jesus was in fact showing the utmost righteousness and grace, even though He was deliberately provoking them.

How have you been tempted to compromise the truth to avoid conflict?

The Jesus You Can't Ignore, 121–122

The Truth About "Judge Not"

Do not give what is holy to the dogs; nor cast your pearls before swine, lest they trample them under their feet, and turn and tear you in pieces.

MATTHEW 7:6

It is crucial to understand Matthew 7:1 properly. "Judge not, that you be not judged" is not a blanket condemnation of all kinds of judgment—just the hypocritical, superficial, and misguided kinds of judgments the Pharisees made. The context makes clear that this is a call for charity and generosity in the judgments we make: "For with what judgment you judge, you will be judged; and with the same measure you use, it will be measured back to you" (v. 2). It is often necessary to make judgments, and when we do, we must "not judge according to appearance, but judge with righteous judgment" (John 7:24).

Jesus' own words make it clear that He expects us to make discerning judgments, because He goes on to say, "Do not give what is holy to the dogs; nor cast your pearls before swine" (Matt. 7:6). "Swine" and "dogs" in that verse refer to people who are chronically antagonistic to the gospel—those whose predictable response to sacred things is that they will "trample them under their feet, and turn and tear [the messenger] in pieces" (v. 6). Obviously, in order to obey that command, we have to know who the swine and dogs are. So an underlying assumption is that we *must* judge carefully and biblically.

But what is most intriguing here is that Jesus was clearly alluding to the Pharisees and others like them, not to the Gentiles and moral pariahs who were normally labeled "swine" and "dogs" by Israel's religious elite.

When have you seen sacred truths trampled on by people who are hostile to the gospel?

The Jesus You Can't Ignore, 144–145

The Truth About Homosexuality

For this reason God gave them up to vile passions. For even their women exchanged the natural use for what is against nature. Likewise also the men, leaving the natural use of the woman, burned in their lust for one another.

ROMANS 1:26–27

Scripture is clear. The Bible condemns homosexuality in explicit and undeniable terms. The Old Testament law grouped homosexuality with incest, bestiality, and other perversions, and the penalty for its practice was death (Lev. 20:13, cf. vv. 11–16). In Romans 1, Paul clearly teaches that homosexual practices are "indecent acts" (v. 27 NASB), driven by "vile passions" (v. 26). The apostle listed homosexuality with the lowest forms of human degradation: "those who are lawless and rebellious . . . , the ungodly and sinners . . . , the unholy and profane . . . , those who kill their fathers or mothers . . . , murderers and immoral men and *homosexuals* and kidnappers and liars and perjurers, and whatever else is contrary to sound teaching" (1 Tim. 1:9–10 NASB, emphasis added). He wrote, "Do you not know that the unrighteous will not inherit the kingdom of God? Do not be deceived. Neither fornicators, nor idolaters, nor adulterers, nor *homosexuals*, nor sodomites, nor thieves, nor covetous, nor drunkards, nor revilers, nor extortioners will inherit the kingdom of God" (1 Cor. 6:9–10, emphasis added).

Is there no hope for homosexuals? Thankfully, there *is* hope. Those who repent and are reborn in Christ can be freed from the sins that would otherwise destroy them. Immediately after giving that long list of the kinds of people who will not inherit the kingdom, Paul wrote to the Corinthian believers, "*Such were some of you*. But you were washed, but you were sanctified, but you were justified in the name of the Lord Jesus and by the Spirit of our God" (v. 11, emphasis added).

How has God's grace transformed you from shameful behavior?

The Vanishing Conscience, 70–71

Signs of the Love of Money

For the love of money is a root of all kinds of evil, for which some have strayed from the faith in their greediness, and pierced themselves through with many sorrows.

1 TIMOTHY 6:10

When a person is a lover of money, one or more of the following danger signs will often appear. First, the person will be bent on making money any way possible. He may have little regard for using only honest means or working hard. Christians, on the other hand, will strive to work honestly and with diligent excellence, knowing that God may reward them with abundant earnings, but that He is not so obligated.

Second, a person is a lover of money if he never seems to have enough. But the one freed from such enslavement will agree with Paul, "I have learned to be content in whatever circumstances I am" (Phil. 4:11 NASB).

Third, if someone loves money, he will likely flaunt it. He derives inordinate pleasure in showing off his luxury purchases—and today many of those likely were made with an overextended credit card.

Fourth, lovers of money usually hate to give it to others, no matter how much those people might need it. And if they give any money at all, it is usually a small amount given with the intent of bringing them some honor.

The final red flag, closely related to the first one, is that people who love money are often willing to sin to acquire more or keep as much as they can of what they have. They may lie on their tax returns, pad their expense accounts, or steal from their workplace. They are willing to compromise their principles for riches, which reveals a heart that loves money more than God, righteousness, and truth.

Which of these signs, if any, do you see in your own life?

Whose Money Is It Anyway? 23–24

Holy Hatred of Sin

"There is no peace," says the Lord, "for the wicked."

Isaiah 48:22

We desperately need to recover a holy hatred of sin. We need to do this corporately as a church, but we also need to do it individually as believers. Sin is surely not a pleasant subject to study or preach on, but it is necessary. Here in the midst of an increasingly worldly church it is *critical*. We must see our sin for what it is. An inadequate view of one's own sinfulness is spiritually debilitating. Those who don't see themselves as despicably sinful will never take the necessary steps to lay sin aside.

God has clearly indicted us for our own sin and assigned full responsibility to each individual sinner. The proof of that is the biblical doctrine of hell—the awful reality that each damned and unforgiven sinner will pay forever in hell the terrible price for his or her own sins. In no way can this guilt be escaped by blaming others. Clearly, God does not see us as a race of victims! If He saw us as victims, He would punish someone else. But every condemned sinner will pay the full price in eternal torment for his or her own deeds—because each one is fully responsible.

No one's conscience will be silent then. It will turn on the sinner with a fury, reminding him that he alone is responsible for the agonies he will suffer eternally.

If you find your conscience vanishing, you must realize the seriousness of your condition and repent; beseech God for a clear, functioning conscience; and set yourself to the task of laying aside sin in your own life.

In what areas of your life have you treated your sin too lightly?

The Vanishing Conscience, 204–205

Fighting for the Truth and Love

I know your works, your labor, your patience, and that you cannot bear those who are evil. And you have tested those who say they are apostles and are not, and have found them liars . . . Nevertheless I have this against you, that you have left your first love.

Revelation 2:2, 4

Truth is under heavy attack, and there are too few courageous warriors who are willing to fight. When we stand before the judgment seat of Christ, believers from this generation will not be able to justify their apathy by complaining that the strife of conflict over truth just seemed "too negative" for the kind of culture we lived in—or that the issues were "merely doctrinal" and therefore not worth the effort.

Remember, Christ rebuked the churches in Revelation 2–3 that had tolerated false teachers in their midst (2:14–16, 20–23). He expressly *commended* the Ephesian church for examining the claims of certain false apostles and exposing them as liars (Rev. 2:2). Churches have a clear duty to guard the faith against false teachers who infiltrate. Christ Himself demands it.

At the same time, we need to notice carefully that a polemical defense of the faith by no means guarantees a healthy church, much less a healthy individual Christian. Christ also *rebuked* the doctrinally sound Ephesians for departing from their first love (Rev. 2:4). As vital as it is for us to enlist in the Truth War and do battle for our faith, it is even more important to remember why we are fighting—not merely for the thrill of vanquishing some foe or winning some argument, but out of a genuine love for Christ, who is the living, breathing embodiment of all that we hold true and worth fighting for.

What can you do to inspire others to defend the truth with both courage and love?

The Truth War, xxvi–xxvii

You Are Not of the World

I have given them Your word; and the world has hated them because they are not of the world, just as I am not of the world.

JOHN 17:14

The world rejects Jesus' disciples because they are no longer a part of its system. Jesus told the apostles, "If you were of the world, the world would love its own. Yet because you are not of the world, but I chose you out of the world, therefore the world hates you" (John 15:19). "World" is the English translation of *kosmos*, a common word in Greek. Here it means the evil, sinful system begun by Satan and acted out by men. The *kosmos* is the result and expression of human depravity. It is set against Christ, His people, and His kingdom, and Satan and his evil minions control it.

This evil world system is incapable of genuine love. When Jesus said the world loves its own, He was saying that a worldly individual loves himself and his own things. He loves others only if it is to his advantage. The world's love is always selfish and superficial.

The world sets itself against those who love and follow Jesus, those who declare their faith in Him and show it by their words and deeds. It does not generally persecute those who are part of its system. Jesus said to His earthly brothers who did not follow Him during His ministry, "The world cannot hate you, but it hates Me because I testify of it that its works are evil" (John 7:7).

The unavoidable fact is that people who don't know Jesus Christ are part of a system that is anti-God, anti-Christ, and satanic. That system fights against God and His principles and is opposed to all that is good, godly, and Christlike.

How have you responded to people who fight against God in this way?

Welcome to the Family, 69–70

Watch Over Your Heart

Would not God search this out? For He knows the secrets of the heart.

Psalm 44:21

It is relatively easy to confess and forsake deeds of sin, sins of omission, and unintentional sin. But the sins of our thought life are soul-coloring sins, character-damaging sins. Because they work so directly against the conscience and will, dealing with them honestly and thoroughly is one of the most difficult aspects of mortifying our sin. If we ever want to see real progress in sanctification, however, this is an area where we must attack and destroy our sinful habits with a vengeance. If we allow our thoughts to be influenced by the values of the world, our conscience will surely be dulled. Listening to and entertaining the claims of bad theologies or the self-esteem credo of modern psychology will surely deaden the conscience. Not only thoughts about lust, envy, and the other traditional sins, but also thoughts about the myriad false values and idols of an unbelieving world can be devastating obstacles to a pure mind.

The Old Testament sage wrote, "Watch over your heart with all diligence, for from it flow the springs of life" (Prov. 4:23 NASB).

David wrote, "You understand my thought afar off . . . and are acquainted with all my ways. For there is not a word on my tongue, but behold, O Lord, You know it altogether" (Ps. 139:2–4). Why, then, would we ever feel free to indulge in gross sins in our imagination—sins we would never act out before others—when we know that God is the audience to our thoughts?

What areas of your thought life need to be purified?

The Vanishing Conscience, 185

Consideration Is Key

Therefore, as the elect of God, holy and beloved, put on tender mercies, kindness, humility, meekness, longsuffering.

COLOSSIANS 3:12

Paul tells believers that they should be "showing all humility to all men" (Titus 3:2). The word rendered *humility*, probably more clearly translated *consideration* (as in the NASB), always has a New Testament meaning of genuine concern for others.

Scripture clearly describes Jesus as the One supremely characterized by humility, or consideration for everyone—the same trait that should identify His followers. First, the Greek translation of Zechariah 9:9 portrays Him that way: "He is just and having salvation, lowly and riding on a donkey, a colt, the foal of a donkey" (see also Matt. 11:29; 21:5).

All our dealings with unbelievers should display this kind of attitude, as the apostle Peter wrote, "Sanctify the Lord God in your hearts, and always be ready to give a defense to everyone who asks you a reason for the hope that is in you, with meekness and fear" (1 Peter 3:15).

Therefore it is understandable that *consideration* is one aspect of the fruit of the Spirit (translated again as "gentleness" in Galatians 5:23).

Sincere, heartfelt "humility [consideration, meekness, gentleness] to all men" is foundational for our Christian walk in a pagan society. Our duty as we relate to an increasingly secular and ungodly culture is not to lobby for certain rights, the implementation of a Christian agenda, or the reformation of the government. Rather, God would have us continually to remember Paul's instructions to Titus and live them out as we seek to demonstrate His power and grace that can regenerate sinners.

What does this attitude of consideration look like?

Why Government Can't Save You, 134–135

A True Perspective

Who is a God like You, pardoning iniquity and passing over the transgression of the remnant of His heritage? He does not retain His anger forever, because He delights in mercy.

MICAH 7:18

It's vital to see the parable of the prodigal son as much as possible through the eyes of someone in the culture of first-century Judaism. To them, the idea that God would freely accept and forgive repentant sinners (including the very worst of them) was a shocking and revolutionary concept. That's why Christ's practice of immediately receiving such people into His fellowship was such a public scandal. Almost no one in that society could conceive of God as reaching out to sinners. Most thought His only attitude toward sinners was stern disapproval, and it was therefore the repentant sinner's duty to work hard to redeem himself and do his best (mainly through legal obedience) to gain whatever degree of divine favor he could earn.

In our culture, the tendency usually goes to the opposite extreme. Too many people today take God's forgiveness for granted. They think of Him as so unconcerned about sin that things such as redemption, atonement, and the wrath of God are unsophisticated, crude, outmoded concepts.

Both perspectives are seriously deficient. God *is* angry over sin (Ps. 7:11), and He *will* punish evildoers with extreme severity (Isa. 13:9–13). Scripture is clear about that. But at the same time, God is "full of compassion, and gracious, longsuffering and abundant in mercy and truth" (Ps. 86:15). He is eager to forgive, and He loves mercy (Ex. 34:6–7; Mic. 7:18). More important, His forgiveness is not conditioned on something we do to earn it. He justifies fully and freely because of what Christ has done for sinners.

Where in your life have you been either unaware of grace or too lenient on your own sin?

A Tale of Two Sons, 20–21

Commitment to Love

Jesus said to him, "'You shall love the LORD your God with all your heart, with all your soul, and with all your mind.' This is the first and great commandment. And the second is like it: 'You shall love your neighbor as yourself.' On these two commandments hang all the Law and the Prophets."

MATTHEW 22:37–40

Loving your neighbor as yourself involves the same virtue as loving the Lord with all your being; there's no difference in sincerity, commitment, or dedication. It is by choice—intentional and active—not merely sentimental and emotional. And it is measured, Jesus said, by love for "yourself."

If you're hungry, you feed yourself; when you're thirsty, you get a drink; and when you're sick, you take medicine or see a doctor—all because you are consumed with caring for *yourself*. You don't just think or talk about what you need; if you have the power to meet your needs you meet them. A Christian looks out for others with the same level of attention and effort.

This dual command sums up the basic requirement of Judaism as well as Christianity: to love God and to love your fellow man. Jesus said that everything God required of believers in both the Old and New Testaments is based on them.

When a person comes to Christ, he must count the cost of becoming a Christian. He needs to know there is a commitment to obedience, to the law of God, and to love God and His people. So the command to love ought to be clear from the beginning because it is part of the covenant of obedience you take when you become a Christian: you will obey the lordship of Jesus Christ, and that means you will love the brethren. God will work in you so your obedience is not burdensome and your love won't be forced or superficial.

How can you be more loving toward your "neighbor"?

Welcome to the Family, 57–58, 60–61

MARCH

THE CROSS AND EASTER

The Ultimate Example of Obedience

Imitate me, just as I also imitate Christ.

1 CORINTHIANS 11:1

Though we can't obey God perfectly, we can and do try to pattern our lives after the one Person in history who could obey with perfection—Jesus Christ. He shows you by example what to do if you will only follow Him.

First John 2:6 tells us, "He who says he abides in Him ought himself also to walk just as He walked." John used the word *abides* to mean "knowing Him," "walking in the light," and "being in fellowship." All those terms indicate salvation. The point is that if you declare yourself to be a Christian, you ought to show a pattern of walking in the same manner as He walked. That doesn't mean your life will be exactly like His, but you will walk with a desire to please God as He did.

Philippians 2:8 says of Jesus: "Being found in appearance as a man, He humbled Himself and became obedient to the point of death, even the death of the cross." Jesus was in the form of God, but He did not insist on hanging on to that glory and privilege. Instead, He was willing to temporarily set them aside and humble Himself. That is the greatest illustration of humility ever. Jesus said, "I have come down from heaven, not to do My own will, but the will of Him who sent Me" (John 6:38). His entire attitude was marked by a spirit of obedience. And that is the pattern of loving obedience we are to imitate. Obedience to Christ and His Word is the ultimate proof of the reality of your love for Him.

What can you do this week to follow Jesus' example more closely?

Welcome to the Family, 19–20

A Truth to Be Remembered

And walk in love, as Christ also has loved us and given Himself for us, an offering and a sacrifice to God for a sweet-smelling aroma.

EPHESIANS 5:2

Every true Christian knows that Christ died for our sins. That truth is so rich that only eternity will reveal its full profundity. But in the mundane existence of our daily lives, we are too inclined to take the Cross of Christ for granted. We mistakenly think of it as one of the elementary facts of our faith. We therefore neglect to meditate on this truth of all truths, and we miss the real richness of it. If we think of it at all, we tend to dabble too much in the shallow end of the pool, when we ought to be immersing ourselves in its depths daily. Many wrongly think of Christ as merely a victim of human injustice, a martyr who suffered tragically and unnecessarily. But the truth is that His death was God's plan. In fact, it was the key to God's eternal plan of redemption. Far from being an unnecessary tragedy, the death of Christ was a glorious victory—the most gracious and wonderful act of divine benevolence ever rendered on behalf of sinners. It is the consummate expression of God's love for them.

Yet here also we see the wrath of God against sin. What is too often missed in all our songs and sermons about the Cross is that it was the outpouring of divine judgment against the person of Christ—not because He deserved that judgment, but because He bore it on behalf of those whom He would redeem. In the words of Isaac Watts, "Did e'er such love and sorrow meet, or thorns compose so rich a crown?"

How has your appreciation for Christ changed as you've reflected on His death?

The Murder of Jesus, xiv–xv

Our True Substitute

For He made Him who knew no sin to be sin for us, that we might become the righteousness of God in Him.

2 CORINTHIANS 5:21

Everything Scripture says about Christ's role as our Savior depends on the fact that He is fully and completely a man. Hebrews 2:17 underscores the point: "In all things He had to be made like His brethren, that He might be a merciful and faithful High Priest in things pertaining to God, to make propitiation for the sins of the people."

Our Lord was not merely playing at being human. He was human in the fullest sense. He took on all our infirmities except for our sin. And in the garden, His humanity manifested itself as clearly as at any time ever in His ministry. We can certainly understand His emotions: horror at the prospect of what God wanted Him to do; consternation over the reality of what that would cost Him; and a very real desire to avoid God's wrath if there was any possible way. All of that contributed to the overwhelming sense of sorrow He was feeling as He anticipated the cross.

In short, Jesus was grieved because He knew that all the guilt of all the sin of all the redeemed of all time would be imputed to Him, and He would bear the full brunt of divine wrath on behalf of others. The holy Son of God who had never known even the most insignificant sin would become sin—an object of God's fury (2 Cor. 5:21). The thought of it literally made Him sweat blood.

How does Jesus' experience in the garden affect the way you face temptation?

The Murder of Jesus, 72–73

The True Passover Lamb

For indeed Christ, our Passover, was sacrificed for us. Therefore let us keep the feast, not with old leaven, nor with the leaven of malice and wickedness, but with the unleavened bread of sincerity and truth.

1 CORINTHIANS 5:7–8

Passover was the first feast of the Jewish calendar, held every year "on the fourteenth day of the first month at twilight" (Lev. 23:5). It was then that every family in Israel commemorated the nation's deliverance from Egypt with the sacrifice of a spotless lamb.

Four days prior to Passover, on 10 Nisan, each family in Israel was to select a spotless sacrificial lamb and separate that lamb from the rest of the herds until Passover, when the lamb was to be slain (Ex. 12:3–6).

Historical records of Jesus' time indicate that as many as a quarter million lambs were slain in a typical Passover season, requiring hundreds of priests to carry out the task. Since all the lambs were killed during a two-hour period just before twilight on 14 Nisan (Ex. 12:6), it would have required about six hundred priests, killing an average of four lambs per minute, to accomplish the task in a single evening.

The amount of blood resulting from all those sacrifices was enormous. The blood was permitted to flow off the steep eastern slope of the temple mount and into the Kidron Valley, where it turned the brook bright crimson for a period of several days. It was a graphic reminder of the awful price of sin.

Of course, all that blood and all those animals could not actually atone for sin (Heb. 10:4). The lambs only symbolized a more perfect sacrifice that God Himself would provide to take away sins. That is why John the Baptist looked beyond those animal sacrifices and pointed to the true "Lamb of God who takes away the sin of the world" (John 1:29).

How are you tempted to gain forgiveness apart from Christ's once-for-all sacrifice?

The Murder of Jesus, 25–27

The Last Supper and Communion

Then He took the cup, and gave thanks, and gave it to them, saying, "Drink from it, all of you. For this is My blood of the new covenant, which is shed for many for the remission of sins."

MATTHEW 26:27–28

At the Last Supper, Christ was already establishing in their minds the theological meaning of His death. He wanted them to understand when they saw Him bleeding and dying at the hands of Roman executioners that He was not a hapless victim of wicked men, but He was sovereignly fulfilling His role as the Lamb of God—the great Passover Lamb—who takes away sin. And in instituting the ordinance as a remembrance of His death, He made the communion cup a perpetual reminder of this truth for all believers of all time. The point was not to impute some magical transubstantiated property to the red fluid (as Roman Catholic theology suggests), but to signify and symbolize His atoning death.

Thus as the last Passover drew to a close, a new ordinance was instituted for the church. And Jesus told the disciples that this would be the last cup He would drink with them until He drank it anew in the Father's kingdom (Matt. 26:29). By saying that, He not only underscored how imminent His departure was, but He also assured them of His return. By implication He also reassured them that they would all be together with Him in that glorious kingdom.

They could not have understood the full import of His words that evening. Only after His death and resurrection did most of these truths become clear to them. They undoubtedly sensed that something momentous was occurring, but they would have been at a loss to explain it that evening.

What thoughts and feelings might you have experienced if you had been among the disciples at the Last Supper?

The Murder of Jesus, 43

True Humility

For I have given you an example, that you should do as I have done to you.

John 13:15

John records that Jesus "rose from supper and laid aside His garments, took a towel and girded Himself. After that, He poured water into a basin and began to wash the disciples' feet, and to wipe them with the towel with which He was girded" (John 13:4–5). Taking the role of the lowest servant, Christ thus transformed the washing ceremony into a graphic lesson about humility and true holiness. He washed the disciples' feet, illustrating that even believers with regenerate hearts need periodic washing from the external defilement of the world.

His act was a model of true humility. Foot washing was a task typically delegated to the lowest slave. Normally in a hired banquet room like this, an attendant would be provided to wash guests' feet when they entered. To omit this detail was considered a gross discourtesy (cf. Luke 7:44). Foot washing was necessary because of the dust and mud and other filth one encountered as a pedestrian on the unpaved roads in and around Jerusalem. But evidently there was no servant to perform the task when Jesus and the disciples arrived at the Upper Room, so instead of humbling themselves to perform such a demeaning task for one another, the disciples had simply left their feet unwashed. Christ's gesture was both a touching act of self-abasement and a subtle rebuke to the disciples (cf. John 13:6–9). It was also a pattern for the kind of humility He expects of all Christians (v. 15; cf. Luke 22:25–26).

Who can you serve with this kind of humility?

The Murder of Jesus, 31–32

The Failure of the Disciples

"Awake, O sword, against My Shepherd, against the Man who is My Companion," says the LORD *of hosts. "Strike the Shepherd, and the sheep will be scattered; then I will turn My hand against the little ones."*

ZECHARIAH 13:7

Some might be tempted to assume that it reflects poorly on Jesus' leadership that all His followers would forsake Him at His arrest. Perhaps that is the very reason all the gospel writers included Jesus' prediction of their denial. Here again we have proof of Jesus' omniscience and His sovereign control over the events that were taking place. It was inexcusable that the disciples were caught off guard. But Jesus knew perfectly what was about to happen. His sovereignty is thus magnified by the weakness of His disciples. His faithfulness is shown in stark contrast to their unfaithfulness. His strength is made perfect in their weakness.

Christ not only knew that the disciples would abandon Him; He also knew that His prediction of their failure would go unheeded. He had already prayed for them, that their faith would not fail (Luke 22:32). And His prayer—like all His prayers—would be answered in God's perfect plan and timing. None of these events were accidental. Everything came to pass exactly as Christ foretold. All of this underscores His absolute sovereignty. Not one event that evening came as a surprise to Him. The actions of His disciples, the actions of Judas, and the actions of the arresting soldiers were all known to Him before they occurred.

Matthew, who wrote as an eyewitness to these events, noted that Jesus Himself foretold the disciples' abandonment as a fulfillment of Old Testament prophecy. When He predicted their failure, He cited Zechariah 13:7. This, like so many details associated with Jesus' crucifixion, "was done that the Scriptures of the prophets might be fulfilled" (Matt. 26:56).

How does Christ respond in the times you lack the courage to stay faithful to Him?

The Murder of Jesus, 54–55

What Judas's Life Teaches Us

Now I pray to God that you do no evil, not that we should appear approved, but that you should do what is honorable.

2 CORINTHIANS 13:7

We can draw some important lessons from the life of Judas. *First*, Judas is a tragic example of lost opportunity. He heard Jesus teach day in and day out for some two years. He could have asked Jesus any question he liked. Yet in the end Judas was damned because of his own failure to heed what he heard.

Second, Judas is the epitome of wasted privilege. He was given the highest place of privilege among all the Lord's followers, but he squandered that privilege—cashed it in for a fistful of coins he decided he did not really want after all. What a stupid bargain!

Third, Judas is the classic illustration of how the love of money is a root of all kinds of evil (1 Tim. 6:10).

Fourth, Judas exemplifies the ugliness and danger of spiritual betrayal. Judas's life is a reminder to each of us about our need for self-examination (cf. 2 Cor. 13:5).

Fifth, Judas is proof of the patient, forbearing goodness and loving-kindness of Christ. "The LORD is good to all, and His tender mercies are over all His works" (Ps. 145:9). He even shows His loving-kindness to a reprobate like Judas. Remember, Jesus was still calling him "Friend," even in the midst of Judas's betrayal.

Sixth, Judas demonstrates how the sovereign will of God cannot be thwarted by any means.

Seventh, Judas is a vivid demonstration of the deceitfulness and fruitlessness of hypocrisy. He is the branch spoken of in John 15:6 that does not abide in the True Vine.

Which of these lessons do you need most right now?

Twelve Ordinary Men, 197–198

The Agony in the Garden

Jesus therefore, knowing all things that would come upon Him, went forward and said to them, "Whom are you seeking?"

JOHN 18:4

When Jesus entered Gethsemane, He knew He would be arrested there and taken through a series of trials and humiliations that would carry Him relentlessly to the cross. In fact, when the apostle John describes the arrival of the soldiers for Jesus' arrest, he records this fact (John 18:4).

Again and again we see that all the Gospel writers deliberately stress Jesus' sovereign omniscience throughout the crucifixion narratives. Their focus never strays far from the fact of His absolute foreknowledge and control of everything that was occurring around Him. All the gospel writers made it clear that Jesus knew "all things that would come upon Him." Nothing that night was accidental. Nothing took Him by surprise. He was fully aware of everything that was happening. Nothing was out of His and the Father's control.

This also means that Jesus understood fully all that His dying would entail. He knew in advance about all the pain and agony and taunting and humiliation He would have to bear. Before He ever set foot in that garden, He knew the awful truth about what He would have to endure. But He was nonetheless prepared to submit Himself completely and unreservedly to the Father's will, in order to accomplish the eternal plan of redemption.

In His prayer that night He grappled with these very issues in the most candid terms. It is one of the most astonishing and mysterious passages in all of Scripture. It reveals His own striving with the terrifying reality of what He was about to endure. Here we have an amazing window into the heart of the God-man.

When has Jesus' sovereign omniscience given you strength to face trials?

The Murder of Jesus, 63

The Prayer of Jesus

He went a little farther and fell on His face, and prayed, saying, "O My Father, if it is possible, let this cup pass from Me; nevertheless, not as I will, but as You will."

Matthew 26:39

When Christ prays, "not as I will, but as You will," we are not to think that there is any disparity between the will of the Father and the will of the Son. Instead, what we see here is the Son consciously, deliberately, voluntarily subjugating all His natural human feelings to the perfect will of the Father. The prayer is the consummate example of how Christ in His humanity always surrendered His will to the will of the Father in all things—precisely so that there would be no conflict between the divine will and His human feelings.

There's a poignant lesson here. Remember that Christ had no sinful appetites, no desires that were perverted by sin, no inclination ever to do wrong. Yet if He needed to submit His appetites and passions to the will of God with such deliberate, purposeful dedication, how much more do we need to be deliberate in surrendering our hearts, our souls, our minds, and our strength to God? All our infirmities, our desires, our appetites, and our very wills must be consciously submitted to the will of God if we expect to be able to live our lives to the glory of God.

Christ's submission to the Father's will was an expression of His eternal love for the Father. As abhorrent and mysterious as it is to think of the Son's dying and the Father's pouring out His wrath on the Son, the underlying purpose of redemption was a pure expression of love between Father and Son. And thus in eternity past the Son willingly, deliberately submitted Himself to the Father's will, and the path to the cross was set.

How do you react to Christ's willing obedience to God in the garden?

The Murder of Jesus, 77–80

No Other Way

[He] has saved us and called us with a holy calling, not according to our works, but according to His own purpose and grace which was given to us in Christ Jesus before time began.

2 TIMOTHY 1:9

Jesus asked to be relieved of the cup only if there were some other way to accomplish the plan of God. God's response to this prayer proves definitively that there was no possible way to achieve the redemption of sinners short of the sacrifice of His own Son. God did not send Christ to die frivolously. If there had been another way, He would have done it. But there was no other way, and that is why the cup did not pass from Christ.

This reveals the mystery of what took place in eternity past between the members of the Godhead. As God the Father and God the Son covenanted together with the Holy Spirit to redeem the elect, it was agreed that Christ would become a man and die to pay the atoning price.

The apostle Paul spoke of this in his epistle to Titus. He opens with these words: "Paul, a bondservant of God and an apostle of Jesus Christ, according to the faith of God's elect and the acknowledgment of the truth which accords with godliness, in hope of eternal life which God, who cannot lie, *promised before time began*" (Titus 1:1–2, emphasis added). If God promised eternal life before time began—before there were any creatures to make such a promise to—to whom did He promise it? It is clear that this describes a covenant that took place between the members of the Godhead for the redemption of the elect.

As His part in the covenant for our redemption, Christ agreed to come to earth for the express purpose of dying as a sacrifice for sin.

How has Christ been faithful to you?

The Murder of Jesus, 77–79

According to the Plan

For truly against Your holy Servant Jesus, whom You anointed, both Herod and Pontius Pilate, with the Gentiles and the people of Israel, were gathered together to do whatever Your hand and Your purpose determined before to be done.

ACTS 4:27–28

Finally having accomplished the evil goal they had so long sought, the members of the Sanhedrin began to vent their satanic hatred of Jesus openly. "They spat in His face and beat Him; and others struck Him with the palms of their hands, saying, 'Prophesy to us, Christ! Who is the one who struck You?'" (Matt. 26:67–68). According to Luke, they blindfolded Him before striking Him and ordering Him to prophesy about who hit Him. Luke adds that there were "many other things they blasphemously spoke against Him" (Luke 22:65).

Christ bore all such abuse with a quiet and majestic grace that is quite remarkable. As always, "when He was reviled, [He] did not revile in return; when He suffered, He did not threaten, but committed Himself to Him who judges righteously" (1 Peter 2:23). He would soon be bearing others' sins; meanwhile He also patiently suffered their hateful abuse.

Isaiah's prophecy, written at least seven hundred years earlier, perfectly described this moment. "He is despised and rejected by men, a Man of sorrows and acquainted with grief. And we hid, as it were, our faces from Him; He was despised, and we did not esteem Him" (Isa. 53:3). Isaiah thus prophetically foretold the whole world's sinful apathy toward Jesus Christ. No one came to His defense. No one spoke in His favor. He was left to bear His affliction all alone.

And thus Christ was unjustly condemned to die. His trial before the Sanhedrin had gone exactly according to Caiaphas's evil plan. At the same time, the plan of God was right on schedule as well.

Why did Jesus suffer abuse patiently?

The Murder of Jesus, 117–118

Two Things Both True

But as for you, you meant evil against me; but God meant it for good, in order to bring it about as it is this day, to save many people alive.

GENESIS 50:20

When Jesus chose Judas, He *knew* Judas would be the one to fulfill the prophecies of betrayal.

And yet Judas was in no sense coerced into doing what he did. No invisible hand forced him to betray Christ. He acted freely and without external compulsion. He was responsible for his own actions. Jesus said he would bear the guilt of his deed throughout eternity. His own greed, his own ambition, and his own wicked desires were the only forces that constrained him to betray Christ.

How do we reconcile the fact that Judas's treachery was prophesied and predetermined with the fact that he acted of his own volition? There is no need to reconcile those two facts. They are not in contradiction. God's plan and Judas's evil deed concurred perfectly. Judas did what he did because his heart was evil. God, who "works all things according to the counsel of His will" (Eph. 1:11), had foreordained that Jesus would be betrayed and that He would die for the sins of the world. Jesus Himself affirmed both truths in Luke 22:22: "Truly the Son of Man goes as it has been determined, but woe to that man by whom He is betrayed!"

God ordained the events by which Christ would die, and yet Judas carried out his evil deed by his own choice, unfettered and uncoerced by any external force. Both things are true. The perfect will of God and the wicked purposes of Judas concurred to bring about Christ's death. Judas did it for evil, but God meant it for good (cf. Gen. 50:20). There is no contradiction.

What good have you seen God bring out of evil circumstances?

Twelve Ordinary Men, 185

Who Killed Jesus?

Then the soldiers of the governor took Jesus into the Praetorium and gathered the whole garrison around Him. . . . And when they had mocked Him, they took the robe off Him, put His own clothes on Him, and led Him away to be crucified.

MATTHEW 27:27, 31

Over the years the Jewish people have usually borne the brunt of the blame. The expression "Christ killers" has often been employed as a racial epithet by misguided zealots and hate-mongers. And sadly, the charge of killing Jesus has frequently been employed to justify everything from hate crimes to holocausts against the Jewish people.

But were the Jews any more culpable than others for Christ's death? Certainly not. It was, after all, Pontius Pilate, a Gentile Roman governor, who sentenced Him to death. And he did so in collusion with Herod Antipas, who (although he bore the title "King of the Jews") was no Jew, but rather an Idumean—a foreign ruler, hated by the Jews, whose throne was granted by Caesar. Furthermore, crucifixion was a Roman method of execution, authorized and carried out by Roman, not Jewish, authorities. Roman soldiers drove the nails through Christ's hands and feet. Roman troops erected the cross (Matt. 27:27–35). A Roman spear pierced His side (John 19:34). Gentile hands therefore played an even more prominent role in the actual murder of Jesus than the Jews did.

In fact, the murder of Jesus was a vast conspiracy involving Rome, Herod, the Gentiles, the Jewish Sanhedrin, and the people of Israel—diverse groups who apart from this event were seldom fully in accord with one another. In fact, it is significant that the crucifixion of Christ is the only historical event where all those factions worked together to achieve a common goal. All were culpable. All bear the guilt together. The Jews as a race were no more or less blameworthy than the Gentiles.

When have you been tempted to cooperate with others to do wrong?

The Murder of Jesus, 3–5

The Truth About Crucifixion

[Thomas] said to them, "Unless I see in His hands the print of the nails, and put my finger into the print of the nails, and put my hand into His side, I will not believe."

JOHN 20:25

Then they crucified Him" (Matt. 27:35). These four words reveal the tremendous pain Jesus endured on the cross.

None of the gospel accounts gives a detailed description of the method used on Him. But we can glean quite a lot of information from the incidental details that are given. From Thomas's remark to the other disciples after the crucifixion we learn that Christ was nailed to the cross, rather than being lashed by leather thongs, as was sometimes done.

We also can glean from secular accounts of crucifixion in Jesus' time some of the details about how crucifixion victims died. Christ would have been nailed to the cross as it lay flat on the ground. The nails used were long, tapered iron spikes, similar to modern railroad spikes, but much sharper. The nails had to be driven through the wrists (not the palms of the hands), because neither the tendons nor the bone structure in the hands could support the body's weight. Nails in the palms would simply tear the flesh between the bones. Nails through the wrists would usually shatter carpal bones and tear the carpal ligaments, but the structure of the wrist was nonetheless strong enough to support the weight of the body. As the nail went into the wrist, it would usually cause severe damage to the sensorimotor median nerve, causing intense pain in both arms. Finally, a single nail would be driven through both feet, sometimes through the Achilles' tendons. None of the nail wounds would be fatal, but they would all cause intense and increasing pain as the victim's time on the cross dragged on.

What would motivate someone to suffer willingly this way for others?

The Murder of Jesus, 198–199

Forgive Them!

Then the word of God spread, and the number of the disciples multiplied greatly in Jerusalem, and a great many of the priests were obedient to the faith.

ACTS 6:7

Luke records that shortly after the cross was raised on Calvary—while the soldiers were still gambling for Jesus' clothing—Jesus prayed to God for forgiveness on their behalf: "And when they had come to the place called Calvary, there they crucified Him, and the criminals, one on the right hand and the other on the left. Then Jesus said, 'Father, forgive them, for they do not know what they do'" (Luke 23:33–34).

Certainly any mortal man would have desired only to curse or revile his killers under these circumstances. One might even think that God incarnate would wish to call down some thunderous blast of judgment against men acting so wickedly. But Christ was on a mission of mercy. He was dying to purchase forgiveness for sins. And even at the very height of His agony, compassion was what filled his heart.

How was Jesus' prayer answered? In innumerable ways. The first answer came with the conversion of one of the thieves on the cross next to Jesus (vv. 40–43). Another followed immediately, with the conversion of a centurion, one of the soldiers who had crucified Christ (v. 47). Other answers to the prayer came in the weeks and months that followed the crucifixion—particularly at Pentecost—as untold numbers of people in Jerusalem were converted to Christ. No doubt many of them were the same people who had clamored for Jesus' death and railed at Him from the foot of the cross. We're told in Acts 6:7, for example, that a great number of the temple priests later confessed Jesus as Lord.

When has God's forgiveness most surprised you?

The Murder of Jesus, 209–211

A Picture of Salvation

Then [the criminal] said to Jesus, "Lord, remember me when You come into Your kingdom." And Jesus said to him, "Assuredly, I say to you, today you will be with Me in Paradise."

LUKE 23:42–43

No sinner was ever given more explicit assurance of salvation. This most unlikely of saints was received immediately and unconditionally into the Savior's kingdom. The incident is one of the greatest biblical illustrations of the truth of justification by faith. This man had done nothing to *merit* salvation. Indeed, he was in no position to do anything meritorious. Already gasping in the throes of his own death agonies, he had no hope of ever earning Christ's favor. But realizing that he was in an utterly hopeless situation, the thief sought only a modest token of mercy from Christ: "Remember me."

Jesus' words to the dying thief conveyed to him an unqualified promise of full forgiveness, covering every evil deed he had ever done. He wasn't expected to atone for his own sins, do penance, or perform any ritual. He wasn't consigned to purgatory—though if there really were such a place, and if the doctrines that invariably accompany belief in purgatory were true, this man would have been assured a long stay there. But instead, his forgiveness was full, and free, and immediate: "Today you will be with Me in Paradise."

How does your experience of coming to Christ compare with the thief's?

The Murder of Jesus, 213–214

Mary and the Cross

Therefore He is also able to save to the uttermost those who come to God through Him, since He always lives to make intercession for them.

Hebrews 7:25

Mary seemed to understand that her steadfast presence at Jesus' side was the only kind of support she could give Him at this dreaded moment. But even that was merely a public show of support. Mary's personal suffering did not represent any kind of participation in His atoning work. Her grief added no merit to His suffering for others' guilt. *He* was bearing the sins of the world. She could not assist with that. Nor did He need her aid as any kind of "co-redemptrix" or "co-mediatrix." "There is one God and one Mediator between God and men, the Man Christ Jesus" (1 Tim. 2:5). Mary herself did not try to intrude into that office.

As a matter of fact, in the waning hours of Jesus' life, it was *Jesus* who came to *her* aid. Already in the final throes of death, He spotted Mary standing nearby with a small group of women and John, the beloved disciple. For the final time, Jesus acknowledged His human relationship with Mary. In his own gospel account, John describes what happened: "When Jesus therefore saw His mother, and the disciple whom He loved standing by, He said to His mother, 'Woman, behold your son!' Then He said to the disciple, 'Behold your mother!' And from that hour that disciple took her to his own home" (John 19:26–27).

So one of Jesus' last earthly acts before yielding up His life to God was to make sure that for the rest of her life, Mary would be cared for.

How would Jesus' compassion from the cross have affected you if you had been in Mary's place?

Twelve Extraordinary Women, 125–126

It Is Finished!

Not that He should offer Himself often, as the high priest enters the Most Holy Place every year with blood of another . . . but now, once at the end of the ages, He has appeared to put away sin by the sacrifice of Himself.

HEBREWS 9:25–26

So when Jesus had received the sour wine, He said, 'It is finished!'" (John 19:30). In the Greek text, "It is finished" is a single word: *Tetelestai*!

It was a triumphant outcry, full of rich meaning. He did not mean merely that His earthly life was over. He meant that the work the Father had given Him to do was now complete. As He hung there, looking every bit like a pathetic, wasted victim, He nonetheless celebrated the greatest triumph in the history of the universe. Christ's atoning work was finished; redemption for sinners was complete; and He was triumphant.

Christ had fulfilled on behalf of sinners everything the law of God required of them. Full atonement had been made. Everything the ceremonial law foreshadowed had been accomplished. God's justice was satisfied. The ransom for sin was paid in full. The wages of sin were settled forever. All that remained was for Christ to die so that He might rise again.

That is why nothing can be added to the work of Christ for salvation. No religious ritual—neither baptism, nor penance, nor any other human work—needs to be added to make His work effectual. No supplemental human works could ever augment or improve the atonement He purchased on the cross. The sinner is required to contribute nothing to earn forgiveness or a right standing with God; the merit of Christ alone is sufficient for our full salvation. *Tetelestai!* His atoning work is done. All of it.

How can you respond when another believer tries to add human effort to Christ's saving work?

The Murder of Jesus, 222–223

The True Meaning of the Cross

For Christ also suffered once for sins, the just for the unjust, that He might bring us to God, being put to death in the flesh but made alive by the Spirit.

1 Peter 3:18

Christ was not merely providing an example for us to follow. He was no mere martyr being sacrificed to the wickedness of the men who crucified Him. He wasn't merely making a public display so that people would see the awfulness of sin. He wasn't offering a ransom price to Satan—or any of the other various explanations religious liberals, cultists, and pseudo-Christian religionists have tried to suggest over the years.

Here's what was happening on the cross: God was punishing His own Son as if He had committed every wicked deed done by every sinner who would ever believe. And He did it so that He could forgive and treat those redeemed ones as if they had lived Christ's perfect life of righteousness.

Scripture teaches this explicitly: "He made Him who knew no sin to be sin for us, that we might become the righteousness of God in Him" (2 Cor. 5:21). "Surely He has borne our griefs and carried our sorrows; yet we esteemed Him stricken, smitten by God, and afflicted. But He was wounded for our transgressions, He was bruised for our iniquities; the chastisement for our peace was upon Him, and by His stripes we are healed" (Isa. 53:4–5). "He had done no violence, nor was any deceit in His mouth. Yet it pleased the Lord to bruise Him; He has put Him to grief . . . [in order to] make His soul an offering for sin" (vv. 9–10).

How would you convey God's punishment of Christ to an unbeliever?

The Murder of Jesus, 219–220

A Death Like No Other

Therefore My Father loves Me, because I lay down My life that I may take it again. No one takes it from Me, but I lay it down of Myself. I have power to lay it down, and I have power to take it again. This command I have received from My Father.

JOHN 10:17–18

Christ died as no other man has ever died. In one sense He was murdered by the hands of wicked men (Acts 2:23). In another sense it was the Father who sent Him to the cross and bruised Him there, putting Him to grief—and it pleased the Father to do so (Isa. 53:10). Yet in still another sense, no one took Christ's life. He gave it up willingly for those whom He loved (John 10:17–18).

When He finally expired on the cross, it was not with a wrenching struggle against His killers. He did not display any frenzied death throes. His final passage into death—like every other aspect of the crucifixion drama—was a deliberate act of His own sovereign will, showing that to the very end, He was sovereignly in control of all that was happening. John says, "Bowing His head, He gave up His spirit" (John 19:30). Quietly, submissively, He simply yielded up His life.

Everything had come to pass exactly as He said it would. Not only Jesus, but also His killers, and the mocking crowd, together with Pilate, Herod, and the Sanhedrin—all had perfectly fulfilled the determined purpose and foreknowledge of God to the letter.

And thus Christ calmly and majestically displayed His utter sovereignty to the end. It seemed to all who loved Him—and even many who cared little for Him—like a supreme tragedy. But it was the greatest moment of victory in the history of redemption, and Christ would make that fact gloriously clear when He burst triumphantly from the grave just days later.

How might Christ's sovereign control over His death strengthen you in your own trials?

The Murder of Jesus, 223–224

The Key to the Resurrection

That I may know Him and the power of His resurrection, and the fellowship of His sufferings, being conformed to His death, if, by any means, I may attain to the resurrection from the dead.

PHILIPPIANS 3:10–11

The Resurrection is one of history's most carefully scrutinized and best-attested facts. The enemies of the gospel from the apostles' day until now have tried desperately to impeach the eyewitness testimony to Jesus' resurrection. They have not been able to do so, nor will they.

Still, it is vital to see that the early church's preaching focused as much on the death of Christ as on His resurrection. Paul wrote, "We preach Christ crucified" (1 Cor. 1:23); "I determined not to know anything among you except Jesus Christ and Him crucified" (2:2); and "God forbid that I should boast except in the cross of our Lord Jesus Christ" (Gal. 6:14).

Why did Paul place so much emphasis on the death of Christ, rather than always stressing the triumph of the resurrection above even His death? Because, again, without the atoning work Christ did on the cross, His resurrection would be merely a wonder to stand back and admire. But it would have no personal ramifications for us. However, "if we died with Christ,"—that is, if He died in our place and in our stead—then "we believe that we shall also live with Him" (Rom. 6:8). Because of the death He died, suffering the penalty of sin on our behalf, we become partakers with Him in His resurrection as well.

So don't ever pass over the meaning of the death of Christ on your way to celebrate the resurrection. It is the cross that gives meaning to the resurrection life.

What can you do regularly to appreciate the meaning of the cross?

The Murder of Jesus, 242

Proof of Jesus' Divinity

He also presented Himself alive [to the apostles] after His suffering by many infallible proofs, being seen by them during forty days and speaking of the things pertaining to the kingdom of God.

Acts 1:3

John 20:26 says that eight days passed after Jesus appeared to the disciples again. Finally Thomas's ragged grief had eased a bit, apparently. Because when the apostles returned to the room where Jesus appeared to them, this time Thomas was with them. Once again, "Jesus came, the doors being shut, and stood in the midst, and said, 'Peace to you!'" (v. 26).

No one needed to tell Jesus what Thomas had said, of course. He looked right at Thomas and said, "Reach your finger here, and look at My hands; and reach your hand here, and put it into My side. Do not be unbelieving, but believing" (v. 27).The Lord was amazingly gentle with him. Thomas had erred because he was more or less wired to be a pessimist. But it was the error of a profound love. It was provoked by grief, brokenheartedness, uncertainty, and the pain of loneliness. No one could feel the way Thomas felt unless he loved Jesus the way Thomas loved Him. So Jesus was tender with him. He understands our weaknesses (Heb. 4:15). So He understands our doubt. He sympathizes with our uncertainty. He is patient with our pessimism. And while recognizing these as weaknesses, we must also acknowledge Thomas's heroic devotion to Christ, which made him understand that it would be better to die than to be separated from his Lord. The proof of his love was the profoundness of his despair.

Then Thomas made what was probably the greatest statement ever to come from the lips of the apostles: "My Lord and my God!" (John 20:28). Let those who question the deity of Christ meet Thomas.

When has Jesus shown patience with your doubts?

Twelve Ordinary Men, 163–164

The Message of the Cross

But we preach Christ crucified, to the Jews a stumbling block and to the Greeks foolishness, but to those who are called, both Jews and Greeks, Christ the power of God and the wisdom of God.

1 CORINTHIANS 1:23–24

What Paul was saying in 1 Corinthians was that the gospel collides with our emotions; it collides with our minds; it collides with our relationships. It smashes into our sensibilities, our rational thinking, and our tolerances. It's hard to believe.

The cross in itself proclaims a verdict on fallen man. The cross says that God requires death for sin, while it proclaims to us the glory of substitution. It rescues the perishing. The perishing are the damned, the doomed, the ruined, the destroyed; they are the lost, under the judgment of God for endless violations of His holy law. And if you and I don't embrace the substitute, then we bear that death ourselves, and that is a death that lasts forever.

The message of the cross is not about felt needs. It is not about Jesus loving you so much He wants to make you happy. It is about rescuing you from damnation, because that is the sentence that rests upon the head of every human being. And so the gospel is an offense every way you look at it. There's nothing about the cross that fits in comfortably with how man views himself.

The gospel confronts man and exposes him for what he really is. It ignores the disappointment that he feels. It offers him no relief from the struggles of being human. Rather it goes to the profound and eternal issue of the fact that he is damned and desperately needs to be rescued. Only death can accomplish rescue, but God, in His mercy, has provided a Substitute.

How do you respond to this message?

Hard to Believe, 33

God's Sovereignty in the Cross

Yet it pleased the LORD to bruise Him; He has put Him to grief. When You make His soul an offering for sin, He shall see His seed, He shall prolong His days, and the pleasure of the LORD shall prosper in His hand.

ISAIAH 53:10

For all the evil in the crucifixion, it brought about an infinite good. In fact, here was the most evil act ever perpetrated by sinful hearts: the sinless Son of God—holy God Himself in human flesh—was unjustly killed after being subjected to the most horrific tortures that could be devised by wicked minds. It was the evil of all evils, the worst deed human depravity could ever devise, and the most vile evil that has ever been committed. And yet from it came the greatest good of all time—the redemption of unnumbered souls, and the demonstration of the glory of God as Savior. Though the murderers meant evil against Christ, God meant it for good, in order to save many (cf. Gen. 50:20).

The cross is therefore the ultimate proof of the utter sovereignty of God. His purposes are always fulfilled in spite of the evil intentions of sinners. God even works His righteousness through the evil acts of unrighteous agents. Far from making Him culpable for their evil, this demonstrates how all He does is good, and how He is able to work all things together for good (Rom. 8:28)—even the most wicked deed the powers of evil have ever conspired to carry out.

Furthermore, if God was sovereignly in control when the unlawful hands of murderous men put His beloved Son on a cross, why would anyone balk at the notion that God is still sovereignly in control even when lesser evils occur? The cross, therefore, establishes God's absolute sovereignty beyond question.

From what difficult situations in your life is God bringing good?

The Murder of Jesus, 7–8

False Methods of Atonement

Therefore by the deeds of the law no flesh will be justified in His sight, for by the law is the knowledge of sin.

ROMANS 3:20

It is quite true that sin *must* be atoned for. Don't imagine for a moment that when God forgives sin, He simply looks the other way and pretends the sin never occurred. Moses' law was filled with bloody sacrifices precisely to make that truth inescapable.

The Pharisees' misunderstanding about what is required to make full atonement for sin lay at the root of their errant theology.

They were convinced sinners needed to do good works to help atone for their own sins. They had even enshrined their own intricate system of finely detailed traditions as the *chief* means by which they thought it possible to acquire the kind of merit they believed would balance out the guilt of sin. That is why they were obsessed with ostentatious works, religious rituals, spiritual stunts, ceremonial displays of righteousness, and other external and cosmetic achievements.

Here was the problem with that: even *authentically* good works could never accomplish what the Pharisees hoped their ceremonial traditions would accomplish. That was made perfectly clear by the Law itself. The Law demanded no less than absolute perfection (Matt. 5:19, 48; James 2:10). And it was filled from start to finish with threats and curses against anyone who violated it at any point. The reason we need atonement is that we are fallen sinners who *cannot* keep the Law adequately.

In fact, the Law itself made perfectly clear that the price of full atonement was more costly than any mere human could ever possibly pay: "The soul who sins shall die" (Ezek. 18:4).

Where have you used religious behavior to cover up sin and appear righteous?

A Tale of Two Sons, 119–120

Purchased by Christ

For the law of the Spirit of life in Christ Jesus has made me free from the law of sin and death.

ROMANS 8:2

The Son of God came so "that through death He might render powerless him who had the power of death, that is, the devil, and might free those who through fear of death were subject to slavery all their lives" (Heb. 2:14–15 NASB).

The glorious theme of redemption—that believers were purchased by our Lord through His death—echoes throughout the New Testament. But unlike the slaves of Roman times, we "were not redeemed with perishable things like silver or gold from [our] futile way of life" (1 Peter 1:18 NASB), nor were we redeemed through "the blood of goats and calves" (Heb. 9:12). Rather, our redemption is Jesus Christ Himself, who in death "gave Himself for us, that He might redeem us from every lawless deed and purify for Himself His own special people, zealous for good deeds" (Titus 2:14). Now, as His possession, we who were formerly slaves to sin are slaves of a new Lord and Master.

Our redemption in Christ results in both *freedom* from sin and *forgiveness* for sin. Not only are we liberated from bondage to our former master; we are also exempt from sin's deadly consequences—namely, the eternal wrath of God. As Paul exclaimed in Romans 8:1–2 (NASB), "Therefore there is now no condemnation for those who are in Christ Jesus. For the law of the Spirit of life in Christ Jesus has set you free from the law of sin and of death." Because we are in Him, all of our sins—past, present, and future—have been "forgiven [us] for His name's sake" (1 John 2:12).

How have you experienced freedom from sin because of the death of Christ?

Slave, 138–139

March 28

The Blood of Jesus

And according to the law almost all things are purified with blood, and without shedding of blood there is no remission.

Hebrews 9:22

There is, unfortunately, much superstition and misunderstanding about the significance of Christ's blood. One popular book written several years ago by a well-known evangelical author suggests that there was something unique about the chemistry of Christ's blood. He surmised that Christ's blood was not human blood. Instead, he said, the blood coursing through Jesus' veins was the blood of God.

Other Christians have misconstrued familiar songs about the blood of Christ (such as "There Is Power in the Blood" or "There Is a Fountain Filled with Blood"). They imagine that there is some supernatural property in Christ's blood that makes it spiritually powerful. A few even suppose that the literal blood of Christ is applied by some mystical means to each believer at conversion, and then collected again so that it can be perpetually applied and reapplied. And many people believe that just mentioning the blood of Christ is a powerful means of stifling demonic activity—like a Christian abracadabra. Fanciful ideas such as those spring from the same superstitious thinking that spawned the notion of transubstantiation.

When the Scriptures say we are redeemed by Christ's blood, we are not to think that His plasma or corpuscles have some supernatural property. His blood was normal human blood, just as His entire body was fully human in every aspect. The "power in the blood" that we sing about lies in the atonement He wrought by the shedding of His blood, not in the actual fluid itself.

So when the Bible speaks about the blood of Christ, it uses the expression as a metonymy for His atoning death.

How would you explain the meaning of Christ's blood to someone who misunderstood it?

The Murder of Jesus, 41–42

Hoping in Truth

Let us therefore come boldly to the throne of grace, that we may obtain mercy and find grace to help in time of need.

Hebrews 4:16

"This hope we have as an anchor of the soul, both sure and steadfast, and which enters the Presence behind the veil, where the forerunner has entered for us, even Jesus" (Heb. 6:19–20). Our hope as Christians is solid and unshakable, embodied in Christ Himself, who has entered into God's presence in the heavenly Holy of Holies on our behalf (Heb. 4:14–16).

In his first epistle, the apostle Peter offered further evidence of the security of our hope: "Blessed be the God and Father of our Lord Jesus Christ, who according to His abundant mercy has begotten us again to a living hope through the resurrection of Jesus Christ from the dead" (1:3). Our hope is based on the resurrection of Christ. On the contrary, "if Christ is not risen, your faith is futile; you are still in your sins" (1 Cor. 15:17). The resurrection is the crown of Christ's atoning work. By His death and resurrection, He bore our sins, satisfied the righteousness of God, conquered death, and guaranteed us a living hope in the next life. Those riches are ours through a spiritual rebirth in Him.

Even though our hope is in the future, it is guaranteed now. For us, future glory is a present fact. That's why we will persevere while we wait eagerly for our glorification. No matter what trials and struggles we encounter while we wait, we can be sure God will fulfill His calling of us and bring us to glory.

How would you encourage a fellow believer whose hope was faltering?

Welcome to the Family, 114–116

The True Gospel

And when they had preached the gospel to that city and made many disciples, they returned . . . exhorting them to continue in the faith, and saying, "We must through many tribulations enter the kingdom of God."

ACTS 14:21–22

The true gospel is a call to self-denial. It is not a call to self-fulfillment. And that puts it in opposition to the contemporary evangelical gospel, where ministers view Jesus as a utilitarian genie. You rub the lamp, and He jumps out and says you have whatever you want; you give Him your list and He delivers.

Jesus said it unmistakably and inescapably, "If anyone desires to come after Me, let him deny himself, and take up his cross, and follow Me. For whoever desires to save his life will lose it, and whoever loses his life for My sake will find it" (Matt. 16:24–25). It's not about exalting me, it's about *slaying* me. It's the death of self. You win by losing; you live by dying. And that is the heart message of the gospel. That is the essence of discipleship.

The passage mentions nothing about improving your self-esteem, being rich and successful, feeling good about yourself, or having your felt needs met, which is what so many churches are preaching these days in order to sugarcoat the truth.

So who's right? Is the message of Christianity self-fulfillment, or is it self-denial? It can't be both. If it's just a matter of opinion, I'll do my thing and you do yours, and we'll both cruise contentedly along in separate directions. But Christianity, the genuine gospel of Jesus Christ, is not a matter of opinion. It is a matter of truth. What you want, or I want, or anybody else wants, makes no difference whatsoever. It is what it is—by God's sovereign will.

What areas of self-fulfillment do you need to give up to follow Jesus more closely?

Hard to Believe, 3–6

A Truth Hard to Find and Hard to Swallow

I also count all things loss for the excellence of the knowledge of Christ Jesus my Lord, for whom I have suffered the loss of all things, and count them as rubbish, that I may gain Christ.

Philippians 3:8

Because narrow is the gate," Jesus said in Matthew 7:14, "and difficult is the way which leads to life, and there are few who find it." I agree that we have a hard time finding it, especially today. You could go to church after church after church and never find it. It's a very narrow gate.

The same teaching appears in Luke 13:23–24: "Then one said to Him, 'Lord, are there few who are saved?' And He said to them, 'Strive to enter through the narrow gate, for many, I say to you, will seek to enter and will not be able.'" It's hard to find, and it's hard to get through.

Why is it so hard to find today, and why is it so hard to get through? It's hard to find because so many churches have strayed from teaching the truth of the gospel. And it's even harder, once we've heard the truth, to submit to it. Man worships himself. He's his own god. What we need to tell people is not "Come to Christ and you'll feel better about yourself," or "Jesus wants to meet whatever your needs are." Jesus doesn't want to meet our felt needs—our worldly, earthly, human desires. He wants us to be willing to say, "I will abandon all the things I think I need for the sake of Christ."

It's hard to get through the narrow gate because it's so hard for us to deny ourselves.

When have you found it hard to swallow Christ's command to deny yourself for His sake?

Hard to Believe, 14

APRIL

GROWING AS A CHRISTIAN

Knowledge Is Essential

My people are destroyed for lack of knowledge.

HOSEA 4:6

It is popular in some circles to denigrate knowledge and elevate passion, mysticism, brotherly love, blind faith, or whatever. Christian doctrine is often set against practical Christianity, as if the two were antithetical. Truth is ignored and harmony exalted. Knowledge is scorned while feeling is elevated. Reason is rejected and sentiment put in its place. That eats away at genuine spiritual maturity, which is always grounded in sound doctrine (cf. Titus 1:6–9).

Knowledge alone is no virtue, of course. If someone "knows to do good, and does not do it, to him it is sin" (James 4:17). Knowledge without love corrupts the character: "Knowledge puffs up, but love edifies" (1 Cor. 8:1).

But *lack* of knowledge is even more deadly. Hosea recorded the Lord's complaint against Israel's spiritual leaders: "My people are destroyed for lack of knowledge. Because you have rejected knowledge, I also will reject you from being My priest. Since you have forgotten the law of your God, I also will forget your children" (Hos. 4:6 NASB).

All spiritual growth is based on *knowledge of truth*. Sound doctrine is crucial to a successful spiritual walk (Titus 2:1, ff.). Paul told the Colossians that the new self is renewed to true knowledge (Col. 3:10). Knowledge is foundational to our new position in Christ. The entire Christian life is established on knowledge of divine principles, sound doctrine, and biblical truth. Those who repudiate knowledge in effect jettison the most basic means of spiritual growth and health, while leaving themselves vulnerable to a host of spiritual enemies.

In what ways have you gained a knowledge of truth?

The Vanishing Conscience, 214–215

The Only Way to Know the Truth

But the Helper, the Holy Spirit, whom the Father will send in My name, He will teach you all things, and bring to your remembrance all things that I said to you.

John 14:26

We'll never know the deep, saving, spiritual truths of God unless someone reveals them to us. As 1 Corinthians 2:11 says, "No one knows the things of God except the Spirit of God." Paul added in verse 12, "Now we have received, not the spirit of the world, but the Spirit who is from God, that we might know the things that have been freely given to us by God." Those things are forgiveness of sin, salvation, and the hope of eternal life, as well as all the blessings of justification, sanctification, glorification. We can't know them by human reason. We can't find them in a test-tube experiment. We can't figure them out by rationalization. We can know them only through the revelation of the Holy Spirit.

You can't go to heaven unless you know how, and you can't know how except by reading the Bible. That's the only place where men wrote down words the Holy Spirit inspired. All Scripture is given by inspiration of God. Peter described the process: "holy men of God spoke as they were moved by the Holy Spirit" (2 Peter 1:21).

You can't understand the things of God on your own, any more than Adam and Eve could, because you can appraise the essence of the Lord and Creator of the universe only through the power and revelation of the Holy Spirit. Without the Spirit, there is no knowledge. But for those of us whom the Holy Spirit has taught through the Scriptures, we have what 1 Corinthians 2:16 calls "the mind of Christ."

We can know what Christ thinks because the Scriptures reveal it.

How has the knowledge that you have access to the mind of Christ aided you?

Hard to Believe, 203–204

Delighting in God's Law

Unless Your law had been my delight, I would then have perished in my affliction.

PSALM 119:92

Paul delighted in God's law (Rom. 7:22). Emanating from the depths of his soul, Paul had a great love for the law of God. His inner man, the part that "is being renewed day by day" (2 Cor. 4:16) and "strengthened with might through [God's] Spirit" (Eph. 3:16), resonated with God's law.

The author of Psalm 119 also had a deep longing for the things of God. Here are some sample expressions of the psalmist's desire for God's law:

- Verses 81–83: "My soul faints for Your salvation, but I hope in Your word. My eyes fail from searching Your word, saying, 'When will You comfort me?' For I have become like a wineskin in smoke, yet I do not forget Your statutes."
- Verse 92: "Unless Your law had been my delight, I would then have perished in my affliction."
- Verse 97: "O how I love Your law! It is my meditation all the day."
- Verse 113: "I hate the double-minded, but I love Your law."
- Verse 131: "I opened my mouth and panted, for I longed for Your commandments."
- Verse 143: "Trouble and anguish have overtaken me; yet Your commandments are my delights."
- Verse 163: "I hate and despise lying, but I love Your law."
- Verse 165: "Great peace have those who love Your law, and nothing causes them to stumble."
- Verse 174: "I long for Your salvation, O LORD, and Your law is my delight."

How have you shown your delight in God's law?

The Gospel According to the Apostles, 136–137

Surrender Is the Key

Whoever desires to come after Me, let him deny himself, and take up his cross, and follow Me.

Mark 8:34

We can't know Jesus as the Messiah until we surrender to Him. I couldn't know Him as my Savior until I gave up my life to Him. Then I knew. Parading an infinite number of miracles in front of me wouldn't have proved anything. Miracles are beside the point. You will never know whether Jesus can save your soul from hell, give you new life, re-create your soul, plant His Holy Spirit there, forgive your sin, and take you to heaven until you give your life totally to Him. That is self-denial, cross bearing, and following Him in obedience.

There's only one reason why people who know the truth of the gospel are not willing to repent and believe. It is because they will not see themselves as the poor, prisoners, blind, and oppressed. It has nothing to do with the style of music your church offers, the drama and skits you stage, or the quality of your laser light show. It has everything to do with the spiritual deadness and blindness of pride. God offers nothing to people who are content with their own condition, except judgment. If you don't think you are headed for hell, don't think you need forgiveness, you put no value on the gospel of grace.

You can't preach salvation, lead anyone to salvation, or be saved yourself unless you're willing to be humiliated and recognize your sinful condition. Again, it's that matter of self-denial, isn't it?

What do you find most challenging about self-denial?

Hard to Believe, 67–69

The Only Thing of True Value

Then Jesus, looking at him, loved him, and said to him, "One thing you lack: Go your way, sell whatever you have and give to the poor, and you will have treasure in heaven; and come, take up the cross, and follow Me."

MARK 10:21

The heart and soul of the Christian life is our love for Christ. Our salvation begins with Him, our sanctification progresses with Him, and our glorification ends with Him. He is the reason for our being, and thus He is more precious to us than anyone or anything.

Paul knew well that the heart of the Christian life is building an intimate knowledge of Christ when he said, "I count all things to be loss in view of the surpassing value of knowing Christ Jesus my Lord (Phil. 3:8 NASB). That was both his passion and his goal (v. 14).

The essence of salvation is an exchange of something worthless for something valuable. That's what happens to those whom God chooses to bring into His kingdom. The person who comes to God is willing to give up whatever He requires, no matter how high the price. When confronted with his sin in light of the glory of Christ—when God takes the blinders off of his eyes—the repentant sinner suddenly realizes that nothing he held dear is worth keeping if it means losing Christ.

At some point in your life, you discovered that Jesus Christ was far more valuable than anything you had. All possessions, fame, and desires became worthless compared to Christ. So you trashed all and turned to Him as your Savior and Lord. He became the supreme object of your affections. Your new desire is to know Him, to honor Him, serve Him, obey Him, and be like Him.

Is there anything you're tempted to cling to more than God? Why or why not?

Welcome to the Family, 9–10

The Desire for Truth

O God, You are my God; early will I seek You; my soul thirsts for You; my flesh longs for You in a dry and thirsty land where there is no water.

PSALM 63:1

Every Christian should want to grow in his relationship to God—to become more Christlike in character. We don't want to be limited in our Christian experience. We want to grow and enjoy the fullness of spiritual life. But that can happen only through daily intake of God's Word. The apostle Peter described the attitude we should have toward our growth through the Bible: "As newborn babes, desire the pure milk of the word, that you may grow thereby" (1 Peter 2:2).

In the Greek, the term translated "long for" refers to intense, recurring craving, the way babies crave milk. They don't care if it's from a bottle or directly from Mom, what color their room is, or even what time of day it is—they want milk and if they don't get it soon enough, they scream and cry. Believers should have that same kind of single-minded craving for the Word of God.

Peter did not say "read the Bible," or "study" it, or "meditate on it"; he said *desire* it. That's what Paul called "the love of the truth" (2 Thess. 2:10). In effect, it produces an attitude in your heart that says, "I want the Word more than I want anything else."

Our desire must be just as strong. Consider the passion for truth outlined in Proverbs 2:1–6. If you seek divine truth as earnestly as some people search after material riches, you will find it, because God has made it available.

In what ways have your actions reflected the passionate desire mentioned above?

Welcome to the Family, 34–35

Growing Out of Immaturity

Solid food belongs to those who are of full age, that is, those who by reason of use have their senses exercised to discern both good and evil.

Hebrews 5:14

The tendency to stall in a state of immaturity also existed in New Testament times. Paul appeals repeatedly to Christians to grow up spiritually. In Ephesians 4:14–15, he writes, "We should no longer be children, tossed to and fro and carried about with every wind of doctrine, by the trickery of men, in the cunning craftiness of deceitful plotting, but, speaking the truth in love, may *grow up* in all things into Him who is the head—Christ" (emphasis added).

How do we grow spiritually? By "speaking the truth in love" to one another. We grow under the truth. It is the same truth by which we are sanctified, conformed to the image of Christ, made to be mature spiritually (John 17:17, 19). As we absorb the truth of God's Word, we grow up and are built up. We might say accurately that the process of spiritual growth is a process of training for discernment.

Hebrews 5:12–6:1 underscores all this.

The writer of Hebrews is telling his readers, "You're babies. You've been around long enough to be teachers, but instead I have to feed you milk. I have to keep giving you elementary things. You can't take solid food. You're not accustomed to the rich things of the Word—and that is tragic."

Notice that in verse 14 (NASB) he says that discernment and maturity go hand in hand: "Solid food is for the mature, who because of practice have their senses trained to discern good and evil." Knowing and understanding the Word of righteousness—taking in solid food—trains your senses to discern good and evil.

What are you doing to grow to spiritual maturity?

The Truth War, 212–213

Purified by Trials

My brethren, count it all joy when you fall into various trials, knowing that the testing of your faith produces patience.

JAMES 1:2–3

While Jesus was inside the high priest's house on trial for His life, Peter, too, was facing the trial of his life, but in a different sense. Satan was sifting him like wheat (Luke 22:31). The imagery of that expression refers to the violent shaking of a tray of grain, which causes the chaff to be thrown into the air and blown away with the wind, leaving behind pure kernels of grain.

God often permits us to be tested by various trials. The purifying process that results is essential—and for true believers, it is always ultimately beneficial (James 1:2–4). But the violent shaking required for the sifting process is inherently unsettling and often quite painful. In fact, as far as Peter was concerned, the pain of the purifying process was more analogous to the fiery heat of the smelter's crucible than the shaking of a tray of wheat. Years later, Peter would encourage others in the midst of the refiner's fire: "You greatly rejoice, though now for a little while, if need be, you have been grieved by various trials, that the genuineness of your faith, being much more precious than gold that perishes, though it is tested by fire, may be found to praise, honor, and glory at the revelation of Jesus Christ" (1 Peter 1:6–7).

Peter's trial certainly purified his faith—even despite his horrible failure. In years to come the memory of that awful night (and his subsequent restoration by a forgiving Master) would no doubt embolden him to face more and even greater trials without ever again denying Christ. In fact, Peter would ultimately forfeit his very life for Christ's sake.

How has your faith been tested over the years?

The Murder of Jesus, 121–122

Producing True Fruit

I am the true vine, and My Father is the vinedresser.

John 15:1

The vine-and-branches concept is an ideal metaphor for the Christian life. As a branch is nothing apart from the vine, so we can do nothing apart from Christ. A branch draws all of its strength from the vine, and we become strong by drawing from His strength.

In John 15, Christ is the Vine and the Father is the Vinedresser. The Father prunes the fruit-bearing branches to make them bear more fruit, removing and burning the fruitless branches so that the fruitfulness of the vine is increased. The branches that abide in the Vine—those who are truly in Christ—are blessed; they grow and bear fruit, and the Father lovingly tends them.

Don't even think you can bear spiritual fruit alone. In nature, a branch can bear no fruit apart from its vine. Even the strongest branches, cut off from the vine, become more helpless than the weakest. Similarly, spiritual fruit bearing is not a matter of being strong or weak, good or bad, brave or cowardly, clever or foolish, experienced or inexperienced.

To bear genuine fruit, you must get as close to the true Vine, our Lord Jesus Christ, as you can. Strip away all the things of the world. Put aside the sins that distract you and sap your energy, and everything that robs you of a deep, personal, loving relationship with Jesus. Stay in God's Word. Having done that, don't worry about bearing fruit. It is not your concern. Get close to Jesus Christ, and His energy in you will produce fruit.

What spiritual fruit has the Holy Spirit produced in your life?

Welcome to the Family, 77–78

True Growth Is Gradual

Sanctify them by Your truth. Your word is truth.

John 17:17

The Bible clearly teaches that you can never attain such sinless perfection in this life. Proverbs 20:9 challenges us: "Who can say, 'I have made my heart clean, I am pure from my sin'?" The apostle John affirmed, "If we say that we have no sin, we deceive ourselves, and the truth is not in us" (1 John 1:8). Sanctification is never complete in this lifetime—that will happen only when we are glorified.

The word *sanctify* comes from the Hebrew and Greek words that mean "set apart." To be sanctified is to be set apart from sin. At conversion, all believers are released from sin's penalty and set apart unto God. Yet the process of separation from the power of sin in your life has just begun. As you grow in Christ, you become further separated from the influence of sin and more consecrated to God. The sanctification that takes place at conversion initiates a lifelong process of distancing yourself further and further from sin and coming gradually and steadily more into conformity with Christlike righteousness.

The more you become like Christ, the more sensitive you are to the remaining corruptions of the flesh. As you mature in godliness, your sins become both more painful and more obvious. The more you put away sin, the more you will notice sinful tendencies you need to eliminate. That is the paradox of sanctification: the holier you become, the more frustrated you will be by the stubborn remnants of your sin.

What changes to your routine or habits have you noticed as a result of the sanctification process?

Welcome to the Family, 38–39

Sanctification Is Never Complete in This Life

But we all, with unveiled face, beholding as in a mirror the glory of the Lord, are being transformed into the same image from glory to glory, just as by the Spirit of the Lord.

2 CORINTHIANS 3:18

Sanctification is a process by which God—working in believers through the Holy Spirit—gradually moves them toward Christlikeness (2 Cor. 3:18). The process of sanctification hones the believer's conscience and keeps it from vanishing. The transformation is gradual, not instantaneous—and never complete in this lifetime.

"For we all stumble in many ways. If anyone does not stumble in what he says, he is a perfect man, able to bridle the whole body as well" (James 3:2 NASB). "For the flesh sets its desire against the Spirit, and the Spirit against the flesh; for these are in opposition to one another, so that you may not do the things that you please" (Gal. 5:17 NASB).

Sanctification is therefore never complete in this lifetime. In heaven alone are the spirits of righteous people made perfect (Heb. 12:23). And at the return of Christ, "when He is revealed, we shall be like Him, for we shall see Him as He is" (1 John 3:2). "We ourselves groan within ourselves, eagerly waiting for the adoption, the redemption of our body" (Rom. 8:23). Those verses describe *glorification*, the immediate and instantaneous completion of our sanctification.

Have you ever believed that you can attain sinless perfection in this lifetime? Why or why not?

The Vanishing Conscience, 129–130

Neither Content nor Perfect

I find then a law, that evil is present with me, the one who wills to do good. For I delight in the law of God according to the inward man.

ROMANS 7:21–22

Maturing Christians never become self-justifying, smug, or satisfied with their progress. They do not pursue self-esteem; they seek instead to deal with their sin. And the more we become like Christ, the more sensitive we are to the remaining corruptions of the flesh. The apostle Paul vividly described his own anguish over this reality in Romans 7:21–24. Romans 7 poses a number of difficult challenges for Bible interpreters, but surely the most difficult question of all is how Paul could say those things *after* he wrote in chapter 6, "Our old self was crucified with Him, in order that our body of sin might be done away with, so that we would no longer be slaves to sin; for he who has died is freed from sin" (Rom. 6:6–7 NASB).

These are vital truths for the Christian to understand. They hold the formula for a healthy spiritual walk, and they give much practical insight into how we should battle sin in our own lives. In Paul's own imagery, dying with Christ (justification) and living with Christ (sanctification) are both necessary results of true faith. Those who think grace makes holiness optional are tragically deceived. Those who think they have experienced all the sanctification they need are equally deluded. Those who think self-esteem is more important than holiness are blind to the truth. If we would know God's principles for dealing with sin, we must understand that it is a life-and-death struggle to the end. To be content with good feelings about oneself is to be content with sin.

How do you keep a balance between a knowledge of sinfulness and the knowledge of grace?

The Vanishing Conscience, 133–134

Reckon the Truth

But God, who is rich in mercy, because of His great love with which He loved us, even when we were dead in trespasses, made us alive together with Christ.

Ephesians 2:4–5

Paul tells us, "Reckon . . . yourselves to be dead indeed unto sin, but alive unto God through Jesus Christ our Lord" (Rom. 6:11 KJV).

Reckoning in this sense goes beyond knowledge. It moves our faith out of the realm of the purely intellectual and makes it supremely practical. Paul is suggesting that our union with Christ ought to be something more than a theoretical truth. We are to count on it, deem it a reality, consider it done—and act accordingly.

Reckoning our old self dead is certainly not an easy thing. So much in our experience seems to argue against the truth we know in our hearts. We may be free from sin's dominion, but our daily battle with sin often seems very much like the old slavery. Nevertheless, we must reckon ourselves dead to sin but alive to God. We cannot live as if the old self were still in control.

It may seem at this point that Paul's advice has something in common with the ideology of the modern "positive thinking" and self-esteem cults. But Paul was not proposing that we play a mere mind game. He was not saying we should seek to convince ourselves of something that is not true.

On the contrary, he was affirming the absolute truth of the believer's union with Christ, and assuring us that we can live our lives in light of that truth. Our old self *is* dead. God's Word declares it. We must regard it as true.

What challenges have you faced in your reckoning your old self dead?

The Vanishing Conscience, 216–217

What Not to Remember

Brethren, I do not count myself to have apprehended; but one thing I do, forgetting those things which are behind and reaching forward to those things which are ahead.

Philippians 3:13

To bring back a lurid memory of a bygone sin is to repeat the sin all over again. Can someone who is truly repentant about a sin still harvest pleasure from the memory of that deed? The answer is yes, because of the deceitfulness of our own hearts and the sinful tendencies of our flesh.

The truth is, we all know what that is like. Sin has a way of impressing itself on our memories with vivid sensations we cannot shake off. As adults we can still remember the sins of our youth as if they occurred only yesterday. Perhaps it was just such thoughts that prompted David to pray, "Do not remember the sins of my youth nor my transgressions" (Ps. 25:7). David himself remembered them all too graphically.

Don't think this problem is unique to sexual sins. Some people like to rehearse memories of the time they got angry and poured out vengeance on someone. Some enjoy thoughts of the time they lied and got away with it. All kinds of tempting memories lodge themselves in us and become new sins every time we remember them with pleasure.

Savoring memories of one's past sin is a particularly heinous form of sin. In Ezekiel 23, the Lord condemned Israel by comparing the nation to a harlot named Oholibah. This was His charge against her: "She multiplied her harlotries, remembering the days of her youth, when she played the harlot in the land of Egypt" (v. 19 NASB).

Satan will take all the garbage out of your past and try to drag it back through your mind so that you relive it.

When are you most tempted to "savor" memories of your past?

The Vanishing Conscience, 188–189

Paying Taxes Is a Christian Duty

Let every soul be subject to the governing authorities. For there is no authority except from God, and the authorities that exist are appointed by God.

Romans 13:1

In Romans 13:7, Paul summarizes the Christian's obligation to human government by enumerating several particulars involved in the tax-paying process and the spirit in which it should be done. "Render therefore to all their due: taxes to whom taxes are due, customs to whom customs, fear to whom fear, honor to whom honor."

First of all, the apostle reinforces Jesus' teaching in Matthew 22:21. Christians have both the moral and spiritual responsibility to pay taxes because that's what God requires of them. Anybody who dodges taxes or underreports what he or she owes is sinning against God as well as committing a crime against their government.

Paul is again referring to the onerous combination of income taxes and property taxes that Rome demanded. The point is simply that believers must pay the variety of taxes (high and low) that might be due to various government officials and agencies. For us that might also involve the willing payment of such regular levies as the sales tax, utility taxes, in some countries the value-added tax, and assorted other occasional and onetime taxes (automobile, capital gains, inheritance).

And he instructs us that such true respect must be accompanied by a sincere honor, or esteem. The respect and honor we pay to those who collect our taxes must be of the highest quality. Just because the whole process of filing and paying taxes (and enduring large withholdings from your paycheck) may be burdensome and distasteful, there is still absolutely no place for a hypocritical or cynical attitude toward our tax officials.

How would you describe your attitude toward the payment of taxes?

Why Government Can't Save You, 63–64

True and False Repentance

For godly sorrow produces repentance leading to salvation, not to be regretted; but the sorrow of the world produces death.

2 Corinthians 7:10

Tears of repentance can in no way atone for sins. (Only Jesus' death can do that.) But genuine sorrow is nonetheless an important sign of true repentance, signifying that a change of mind and heart have truly taken place.

Not all sorrow signifies true repentance, however. "Godly sorrow produces repentance leading to salvation, not to be regretted; but the sorrow of the world produces death" (2 Cor. 7:10). Judas was remorseful over what he had done and tried to return the blood money to the ruling priests (Matt. 27:3–5). His guilt over what he had done finally even motivated him to go out and kill himself. But that kind of sorrow is a worldly sorrow that only leads to death. It may involve sincere remorse over the consequences of one's sin—regret over the loss of prestige or friends or influence. But it reflects no true change of heart, and thus no true grief over the sin itself.

Peter's sorrow was of a different sort. He "wept bitterly" (Matt. 26:75). It was the deepest possible sorrow of heart—mingled with shame over his sinful behavior, hatred of the sin itself, and a desperate longing to be restored to a right relationship with Christ.

Peter's repentance was certainly genuine. He never again denied Christ.

The marvelous way Peter was forgiven and restored by Christ is proof of the thoroughness of Peter's repentance. He never forgot the bitterness of his denial, and thus he never again returned to that sin.

When has "godly sorrow" produced repentance in your life?

The Murder of Jesus, 137–139

Pointless Penance

For such a High Priest was fitting for us . . . who does not need daily, as those high priests, to offer up sacrifices, first for His own sins and then for the people's, for this He did once for all when He offered up Himself.

Hebrews 7:26–27

Let's make an important distinction between self-denial and penance. Self-denial is giving up creature comforts to work toward a worthy goal. Penance is self-punishment in hopes of earning God's favor, which is absolutely, 100 percent impossible—and 100 percent unnecessary. No one can be good enough, or make himself feel bad enough, to earn his way into heaven. But no one has to, because Jesus paid the full price of entry on behalf of all true Christians.

Even so, history gives many, many gruesome examples of tragically misguided penitents. Saint Assepsumas thought he could rid himself of sin through self-inflicted pain, and he wore so many chains that he had to crawl around on his hands and knees.

Agnes de Roucher was the only daughter of one of the wealthiest merchants in Paris, and all the neighborhood admired her beauty and virtue. Her father died, leaving her his entire estate. She determined to become a recluse and spend the remainder of her days in a narrow cell built within the wall of a church. The bishop of Paris, attended by his chaplains and the canons of Notre Dame, entered the cell and celebrated a pontifical mass. Then, after the poor thing had bidden adieu to her friends and relations, Agnes ordered the masons to fill up the opening except for a small hole so she could watch and hear the offices of the church. She was eighteen when she went in and died at age eighty, never having come out. In all that time, no one ever told her Jesus was the key to redemption.

Have you had a tendency toward self-denial or penance? Explain.

Hard to Believe, 145–146

How the Gospel Grows

We have renounced the hidden things of shame, not walking in craftiness nor handling the word of God deceitfully, but by manifestation of the truth commending ourselves to every man's conscience in the sight of God.

2 CORINTHIANS 4:2

The gospel is hard to believe, and the people who bring it to the world are nobodies. The plan is still the same for all who are God's clay pots. Here is Paul's humble, five-point strategy (from 2 Cor. 4): We will not lose heart. We will not alter the message. We will not manipulate the results, because we understand that a profound spiritual reality is at work in those who do not believe. We will not expect popularity, and therefore, we will not be disappointed. And we will not be concerned with visible and earthly success but devote our efforts toward that which is unseen and eternal.

In 2 Corinthians 4:6–7, Paul wrote, "For it is the God who commanded light to shine out of darkness who has shone in our hearts to give the light of the knowledge of the glory of God in the face of Jesus Christ. But we have this treasure in earthen vessels, that the excellence of the power may be of God and not of us." At the end of the day there is no human explanation for the growth of the church. The world thinks we're odd and bizarre. We're the losers. We're the privy pots. And yet, through the mouths of Paul and other misfits across the centuries, the church inexplicably moves in the history of the world with immense power beyond anything else. The gospel alone turns sinners into saints by transplanting men and women from the kingdom of darkness into the kingdom of God's dear Son.

In what ways have you devoted your efforts toward that which is unseen and eternal?

Hard to Believe, 50–51

The Hard Words of Jesus

For whoever desires to save his life will lose it, but whoever loses his life for My sake will save it. For what profit is it to a man if he gains the whole world, and is himself destroyed or lost?

LUKE 9:24–25

Luke 9 cuts to the core of the question of what Christianity is all about. Here, Jesus was with His disciples shortly after miraculously feeding a crowd of five thousand, who had come to hear Him speak, with one modest basket of loaves and fishes. In Luke 9:23–26 we read:

> Then He said to them all, "If anyone desires to come after Me, let him deny himself, and take up his cross daily, and follow Me. For whoever desires to save his life will lose it, but whoever loses his life for My sake will save it. For what profit is it to a man if he gains the whole world, and is himself destroyed or lost? For whoever is ashamed of Me and My words, of him the Son of Man will be ashamed when He comes in His own glory, and in His Father's, and of the holy angels."

It's pretty simple. Anyone who wants to come after Jesus into the kingdom of God—anyone who wants to be a Christian—has to face three commands: 1) deny himself, 2) take up his cross daily, and 3) follow Him. These words are hard to believe. They're not consumer-friendly or seeker-sensitive. Christianity Lite is nowhere to be found. But this is not an obscure passage, or something different from other teachings of Jesus. These are principles that He taught consistently and repeatedly throughout His ministry, over and over again in all different settings.

What does "losing your life for the sake of Christ" look like in your life?

Hard to Believe, 6

No Carry-Ons

Because narrow is the gate and difficult is the way which leads to life, and there are few who find it.

MATTHEW 7:14

You can't go through a turnstile with baggage. To get through the narrow gate that leads to heaven, you leave all your possessions behind and enter empty-handed. It's not the gate of the self-contented, who want to carry all their stuff in with them; it's the gate of the self-denying, who strip off all self-righteousness and self-reliance.

The rich young ruler made it to the gate and asked Jesus what he had to do to enter the kingdom. The Lord told him to drop his matched set of Gucci luggage and come on through. He had found the gate that few people ever find, but he refused to enter because he was too selfish and self-centered to make the sacrifice Jesus asked of him.

The point here is wonderfully expressed in Matthew 18:3, where Jesus says, "Unless you are converted and become as little children, you will by no means enter the kingdom of heaven." The distinctive mark of children is that they are utterly dependent on others and have achieved nothing of merit themselves. As the hymn writer puts it, "Nothing in my hand I bring, simply to Thy cross I cling." Saving faith is more than an act of the mind; it is a disdain for one's sinful self, an admission of unworthiness, a naked plea: "Lord, be merciful to me, a sinner!" Jesus called for a narrow, difficult, radical, dramatic admission of sinfulness; an acknowledgment that we are nothing and have nothing with which to commend ourselves to God. Faith begins when we throw ourselves on His mercy for forgiveness.

How would you explain the value of the "narrow" way to a non-believer?

Hard to Believe, 85–86

The Need for Self-Examination

Examine yourselves as to whether you are in the faith. Test yourselves. Do you not know yourselves, that Jesus Christ is in you?—unless indeed you are disqualified.

2 CORINTHIANS 13:5

We can't take someone's initial positive response to the gospel as absolute assurance that they're saved; nor should we be too quick to dismiss a person's uncertainty or discourage self-examination. The Holy Spirit alone gives genuine assurance: "The Spirit Himself bears witness with our spirit that we are children of God" (Rom. 8:16). Don't usurp His role in someone's life. Don't let false assurance overrule His convicting work.

People can be deceived about their salvation if they fail at self-examination. They get into such a mind-set, one that says everything is grace and forgiveness, that they never really bother to face their sin. They hear somebody say, "You don't have to confess your sin; your sin's already forgiven! Don't worry about that. Just go on and live your life!" It is a kind of antinomianism, an attitude of being against or indifferent to the law of God.

The Lord brings us to His communion table over and over again in order that each professing Christian may examine himself. Second Corinthians 13:5 says, "Examine yourselves as to whether you are in the faith. Test yourselves. Do you not know yourselves, that Jesus Christ is in you?—unless indeed you are disqualified." You need to look at your sin and your motivation for doing what you do. Believe me, if you are genuinely saved, God will confirm that by His Spirit witnessing with your spirit. Raising your hand or walking the aisle has nothing to do with it.

How do you think the Holy Spirit would describe your walk with Christ?

Hard to Believe, 96–97

Confessing with Our Lives

But He will say, "I tell you I do not know you, where you are from. Depart from Me, all you workers of iniquity."

LUKE 13:27

Not everyone who confesses Jesus is going to enter the kingdom of heaven, because not all who confess have been doing the will of the Father. In Matthew 7:23 the Lord made a confession, *homologeo*, of His own: "I never knew you." What a shock! They were banging on the door, saying, "Lord, Lord," and He responded, "Go away, I don't know you."

Of course He *knows* them; He knows everything. This isn't a matter of awareness or recognition. The word *know* in the Bible is used to characterize an intimate personal relationship. For example, in Amos 3:2, God said of Israel, "You only have I known of all the families of the earth." That doesn't mean the only people He knew about were Jews, but that He had an intimate relationship with just them.

The Old Testament says, "Cain knew his wife," and she bore a son (see Gen. 4:17). That doesn't mean he knew who she was, or he knew her name; it means he knew her in the intimate act of marriage. When Mary was pregnant with our Lord, as the divine seed was infused by the Spirit of God, the Bible says Joseph was shocked because he had never "known her" (see Matt. 1:25).

Jesus sends away those who falsely claim to know Him because they "practice lawlessness" (Matt. 7:23). Instead of doing the will of God, and living by these righteous principles Jesus explained in the Sermon on the Mount, they live sinfully. It isn't what you *say* that proves the reality of your faith; it's what you *do*.

In what ways does your life prove the reality of your faith?

Hard to Believe, 103

Dead to Sin

For the death that He died, He died to sin once for all;
but the life that He lives, He lives to God.

Romans 6:10

Christians have died to sin. It is therefore inconceivable to Paul that we might continue to live in the sin from which we were delivered by death. Only a corrupt mind using perverted logic could argue that continuing in sin magnifies God's grace. It is self-evident that death terminates life; it is equally obvious that death to sin must end a life of unbroken transgression.

"Died to sin" speaks of a historical fact referring to our death in the death of Christ. Because we are "in Christ" (Rom. 6:11; 8:1), and He died in our place (Rom. 5:6–8), we are counted dead with Him. We are therefore dead to sin's penalty and dominion. Death is permanent. Death and life are incompatible. So the person who has died to sin cannot continue living in iniquity. Certainly we can commit sins, but we do not live anymore in the dimension of sin and under sin's rule (cf. Rom. 8:2–4). It is not merely that we *should not* continue to live in unbroken sin but that we *cannot*.

The phrase "we who died to sin" does not describe an advanced class of Christians. Paul is speaking here of all believers. His point is that a justified life must be a sanctified life. Practical holiness is as much God's work as any other element of redemption. When we are born again, God not only declares us righteous, but He also begins to cultivate righteousness in our lives. There is no such thing as a true convert to Christ who is justified but who is not being sanctified.

What do you find most challenging about the notion of "dying to sin"?

The Gospel According to the Apostles, 113–114

The True Intent of the Law

Now to him who works, the wages are not counted as grace but as debt.

ROMANS 4:4

The Law was not revealed to Moses until more than half a millennium *after* Abraham lived. Abraham clearly did not become righteous by means of the Law (Rom. 4:13–15).

Justification has never been through ritual *or* law. God's law "is holy, and the commandment holy and righteous and good" (Rom. 7:12; cf. Gal. 3:21). But the Law has never been a means of salvation. "For as many as are of the works of the Law," that is, seek to justify themselves on the basis of keeping the Law, "are under a curse; for it is written, 'Cursed is everyone who does not abide by all things written in the book of the law, to perform them'" (Gal. 3:10 NASB). The Law demands perfection. But the only way to obtain perfect righteousness is by imputation—that is, being justified by faith.

The purpose of the Law was to reveal God's perfect standards of righteousness. At the same time, it sets a standard that is impossible for sinful humans to live up to. That should show us our need for a Savior and drive us to God in faith. Thus the Law is a "tutor to bring us to Christ, that we might be justified by faith" (Gal. 3:24).

God has never recognized any righteousness but the righteousness of faith. The Law cannot save because the Law only brings wrath. The more someone seeks justification through the Law, the more that person proves his or her sinfulness, and the more judgment and wrath is debited to that person's account (cf. Rom. 4:4).

How do you guard against a legalistic attitude toward the Law?

The Gospel According to the Apostles, 102–103

Do the Word!

For as the body without the spirit is dead, so faith without works is dead also.

James 2:26

For if anyone is a hearer of the word and not a doer, he is like a man who looks at his natural face in a mirror; for once he has looked at himself and gone away, he has immediately forgotten what kind of person he was. But one who looks intently at the perfect law, the law of liberty, and abides by it, not having become a forgetful hearer but an effectual doer, this man will be blessed in what he does" (James 1:23–25 NASB).

James is illustrating *the urgency of actively obeying the Word*. If you don't deal with what you see while you are looking into the mirror, you will forget about it later. By Monday morning you may forget the impact of Sunday's sermon. By this afternoon, this morning's readings might be a dim memory. If you do not make the necessary responses while God is convicting your heart, you will probably not get around to it.

Even more pointedly, James is illustrating *the utter uselessness of passively receiving the Word*. Verse 21 spoke of how we are to receive the Word. The conjunction *but* at the beginning of verse 22 is equivalent to *moreover*, or *now*, implying that what follows is not a contrast but an amplification of the command in verse 21. In other words, James is saying it is wonderful to be receptive to the Word—to hear with approval and agreement—but that is not enough. We must receive it as those who would be doers.

How do you demonstrate an active obedience of the Word?

The Gospel According to the Apostles, 144–145

Affirming the Same Truth

Now to Him who is able to establish you according to my gospel and the preaching of Jesus Christ, according to the revelation of the mystery kept secret since the world began . . . be glory.

Romans 16:25, 27

James is not at odds with Paul. In James 1:17–18, James affirms that salvation is a gift bestowed according to the sovereign will of God. Later, he stresses the importance of faith's fruit—the righteous behavior that genuine faith always produces. Paul, too, saw righteous works as the necessary proof of faith.

Those who imagine a discrepancy between James and Paul rarely observe that it was Paul who wrote, "Shall we sin because we are not under law but under grace? May it never be!" (Rom. 6:15 NASB); and "Having been freed from sin, you became slaves of righteousness" (v. 18 NASB). Thus Paul condemns the same error James is exposing here. Paul never advocated any concept of dormant faith.

James and Paul both echo Jesus' preaching. Paul represents the beginning of the Sermon on the Mount (Matt. 5:3); James the end of it (Matt. 7:21). Paul declares that we are saved by faith *without the deeds of the Law*. James declares that we are saved by faith, *which shows itself in works*. Both James and Paul view good works as the proof of faith—not the path to salvation.

James could not be more explicit. He is confronting the concept of a passive, false "faith," which is devoid of the fruits of salvation. He is not arguing for works in addition to or apart from faith. He is showing why and how true, living faith always works. He is fighting against dead orthodoxy and its tendency to abuse grace.

In the past week or month, how have your good works "proven" your faith?

The Gospel According to the Apostles, 153–154

A Weak Conscience

Receive one who is weak in the faith, but not to disputes over doubtful things.

ROMANS 14:1

Scripture indicates that some Christians have weak consciences. A weak conscience is not the same as a seared conscience. A seared conscience becomes inactive, silent, rarely accusing, insensitive to sin. But the weakened conscience usually is hypersensitive and overactive about issues that are not sins. Ironically, a weak conscience is more likely to accuse than a strong conscience. Scripture calls this a weak conscience because it is *too easily wounded*. People with weak consciences tend to fret about things that should provoke no guilt in a mature Christian who knows God's truth.

A weak and constantly accusing conscience is a spiritual liability, not a strength. Many people with especially tender consciences tend to display their overscrupulousness as if it were proof of deep spirituality. It is precisely the opposite. Those with weak consciences tend to be too easily offended and stumble frequently (cf. 1 Cor. 8:13). They are often overly critical of others (Rom. 14:3–4). They are too susceptible to the lure of legalism (Rom. 14:20; cf. Gal. 3:2–5).

Throughout Paul's discussion of those with weak consciences (Rom. 14; 1 Cor. 8–10), he treats the condition as a state of spiritual immaturity—a lack of knowledge (1 Cor. 8:7) and a lack of faith (Rom. 14:1, 23). Paul clearly expected that those with weak consciences would grow out of that immature state, like children inevitably outgrow their fear of the dark. True spiritual growth enlightens the mind and strengthens the heart in faith. It is ultimately the only way to overcome a weak conscience.

How would you encourage someone with a weak conscience?

The Vanishing Conscience, 44–47

Educating Your Conscience

For when Gentiles, who do not have the law, by nature do the things in the law, these, although not having the law, are a law to themselves, who show the work of the law written in their hearts, their conscience also bearing witness.

Romans 2:14–15

If your conscience is too easily wounded, don't violate it; to do so is to train yourself to override conviction, and that will lead to overriding true conviction about real sin. Moreover, violating the conscience is a sin in itself (1 Cor. 8:12, cf. Rom. 14:23). Instead, immerse your conscience in God's Word so it can begin to function with reliable data.

An important aspect of educating the conscience is teaching it to focus on the right object—divinely revealed truth. If the conscience looks only to personal feelings, it can accuse us wrongfully. We are certainly not to order our lives according to our feelings. A conscience fixed on feelings becomes unreliable. Individuals subject to depression and melancholy especially should not allow their conscience to be informed by their feelings. Despondent feelings will provoke unnecessary doubts and fears in the soul when not kept in check by a well-advised conscience. The conscience must be persuaded by God's Word, not by our feelings.

Furthermore, conscience errs when the mind focuses wholly on our faltering in sin and ignores the triumphs of God's grace in us. True Christians experience both realities. Conscience must be allowed to weigh the fruit of the Spirit in our lives as well as the remnants of our sinful flesh. Otherwise the conscience will become overly accusing, prone to unwholesome doubts about our standing before God.

We must subject our conscience to the truth of God and the teaching of Scripture. As we do that, the conscience will be more clearly focused and better able to give us reliable feedback.

What steps have you taken to educate your conscience?

The Vanishing Conscience, 49

Jesus Alone, Not Jesus + Anything

For by grace you have been saved through faith, and that not of yourselves; it is the gift of God, not of works, lest anyone should boast.

Ephesians 2:8–9

Nevertheless even among the rulers many believed in Him, but because of the Pharisees they did not confess Him, lest they should be put out of the synagogue; for they loved the praise of men more than the praise of God" (John 12:42–43). Were they genuine believers—regenerate men—or was their "faith" of the spurious, temporary, nonredemptive kind?

Whatever the nature of their "belief," they still were concerned more about their membership in the synagogues than they were about Christ. It seems certain that the vast majority of them were convinced but uncommitted and therefore not authentic believers—not yet, at least. Some of them may have come to true faith at some later time. Joseph of Arimathea and Nicodemus were Pharisees—council members—who came slowly and haltingly to Christ but who ultimately showed their true commitment to Him at a pivotal moment (Luke 23:50–52; John 19:38–39).

Some of the earliest heretics in the primitive church were former Jewish leaders who had been persuaded of the truth about Christ, but rather than repenting of their own self-righteousness, they had dragged their pharisaical perspective into the church, corrupting the message of Christianity in the process (see Acts 15:1–5). So thoroughly embedded in all their thoughts was a love for the praise of men that even after being persuaded of the truth, some Pharisees were unable to lose the works-based orientation of their religion.

What is the "equation" of your walk? Jesus alone? Jesus + my good works? Explain.

The Jesus You Can't Ignore, 187–188

Christ Brings Divisions

For first of all, when you come together as a church, I hear that there are divisions among you, and in part I believe it.

1 Corinthians 11:18

A central characteristic of a true disciple—and in some ways, almost an unbelievable one, because it goes so radically against our natural longings—is a willingness to forsake family if necessary. In Matthew 10:34 Jesus said: "Do not think that I came to bring peace on earth. I did not come to bring peace but a sword." This is a most dramatic statement. He was saying, "Now, some of you who are real will confess Me when you're brought to the tribunals and the courts of men, and even in the course of day-to-day life. Others of you will deny Me, because it isn't that important to you, and you'll save your necks and your reputations. And that just proves that I have come to bring a sword. I cause divisions. I force people to decisions that separate one from another." The very fact that some confess Christ and some deny Christ indicates that His coming causes divisions. Jesus didn't deny that stark reality; He built on it.

It's as if Jesus was saying there will be a division *for the moment*. The intervention of God in history through the incarnation of Christ was going to split and fracture the world into parties that would pit themselves against one another. So don't be under any illusion as a disciple to think the whole world is going to fall at your feet. You're going to rush home and tell everybody you've become a Christian? You're going to shout the news at school, and everybody's going to line up to join you? It's not going to happen.

When have you seen the reality of the truth described here?

Hard to Believe, 127–129

May

PARENTING

The True Way to Be a Blessing

For whoever is ashamed of Me and My words in this adulterous and sinful generation, of him the Son of Man also will be ashamed when He comes in the glory of His Father with the holy angels.

MARK 8:38

As well as creating war, strife, division, separation, and friction, we do have a positive effect. We are the destiny-determiners in the world. When we bring down the sword that separates, on the one hand are the unbelievers, but on the other hand are the *believers*. And when we preach, live, and give our testimonies, thank God some respond in genuine repentance and self-denying faith.

On the one hand, you create this antagonism by standing fast in the faith; then, on the other hand, you create this marvelous reality that people receive God through you.

When you go out representing God by your life and your lips, by your speaking and your living, those who receive you will receive the reward that you receive. This could be true of a pastor, a teacher, a missionary, an evangelist, or anyone who represents Christ; the one who receives that one will share that one's reward. If the Lord gives me a reward for proclaiming to you, He'll give you the same reward for receiving what I proclaim. We all share.

You want to be a blessing in the world? Then confess Christ before men! Stand up boldly, and don't mitigate your testimony; don't be ashamed of Christ. Don't water down the truth. And let your life become the source of their reward. Then a disciple is a person who determines destiny. Even the least of us shares with the greatest of us in what God does in blessing us.

How are you a blessing in the world?

Hard to Believe, 137–138

The Problem of the Worldly Church

Do not love the world or the things in the world. If anyone loves the world, the love of the Father is not in him.

1 John 2:15

Whole churches have deliberately immersed themselves in "the culture"—by which they actually mean "whatever the world loves at the moment." Thus we now have a new breed of trendy churches whose preachers can rattle off references to every popular icon, every trifling meme, every tasteless fashion, and every vapid trend that captures the fickle fancy of the postmodern, secular mind. Worldly preachers seem to go out of their way to put their carnal expertise on display—even in their sermons. In the name of "connecting with the culture" they boast of having seen all the latest programs on MTV; memorized every episode of *South Park*; learned the lyrics to countless tracks of gangsta rap and heavy metal music; or watched who-knows-how-many R-rated movies. They seem to know every fad top to bottom, back to front, and inside out. They've adopted both the style and the language of the world. They want to fit right in with the world, and they seem to be making themselves quite comfortable there.

Let's face it. Scripture speaks quite plainly against such a mentality (James 4:4). Many of the world's favorite fads are toxic, and they are becoming increasingly so as our society descends further into the death-spiral described in Romans 1. It's like a radioactive toxicity, so while those who immerse themselves in it might not notice its effects instantly, they nevertheless cannot escape the inevitable, soul-destroying contamination. And woe to those who become comfortable with sinful fads of secular society.

How can you guard against a tendency to "love the world"?

The Truth War, 140–141

The True View of the Family

Therefore a man shall leave his father and mother and be joined to his wife, and they shall become one flesh.

Genesis 2:24

According to the Bible, God Himself ordained the family as the basic building block of human society, because He deemed it "not good that man should be alone" (Gen. 2:18). The verse stands out starkly in the biblical Creation narrative, because as Scripture describes the successive days of the Creation week, the text punctuates each stage of Creation with the words: "God saw that *it was good*."

God established the family for all time. God ordained marriage and the family, and therefore they are sacred in His sight.

So it is no mere accident of history that family relationships have always been the very nucleus of all human civilization. According to Scripture, that is precisely the way God designed it to be. And therefore, if the family crumbles as an institution, all of civilization *will* ultimately crumble.

Over the past generation, we have seen that destructive process taking place before our eyes. It seems contemporary secular society has declared war on the family.

As society continues its mad quest to eliminate the family, and as our whole culture therefore unravels more and more, it becomes more important than ever for Christians to understand what the Bible teaches about the family, and to put it into practice in their homes. It may well be that the example we set before the world through strong homes and healthy families will in the long run be one of the most powerful, attractive, and living proofs that when the Bible speaks, it speaks with the authority of the God who created us—and whose design for the family is perfect.

How is your family an example to the world of God's intent for families?

The Fulfilled Family, x–xv

The Key to Parenting

Children, obey your parents in the Lord, for this is right.

Ephesians 6:1

While Christian ministries often discuss parenting and family, statistics still show that, in general, Christian families are not in much better shape than families of their non-Christian neighbors.

Something is clearly wrong.

Part of the problem is that many of the parenting and family programs labeled "Christian" today are not truly Christian. Some are nothing more than secular behaviorism papered over with a religious veneer.

Some Christian parenting programs seem to begin well but quickly move away from biblical principles and into other things. Those other things often receive more stress than more vital issues that are truly biblical. The resulting lists of rules and how-tos quickly supersede the vital biblical principles.

What we desperately need is a return to the biblical principles of parenting. Christian parents don't need new, shrink-wrapped programs; they need to apply and obey consistently the few simple principles that are clearly set forth for parents in God's Word, such as these: Constantly teach your kids the truth of God's Word (Deut. 6:7). Discipline them when they do wrong (Prov. 23:13–14). And don't provoke them to anger (Col. 3:21). Those few select principles alone, if consistently applied, would have a far greater positive impact for the typical struggling parent than hours of discussion about whether babies should be given pacifiers, or what age kids should be before they're permitted to choose their own clothes, or dozens of similar issues that consume so much time in the typical parenting program.

How do you impart biblical principles to your children?

What the Bible Says About Parenting, 11–13

No Breaks in Parenting

You shall teach them to your children, speaking of them when you sit in your house, when you walk by the way, when you lie down, and when you rise up.

Deuteronomy 11:19

God made parenting a full-time responsibility. There are no coffee breaks from our parental duties. This principle was even built into the Law at Sinai. God prefaced His instruction to the Israelites with this solemn charge: "These words, which I am commanding you today, shall be on your heart. You shall teach them diligently to your children, and shall talk of them when you sit in your house, when you walk by the way, when you lie down, and when you rise up" (Deut. 6:6–7).

This is God's own definition of parenting. It means parenting is a full-time assignment in every sense of the expression. No phase of life is exempt. Not one hour of the day is excluded. There is no time-out for the parent who wants to be faithful to this calling.

Some parents think they can compartmentalize their child's life, assign a set number of hours per week to spend on parenting, and then fulfill their duties as parents by making sure the hours they put into the task are "quality time." That whole philosophy is contrary to the spirit of Deuteronomy 6:7, and it is a sure way to guarantee that outside influences will have more influence than the parents in shaping the child's character.

The history of Old Testament Israel is an object lesson about the dangers of neglecting this vital principle. Israel failed miserably when it came to the duty of teaching their children about God's righteousness (see Judges 2:7, 10).

If you have children, what do you find most challenging about parenting?

What the Bible Says About Parenting, 21–22

The True Measure of Success in Parenting

Train up a child in the way he should go, and when he is old he will not depart from it.

Proverbs 22:6

If we measure our success as parents solely by what our children become, there is no inviolable guarantee in Scripture that we will experience absolute success on those terms. Sometimes children raised in fine Christian families grow up to abandon the faith. On the other hand, the Lord graciously redeems many children whose parents are utter failures. The outcome of the child, as a factor taken by itself, is no reliable gauge of the parents' success.

However, the *true* measure of success for Christian parents is the parents' own character. To the degree that we have followed God's design for parenting, we have succeeded as parents before God.

As a general rule, parents who follow biblical principles in bringing up their children will see a positive effect on the character of their children. From a purely statistical point of view, children who grow up in Christ-honoring homes are more likely to remain faithful to Christ in adulthood. The truism of Proverbs 22:6 does apply. God often uses faithful parents as instruments in the salvation of children.

Ultimately, however, your children's salvation is a matter to be settled between them and God. Nothing you can do will guarantee your kids' salvation. To that end you should be praying to God and instructing your child—using all available means to impress the truths of the gospel perpetually on the child's heart. But ultimately a grown child's spiritual fitness alone is not necessarily a reliable gauge of the parents' success.

What is your measure of parenting success?

What the Bible Says About Parenting, 17–19

Good Marriages Make Good Parents

Wives, submit to your own husbands, as to the Lord. . . . Husbands, love your wives, just as Christ also loved the church and gave Himself for her.

Ephesians 5:22, 25

Hannah's love for her husband is the first key to understanding her profound influence as a mother. Contrary to popular opinion, the most important characteristic of a godly mother is not her relationship with her *children*. It is her love for her *husband*. A healthy home environment cannot be built exclusively on the parents' love for their children. The properly situated family has *marriage* at the center; families shouldn't revolve around the children.

Furthermore, all parents need to heed this lesson: what you communicate to your children through your marital relationship will stay with them for the rest of their lives. By watching how mother and father treat each other, they will learn the most fundamental lessons of life—love, self-sacrifice, integrity, virtue, sin, sympathy, compassion, understanding, and forgiveness. Whatever you teach them about those things, right or wrong, is planted deep within their hearts.

That emphasis on the centrality of marriage was very evident between Elkanah and Hannah. With all their domestic issues, they nonetheless had a healthy marriage and an abiding love for each other. Their inability to have children together was like an open wound. But it was an experience that drew out of Elkanah tender expressions of love for his wife. And even in a home environment with a second wife and multiple children—a chaos created by the folly of Elkanah's bigamy and made even more dysfunctional by Peninnah's ill temperament—Hannah and Elkanah clearly loved each other deeply.

What are you teaching your children through your marriage?

Twelve Extraordinary Women, 95–96

The Parent's Top Priority

Then little children were brought to Him that He might put His hands on them and pray.

Matthew 19:13

Your top-priority job as a parent is to be an evangelist in your home. You need to teach your children the law of God; teach them the gospel of divine grace; show them their need for a Savior; and point them to Jesus Christ as the only One who can save them. If they grow up without a keen awareness of their need for salvation, you as a parent will have failed in your primary task as their spiritual leader.

Note this, however: Regeneration is not something you can do for them. Parents who force, coerce, or manipulate their kids may pressure them into a false profession, but genuine faith is something only divine grace can prompt. The new birth is a work of the Holy Spirit (see John 3:8). God works sovereignly in your children's hearts to draw them to Himself. Their salvation is a matter that must ultimately be settled between them and God.

But as parents, you are nonetheless responsible to exalt Christ in your home and point your kids to Him as Savior. You are the first and most important preachers God has given them. They will observe your lives up close, to see whether you seriously believe what you are teaching them. You have a better opportunity than anyone to help frame what they know about Christ. Every moment of their lives is a teaching opportunity (Deut. 6:6–7), and you should use those opportunities to the best advantage for your kids' sake.

How are you pointing your children to the Savior?

What the Bible Says About Parenting, 42–43

Sharing the Gospel with Your Children

Let the word of Christ dwell in you richly in all wisdom, teaching and admonishing one another in psalms and hymns and spiritual songs, singing with grace in your hearts to the Lord.

Colossians 3:16

Leading your children to Christ is a long-term, full-time assignment—the most important duty God has given you as a parent.

Parents more than anyone have ample time to be thorough and clear; to explain and illustrate; to listen to feedback; to correct misunderstanding; and to clarify and review the difficult parts. It is the best possible scenario for evangelism. The wise parents will be faithful, patient, persistent, and thorough. In fact, that is precisely what Scripture demands of every parent (see Deut. 6:6–7).

Don't think of the gospel as something suited only for special evangelistic occasions. Don't assume Sunday school classes or children's Bible clubs will give your children all the gospel truth they need. Look for and seize the many daily opportunities you will have for highlighting and punctuating the gospel truth in your kids' thinking.

Don't rely too much on canned or formulaic gospel presentations. Many of the programmed approaches to child evangelism fail to explain the concepts of sin and the holiness of God. They say nothing of repentance. But then they typically solicit some active response from the child—a show of hands in a group setting, a rote prayer on Mother's lap, or almost anything that may be counted as a positive response. As a consequence, the church is filled with teenagers and adults whose hearts are devoid of real love for Christ, but who think they are genuine Christians because of something they *did* as children.

What opportunities for punctuating the gospel truth have you witnessed this week?

What the Bible Says About Parenting, 48–49

What the Gospel Includes

God, who at various times and in various ways spoke in time past to the fathers by the prophets, has in these last days spoken to us by His Son, whom He has appointed heir of all things.

Hebrews 1:1–2

The gospel is the good news about Christ. There is a sense in which the gospel includes *all* truth about Him. There's no need to think of any aspect of biblical truth as incompatible with or extraneous to the gospel. In fact, since Christ is the sum and the summit of all biblical revelation (Heb. 1:1–3), every truth in Scripture ultimately points to Him. And therefore none of it is out of place in evangelistic contexts. One could accurately say, then, that parents who want to be thorough in evangelizing their children need to teach them *the whole counsel of God*, taking care to show the gospel ramifications in all that truth. That, I believe, is the true spirit of what Deuteronomy 6:6–7 calls for.

No single formula can possibly meet the needs of every unregenerate person anyway. Those who are *ignorant* need to be told who Christ is and why He offers the only hope of salvation (Rom. 10:3). Those who are *careless* need to be confronted with the reality of impending judgment (John 16:11).Those who are *fearful* need to hear that God is merciful, delighting not in the death of the wicked but pleading with sinners to come to Him for mercy (Ezek. 33:11). Those who are *hostile* need to be shown the futility of opposing the will of God (Ps. 2:1–4). Every gospel presentation should include an explanation of Christ's sacrificial death for sin (1 Cor. 15:3). And the message is not the gospel if it does not also recount His burial and the triumph of His resurrection (vv. 4, 17).

How will you share the hope of salvation this week?

What the Bible Says About Parenting, 52–53

Target the Child's Heart

Hear, my children, the instruction of a father, and give attention to know understanding.

PROVERBS 4:1

Parents should be very clear about this: Behavior is not the crucial issue. A change in behavior will not fix the child's root problem. A change in behavior without a change in heart is nothing but hypocrisy.

How can parents nurture the child's heart? To begin with, parents need to help the children understand that they have sinful hearts. Children themselves need to know that all their evil words, thoughts, and deeds spring from sin-tainted hearts, and the only remedy for this is the gospel.

Your child's heart is a battlefield where sin and righteousness are in conflict. Your child's greatest problem is not a lack of maturity. It is not a lack of experience or a lack of understanding. It is a wicked heart. Those other things will exacerbate the heart problem. But the remedies for immaturity, ignorance, and inexperience are no cure for the main problem. Your child will not outgrow his own depravity.

As parents, we must target the children's hearts. The goal of parenting is not behavior control. It is not merely to produce well-mannered children. It is not to teach our kids socially commendable behavior. It is not to make them polite and respectful. It is not to make them obedient. It is not to get them to perform for our approval. It is not to conform them to a moral standard. It is not to give us, as parents, something to be proud of.

The ultimate goal and proper focus of biblical parenting is redemptive.

What goals have you set for conforming your child(ren) to a moral standard?

What the Bible Says About Parenting, 147–148

The Needs of Children

Though He was a Son, yet He learned obedience by the things which He suffered.

Hebrews 5:8

Remember that when Jesus took on a human form, it was not in appearance only. He was a true man. And as a child, He learned things—including obedience (see Heb. 5:8).

As a matter of fact, the way Jesus learned and grew is essentially the same way every child learns and grows. Of course, because He was sinless, He did not require punishment. But He no doubt learned through *positive* instruction and reinforcement from loving parents.

He grew in four ways (Luke 2:52): intellectually ("in wisdom"), physically ("and stature"), socially ("in favor with . . . men"), and spiritually ("in favor with God"). All children have needs in these same four areas.

Our kids have *intellectual needs*, because they are born without any knowledge of what is good for them and what is not. Obedience is the first step toward wisdom.

They have *physical needs*, and the younger they are, the greater those needs.

They have *social needs*, because they have to learn how to interact with others. Babies are concerned with nothing but their own needs, and the only form of communication they know is crying. As they grow, they have to be taught concern for others. Learning to obey their parents is the first vital step in learning all the social skills they will need for life.

Above all, they have *spiritual needs*. Their parents need to teach them the gospel of salvation. They will not learn to love the Lord naturally.

The parents' authority provides a safe environment in which children can grow in all these ways.

How are you working to provide the kind of environment where your child(ren) can grow intellectually, physically, socially, and spiritually?

The Fulfilled Family, 94–96

Teaching Your Children to Be Obedient

He who spares his rod hates his son, but he who loves him disciplines him promptly.

PROVERBS 13:24

Parents *must* teach their children obedience. This is one of the most basic and obvious responsibilities of parenthood. If we are going to raise a generation of faithful children to live righteous lives, they must begin by learning to obey their parents. And it is the parents' solemn responsibility to teach them this. I constantly marvel at how many parents seem practically clueless when it comes to this responsibility. This is by no means an optional aspect of parenting. As the apostle Paul points out in Ephesians 6:2–3, the first of the Ten Commandments accompanied by a promise for those who obeyed it was the fifth commandment: "Honor your father and your mother, that your days may be long upon the land which the LORD your God is giving you" (Ex. 20:12). It is the parents' responsibility to train the child to obey from the time the child learns the sound of the parents' voices.

That involves discipline and, when necessary, chastening and correction. Parents who fail to correct their disobedient children are displaying a shameful lack of love. "He who spares his rod hates his son, but he who loves him disciplines him promptly" (Prov. 13:24). Parents who truly love their children will reprove them when they disobey.

Proper chastening is not merely for retribution; it really is in the child's best interest. Chastening helps conform their minds to wisdom. It removes foolishness from their hearts. It can help deliver them from the misery of sin's consequences up to and including hell.

How do you teach your child(ren) obedience?

What the Bible Says About Parenting, 83–84

True Obedience in Children

Honor your father and your mother, that your days may be long upon the land which the LORD your God is giving you.

Exodus 20:12

The obedience Paul called for in Ephesians 6:1 is above all an attitude, not merely visible behavior. The Greek word for "obey" is *hupakouw*—from a root that means "to hear" or "to heed." It includes the idea of listening attentively as well as obeying. That is why Paul cited the fifth commandment as an exact parallel: "*Honor* your father and mother" (v. 2, emphasis added).

Paul further explained the proper attitude of obedience with the phrase in the middle of verse 1: "Obey your parents *in the Lord*" (emphasis added). In other words, when children rightly obey, they do it as unto the Lord (see also Col. 3:23–24)—because God delegates parents' authority to them. The parents therefore are ministers of God as far as the child is concerned (see also Rom. 13:1–4).

The *attitude* is of supreme importance. If the attitude is right, proper actions will be the natural result. "For as he thinks in his heart, so is he" (Prov. 23:7). If the actions are right but the attitude is wrong, that's nothing but hypocrisy, which dishonors the parents and disgraces the child. In our family, the children were more often disciplined for bad attitudes than bad behavior.

So the message for children is short and simple: obedience—in both attitude and action—is "right" (Eph. 6:1). It is "well pleasing to the Lord" (Col. 3:20). It is honoring to the parents. And it is good for children—protecting them from a world of evil, prolonging their lives, and bringing them an abundance of blessing.

How do you encourage an attitude of obedience in your child(ren)?

The Fulfilled Family, 96–99

Don't Provoke Your Children

And you, fathers, do not provoke your children to wrath, but bring them up in the training and admonition of the Lord.

Ephesians 6:4

The expression "provoke . . . to wrath" is one word in the Greek: *parorgiz*. It applies to every kind of anger, from silent fuming, to indignant outburst, to full-fledged rebellious rage.

Some parents crush their children with *excessive discipline*. I have known parents who seemed to think if discipline is good for a child, extra discipline must be even better. Other parents provoke their children by *inconsistent discipline*. If you overlook an infraction three times and punish the child severely the fourth time, you will confuse and exasperate your child.

Some parents provoke their children with *unkindness*. I cringe when I hear parents deliberately say mean-spirited things to their children. That's a sure way to crush a child's heart and provoke him to resentment.

Another way parents provoke their kids is by *showing favoritism*. Isaac favored Esau over Jacob, and Rebekah preferred Jacob over Esau (Gen. 25:28). The resentment their favoritism provoked caused a permanent split in the family (Gen. 27).

Some parents actually goad their children to exasperation through *overindulgence*. They are too permissive. On the other hand, some parents frustrate their children by *overprotection*. They fence them in, suffocate them, deny them any measure of freedom or trust.

Plenty of parents arouse their children's anger through constant *pressure to achieve*. Other ways parents provoke their children are through neglect, constant criticism, condescension, indifference, detachment, cruelty, sanctimoniousness, hypocrisy, a lack of fairness, or deliberate humiliation. All of those things provoke children to exasperation by *discouragement*.

What steps will you take to avoid the parenting traps discussed above?

The Fulfilled Family, 108–112

Disciplining Without Provoking

But let your "Yes" be "Yes," and your "No," "No." For whatever is more than these is from the evil one.

Matthew 5:37

Here are three simple principles that will be helpful to parents who want to understand how to discipline their children without provoking them to anger:

First, *discipline should be consistent*. "Let your 'Yes' be 'Yes,' and your 'No,' 'No'" (Matt. 5:37). If a parent tells a child not to do something and the child does it anyway, the parent *must* correct the child. To ignore the offense is to sanction the disobedience and encourage more rebellion. Furthermore, don't be severe sometimes and lenient other times. Discipline should always be firm (not necessarily harsh) but always loving and always consistent. Be equally firm with all your children. And keep your word when you make promises.

Second, *the punishment should fit the crime*. Reserve the harshest punishment for instances where the child has willfully disobeyed. Don't punish a child who has merely been careless with the same rigor you might punish an act of overt defiance. Use corporal punishment only for the most serious infractions; don't mete it out automatically with every petty offense.

Finally, remember that *as much as possible, your training should be positive*. Be sure you notice and reward positive behavior at least as often as you punish misbehavior. It's significant, I think, that the fifth commandment itself is reinforced with positive motivation—a promise of blessing to those who obey. Rewards for obedience are perfectly legitimate.

Those principles—like all the biblical principles for families—are simple and straightforward. Parenting isn't complex; what makes it difficult is failing to follow these principles faithfully, diligently, and consistently.

What is your method for disciplining without provocation?

The Fulfilled Family, 119–120

The Truth About Spanking

Foolishness is bound up in the heart of a child; the rod of correction will drive it far from him.

PROVERBS 22:15

The subject of corporal punishment is inexplicably baffling to many parents. Part of the problem is the confusion of the times in which we live. It has been popular for more than half a century to decry corporal punishment as inherently inappropriate, counterproductive, and detrimental to the child.

However, Scripture itself *prescribes* corporal discipline and cautions parents not to abandon the use of the rod. The opinions of self-proclaimed *experts* who disagree frankly amount to little. In the end, the facts will be found to agree with the Word of God.

It is worthwhile to reiterate some truths. Parental discipline should never injure the child. It is never necessary to bruise your children in order to spank them hard enough to make your point. Spanking should always be administered with love and never when the *parent* is in a fit of rage. That sort of discipline is indeed abusive, wrong, and detrimental to the child, because it shatters the environment of loving nurture and instruction Ephesians 6:4 describes.

Furthermore, spanking is by no means the *only* kind of discipline parents should administer. There are many other viable forms of punishing children that, on occasion, can be used in addition to the rod. If the child responds immediately to a verbal rebuke in a given situation, a spanking is probably not necessary. Other punishments, such as withdrawing privileges, can also be used as occasional alternatives to spanking if the situation warrants it.

What is your policy in regard to spanking?

What the Bible Says About Parenting, 152–155

The Truth About Friendships

My son, if sinners entice you, do not consent.

PROVERBS 1:10

No principle in child-rearing may be more vital and yet more neglected than this one: teach your children to select their companions wisely. Solomon wrote, "He who walks with wise men will be wise, but the companion of fools will be destroyed" (Prov. 13:20).

Parents must take the offensive on this. If you do not help your children select, and help them learn to select for themselves, the right kind of companions, the wrong kind of companions will inevitably select them. The responsibility of teaching children how to choose their friends wisely is therefore a fundamental element of successful biblical parenting. The apostle Paul wrote, "Do not be deceived: 'Evil company corrupts good habits'" (1 Cor. 15:33). Your kids' personal moral standards, the language they use, and the activities they engage in, will probably not rise above the lowest common denominator of their companions' standards. Rarely does a child have the capability to elevate himself beyond the constituent group in which he functions.

Every parent must take this duty seriously. Even if you don't live in the kind of neighborhood where gangs might recruit your children, you can be certain that eventually your kids will face tremendous peer pressure to conform to a standard of conduct that is ungodly and sinful. You must teach them to select their companions wisely, so that they will not be intimidated into the wrong kinds of alliances. Don't let your children surround themselves with the wrong kind of peer pressure. Instruct them how to choose companions who lift them up.

How do you encourage your child(ren) to make good friendships?

What the Bible Says About Parenting, 88–90

Teach Your Kids to Guard Their Minds

The peace of God, which surpasses all understanding, will guard your hearts and minds through Christ Jesus.

PHILIPPIANS 4:7

Here's a principle that parents must emphasize more than ever, especially in the age of the Internet: Teach your children to guard their *minds*. Proverbs 4:23 says, "Keep your heart with all diligence, for out of it springs the issues of life." Scripture speaks of "the heart" as the seat of both the emotions and the intellect. It is often used as a synonym for the mind. "As he *thinks* in his heart, so is he" (Prov. 23:7, emphasis added).

Our children must learn to guard their minds diligently. Never in human history have the forces of evil waged a campaign to capture human minds on the scale we are seeing today. As parents, we are partly responsible for guarding our children's minds. The onslaught against righteous thinking comes from several fronts: television, radio, movies, music, the Internet, and nowadays even from school curriculum. So the parent's task is indeed a formidable one.

Parents can and must protect children from exposure to the most unsavory aspects of modern entertainment and media. Monitor what they see and hear. Do not simply turn them loose on the Internet. Don't hand them the television remote and leave the room. It is all right to allow them some choice about what they will watch and listen to, but do not let them make those choices totally unsupervised. You have a right and responsibility to help steer them toward what edifies and away from all that does not. All such choices need to be made with parental guidance, and with the utmost caution.

What do you do to model the type of heart guard your child(ren) need?

What the Bible Says About Parenting, 80–81

Discerning Our Hearts

For if anyone is a hearer of the word and not a doer, he is like a man observing his natural face in a mirror; for he observes himself, goes away, and immediately forgets what kind of man he was.

James 1:23–24

Do you realize that the difference between a sincere, Spirit-controlled, devoted, godly, obedient Christian and a defeated, weak, struggling Christian is what takes place in the mind? They may be attending the same church, active in the same ministries, and externally doing the same things, but one is defeated and the other lives a spiritually fruitful life. The difference is the thought life.

One day the difference will be made manifest. Paul told the Corinthians that when the Lord comes, He "will both bring to light the things hidden in the darkness and disclose the motives of men's hearts" (1 Cor. 4:5 NASB). Jesus said something similar: "Nothing is hidden that shall not become evident, nor anything secret that shall not be known and come to light" (Luke 8:17 NASB). And, "Beware of the leaven of the Pharisees, which is hypocrisy. For there is nothing covered that will not be revealed, nor hidden that will not be known" (Luke 12:1–2).

I urge you to look deeply into the mirror of God's Word (James 1:23–24), which is a powerful "discerner of the thoughts and intents of the heart" (Heb. 4:12 KJV). As Jeremiah counseled Israel, "Wash your heart from evil, O Jerusalem, that you may be saved. How long will your wicked thoughts lodge within you?" (Jer. 4:14). And "let us cleanse ourselves from all filthiness of the flesh and spirit, perfecting holiness in the fear of God" (2 Cor. 7:1).

What has the mirror of God's Word revealed to you recently?

The Vanishing Conscience, 193

The Importance of Loyalty

He walked in all the sins of his father, which he had done before him; his heart was not loyal to the LORD his God, as was the heart of his father David.

1 KINGS 15:3

Loyalty is a great virtue. We often forget that simple truth in the cynical age in which we live. Our society is so rife with corrupt leaders and so hostile to the concept of authoritative truth that loyalty is often perceived as a weakness rather than a merit. Rebellion and defiance have been canonized as virtues instead. "Who can find a faithful man?" (Prov. 20:6).

But Scripture exalts loyalty. Loyalty is owed, first of all, to the Lord and to His truth, but also to those who stand for the truth. Second Chronicles 16:9 says, "The eyes of the LORD run to and fro throughout the whole earth, to show Himself strong on behalf of those whose heart is loyal to Him."

Loyalty is a fragile thing. David prayed, "Give my son Solomon a loyal heart to keep Your commandments and Your testimonies and Your statutes" (1 Chron. 29:19). Solomon himself urged all Israel, "Let your heart therefore be loyal to the LORD our God, to walk in His statutes and keep His commandments, as at this day" (1 Kings 8:61). But Solomon's own moral downfall came because "his heart was not loyal to the LORD his God, as was the heart of his father David" (1 Kings 11:4; 15:3).

No sin in all of Scripture is more despicable than Judas's traitorous act of treachery. Jesus Himself classed Judas's wickedness as more wretched than that of Pilate (John 19:11).

In what ways have you demonstrated loyalty to God recently?

Called to Lead, 69

Teach Your Children About Marriage

Do not stir up nor awaken love until it pleases.

Song of Solomon 3:5

Teach your children to channel their youthful passions toward righteous ends. Especially, teach them to reserve their sexual passions for their spouses alone, and then teach them to be faithful in marriage. Teach your children that the only righteous place to find gratification of their sexual desires is from their own spouses. Solomon wrote an entire book of the Bible—the Song of Solomon—celebrating the joys of the marital relationship. Unfortunately, Solomon himself took multiple wives, destroying the perfect union between one man and one woman that marriage was supposed to be (Gen. 2:24). Nonetheless, Song of Solomon stands as an inspired song about what the ideal marriage relationship is supposed to be.

First Thessalonians 4:3–5 says, "For this is the will of God, your sanctification: that you should abstain from sexual immorality; that each of you should know how to possess his own vessel in sanctification and honor." "Vessel" in that verse could be a reference to the wife, the weaker vessel (1 Peter 3:7), or it could be a reference to the person's own body. Either way, it enjoins faithfulness within the bonds of marriage, which in God's design is a union between *two* people who become *one* flesh (Eph. 5:31).

Parents, don't make the mistake Solomon did. Teach this lesson to your children by example as well as by precept. Show them by the way you treat your spouse and by the things you say to each other that true contentment and full satisfaction are found only within the covenant of marriage.

How will you teach your child(ren) the value of abstinence?

What the Bible Says About Parenting, 96–98

Consequences upon Our Children of Rejecting the Truth

You show lovingkindness to thousands, and repay the iniquity of the fathers into the bosom of their children after them—the Great, the Mighty God, whose name is the Lord *of hosts.*

Jeremiah 32:18

When the Lord met Moses on Sinai to give him the Ten Commandments on tablets of stone, He announced His arrival by saying, "The Lord, the Lord God, merciful and gracious, longsuffering, and abounding in goodness and truth, keeping mercy for thousands, forgiving iniquity and transgression of sin, by no means clearing the guilty, visiting the iniquity of the fathers upon the children and the children's children to the third and fourth generation" (Ex. 34:6–7; see also Deut. 5:9 and Jer. 32:18). Doesn't that mean children are held guilty for the sins of their parents?

No. In fact, Deuteronomy 24:16 says, "Fathers shall not be put to death for their children, nor shall the children be put to death for their fathers; a person shall be put to death for his own sin." The principle underlying that law is given in Ezekiel 18:20: "The soul who sins shall die. The son shall not bear the guilt of the father, nor the father bear the guilt of the son. The righteousness of the righteous shall be upon himself, and the wickedness of the wicked shall be upon himself." This is an emphatic denial that a child is held guilty for the sins of the parent.

Are these contradictory? No. No son bears the *guilt* of his father. But the children of a sinful generation are powerfully affected by the *consequences* of the sins of a society.

How do you help your child(ren) understand the serious consequences of sin?

Safe in the Arms of God, 41–42

Remember Our Weaknesses

And I, brethren, when I came to you, did not come with excellence of speech or of wisdom declaring to you the testimony of God.

1 CORINTHIANS 2:1

Those whom the world holds up as leaders often exude arrogance, cockiness, egotism, and conceit. Those things are not qualities of true leadership; they are actually hindrances to it. The leader who forgets his own weaknesses will inevitably fail.

Paul, by contrast, drew strength from remembering his own weakness, because those things made him more dependent on the power of God. He wrote, "I take pleasure in infirmities, in reproaches, in needs, in persecutions, in distresses, for Christ's sake. For when I am weak, then I am strong" (2 Cor. 12:10). When he came to the end of his human resources, that was when the power of God flowed through him. God, and God alone, was Paul's only true source of sufficiency.

People are not effective in leadership merely because they're naturally talented communicators, because they have creative minds, because they have a flair for persuading people, or because of any other natural talents. From a spiritual perspective, human ingenuity and human cleverness tend to corrupt more than they help.

The apostle Paul had a great mind, but he didn't depend on it. He had wonderful training and he made use of it (or rather, God used it mightily). But he had no confidence whatsoever in the power of human wisdom when used for its own ends. He reminded the Corinthians that God's Word says, "I will destroy the wisdom of the wise, and bring to nothing the understanding of the prudent" (1 Cor. 1:19). For that very reason, Paul's preaching in Corinth had been simple and plain (see 1 Cor. 2:1–5).

How do you walk the balance between reliance on human wisdom and using the mind God gave you?

Called to Lead, 101–102

A Mother's Influence

She watches over the ways of her household, and does not eat the bread of idleness. Her children rise up and call her blessed.

PROVERBS 31:27–28

Hannah serves as an example of the influence a godly mother can have on her children.

No mother was ever more devoted to home and child. She had important work to do—nurturing Samuel, caring for him, and helping him learn the most basic truths of life and wisdom. She taught him his first lessons about YHWH. She made her home an environment where he could learn and grow in safety. And she carefully directed the course of his learning and helped shape his interests.

Hannah seemed to understand how vital those early years are, when 90 percent of personality is formed. "Train up a child in the way he should go, and when he is old he will not depart from it" (Prov. 22:6). She prepared Samuel in those formative years for a lifetime of service to God—the high calling to which she had consecrated him before he was ever born. History tells us that she did her job well. Samuel, obviously a precocious child, grew in wisdom and understanding. Those early years set a course for his life from which he never deviated. The only blot on his record came in his old age, when he made his sons judges and they perverted justice (1 Sam. 8:1–3). Samuel's own failure as a father was the one aspect of his life that obviously owed more to the influence of Eli, the old priest, than to the example of Hannah.

But it is apparent that Hannah's influence on Samuel remained far more of a guiding force in his life than the spiritually feeble example of Eli.

How do you demonstrate a godly influence in your child's life?

Twelve Extraordinary Women, 104–105

Adopted by God

But as many as received Him, to them He gave the right to become children of God, to those who believe in His name.

John 1:12

Becoming a Christian is like being adopted into a new family. The apostle Paul used this comparison in his letter to the Romans: "For as many as are led by the Spirit of God, these are sons of God. For you did not receive the spirit of bondage again to fear, but you have received the Spirit of adoption by whom we cry out, 'Abba, Father.' The Spirit Himself bears witness with our spirit that we are children of God" (8:14–16). As Christians, we have been adopted by God into His family and receive His intimate, fatherly love, grace, and compassion.

Just as husband and wife show love and compassion to a parentless child by making him a member of their family, God grants us grace by bringing us into His family and giving us all the same rights and privileges His other children have. In the Roman culture of Paul's days, an adopted child, especially a son, usually received greater prestige and privilege than the natural children of a family, particularly if the father was disappointed with his own children. That's what happens as a result of your spiritual adoption by God. He graciously and lovingly sought you out and made you His child, solely on the basis of your trust in His eternal Son, Jesus Christ. Because of your adoption, you will share in the full inheritance of Christ Himself.

How do you celebrate your adoption?

Welcome to the Family, viii–ix

From Slaves to Sons

For whom He foreknew, He also predestined to be conformed to the image of His Son, that He might be the firstborn among many brethren.

Romans 8:29

That God, in His grace, would free us from sin and make us His slaves is a wondrous truth to comprehend. What a privilege it is for us to know and obey the heavenly Master! A slave's dignity was derived from the power and position of his owner. In ancient times, the slaves of the king were the most highly respected of all. We belong to the King of kings—God Himself. There can be no higher honor than that. And yet the Lord has bestowed an even greater distinction upon those who are His own.

Having delivered us from the destitution of sin, God not only receives us as His slaves—but He has also welcomed us into His household and made us members of His very family. He not only rescued us, purchased us, befriended us, and took us in; He has also adopted us, thereby transforming those who were formerly children of wrath (Eph. 2:3) into the sons and daughters of righteousness. All of this is possible through the redemptive work of Christ, who is the "only begotten Son" (John 3:16), and the "firstborn among many brethren" (Rom. 8:29; cf. Rev. 1:5).

In ancient Rome, the act of adoption immediately granted the former slave his freedom, permanently placing him into the family of his master. So also, as the adopted children of God, we have been set free from slavery to sin. Moreover, we can rest assured in knowing that we have been given a permanent place in the family of God.

How does the truth of your adoption affect your view of your worth?

Slave, 154–156

Adopted Forever

You were sealed with the Holy Spirit of promise, who is the guarantee of our inheritance until the redemption of the purchased possession, to the praise of His glory.

Ephesians 1:13–14

Jesus told the unbelieving Pharisees, "The slave does not remain in the house forever; the son does remain forever" (John 8:35 NASB). In context, Jesus was warning the Pharisees (who thought they were God's children through Abraham) that they were, in reality, the slaves of sin (v. 34), in desperate need of liberation through the Son of God (v. 36). Only through faith in Christ could sin's slaves be freed from sin. And once freed, they would be adopted into the true family of God—trading something that was temporary for an *eternal* position.

The doctrine of adoption establishes the reality that believers, once saved, are always saved.

If our adoption were not permanent, we would have great reason to fear. Our sin might yet condemn us, but the Holy Spirit testifies to our spirits that we are the children of God (Rom. 8:16), and if we have the Holy Spirit, we have God's unbreakable seal guaranteeing our future inheritance.

Later in Romans 8, Paul further underscored the permanence of our adoption. In verses 29–31, he explained that all those whom God has justified, He will glorify; none will be lost. In verses 32–34, he encouraged believers with the truth that no accusation made against God's elect will ever stick, because all has been forgiven through Christ. Finally, in verses 35–39, the apostle noted that absolutely nothing can separate God's children from His eternal love. Our security in God's family is forever fixed.

How can these truths help settle the question concerning whether or not you can ever lose your salvation?

Slave, 170–172

All Are Prodigals

For all have sinned and fall short of the glory of God.

ROMANS 3:23

When we sin, we show disdain for God's fatherly love as well as His holy authority. We spurn not merely His law, but also His very person. To sin is to deny God His place. It is an expression of hatred against God. It is tantamount to wishing He were dead. It is dishonoring to Him. And since all sin has at its heart this element of contempt for God, even the smallest sin has enough evil to unleash an eternity full of mischief, misfortune, and misery. The fact that the entire world of human evil all stemmed from Adam's simple act of disobedience is vivid proof of that (Rom. 5:12, 19; 1 Cor. 15:21–22).

Moreover, sin *always* bears evil fruit. We cannot take the good gifts God has surrounded us with, barter them away as if they were nothing, and then not expect to reap the consequences of spiritual poverty that are the inevitable result. Here's a shocking reality: the prodigal son is not merely a picture of the worst of sinners; he is a symbol of *every* unredeemed sinner—alienated from God and without a hope in the world (Eph. 2:12). He is a precise and living effigy of the entire human race—fallen, sinful, and rebellious.

It's true: the evil motives that drove the prodigal are the natural tendencies of every human heart.

In other words, we are *all* prodigal sons and daughters. Apart from God's restraining grace, every one of us would have long ago sold our birthright, wasted our lives, and squandered every blessing God has given us—trading away His bountiful, daily goodness in exchange for a brief moment of cheap self-gratification.

How could the notion that all are prodigals change your viewpoint of others?

A Tale of Two Sons, 78–79

Jesus' Emptying Himself for Us

He humbled Himself and became obedient to the point of death, even the death of the cross.

Philippians 2:8

Upon his return, the father of the prodigal son in effect said to the prodigal, "The best of all that I have is yours. You are now fully restored to sonship, and even elevated in our household to a position of honor." Like a king passing his robe and signet ring to a prince, the father did this ceremoniously and publicly, to eliminate any question from anyone's mind about whether he really meant it or not. This was a self-emptying act by the father.

The father here is a symbol of Christ and the way He is described in Philippians 2:6–8. Christ emptied Himself not by ceasing to be God, and not by divesting Himself of His divine nature or attributes, but by taking a real, authentic human nature on Himself and thereby covering His glory with the shroud of His humanity. He thus stepped down from His grandeur and majesty and became a man. He put Himself on our level. Then He humbled Himself even further by suffering the most ignominious kind of death by capital punishment—as if He embodied all the worst traits of the lowest dregs of human society. That's what the phrase "even death on a cross" signifies. It's a far greater act of humiliation than any indignity the father in this parable suffered. So if the behavior of the father in the parable seems exaggerated, don't miss the fact that the disgrace the father bore could not possibly be exaggerated enough to even begin to be in the same league as the humility of Christ.

What do you find most challenging about this level of humility?

Tale of Two Sons, 130

Repentance—a Need for All

In those days John the Baptist came preaching in the wilderness of Judea, and saying, "Repent, for the kingdom of heaven is at hand!"

Matthew 3:1–2

One of the clear implications of the parable of the prodigal son is that *no one* is free from the need for repentance. If the Pharisees needed to repent, despite their obsession with the minute details of the ceremonial law, how much more do we need to repent for not taking the holiness of God as seriously as we should?

Notice that Jesus did not rebuke the Pharisees for counting out little seeds to tithe; He rebuked them for using that kind of thing as a cloak to hide their failure with regard to the more important *moral* aspects of the Law. He told them, "You pay tithe of mint and anise and cummin, and have neglected the weightier matters of the law: justice and mercy and faith. *These you ought to have done, without leaving the others undone*" (Matt. 23:23, emphasis added).

If you can hear the parable of the prodigal son and not identify yourself, you are missing the unspoken point of Jesus' message. It is a call to repentance, and it applies to prodigals (immoral, outcast sinners) and Pharisees (moral, respectable hypocrites) alike. Both the point and the counterpoint of the parable underscore this idea. On the one hand, we see how repentance unleashes heaven's joy. On the other hand, we learn that refusing to see one's own need for repentance is nothing but stubborn, self-righteous opposition to heaven's agenda. Therefore, the parable demands repentance from prodigals and Pharisees.

The promise of redemption for penitent sinners goes hand in hand with that truth.

How have you shown your identification with the prodigal in this parable?

A *Tale of Two Sons*, 36–37

JUNE

MARRIAGE

Filled with the Spirit

And the disciples were filled with joy and with the Holy Spirit.

ACTS 13:52

Many Christians who know and love the Lord Jesus Christ do not live consistently in accordance with His principles. Why? Because they are not filled with the Spirit.

We see what this means in Ephesians 5:18–21. Paul says, *walk in the Spirit*. In other words, let the Spirit of God control you and direct your every step. It's one thing to be a believer and therefore possess the Spirit of God. It's another thing to be possessed by Him so that He controls every aspect of our walk. As Paul said in Galatians 5:25, "If we live in the Spirit, let us also walk in the Spirit."

Here in Ephesians 5, Paul made a negative parallel between being Spirit-filled and being full of wine. "Do not be drunk with wine, in which is dissipation; but be filled with the Spirit" (v. 18). Paul was not suggesting that we can possess the Spirit in varying measures. No one has the Spirit of God in partial measures. But to be "*filled* with the Spirit" is to be *controlled* by the Spirit.

To be filled with the Spirit is simply to be controlled by Him so that His power dominates you in a positive way.

In other words, the Spirit of God is the one who empowers us to live lives of obedience to God. In fact, He is the *only* source of power that enables us to be subject to God's law. Without His power, we cannot even begin to please God or truly obey Him with pure motives or from a sincere heart.

In what tangible ways would someone see that God directs your every step?

The Fulfilled Family, 6–8

Marriage Is an Illustration of the Gospel

This is a great mystery, but I speak concerning Christ and the church. Nevertheless let each one of you in particular so love his own wife as himself, and let the wife see that she respects her husband.

EPHESIANS 5:32–33

The meaning of love is summed up in the word *submission*. The manner of love is "sacrifice"—defined by Christ's self-giving love for His church. What is the motive of the husband's love for his wife?

"This is a great mystery," Paul writes, "but I speak concerning Christ and the church. Nevertheless let each one of you in particular so love his own wife as himself, and let the wife see that she respects her husband" (Eph. 5:32–33). Here is the motive: love's sacredness.

Marriage is a picture of Christ and the church. It is a sacred mystery. In fact, the sacredness of Christ's church is linked to the sacredness of marriage. Christ is the heavenly Bridegroom and the church is His bride (Rev. 21:9). Marriage illustrates this union. The husband is called to be Christlike in his love for his wife because this protects the sacredness of the divine object lesson. The Christian husband therefore displays what he thinks of Christ by the way he treats his wife. And marriage itself is a sacred institution because of what it illustrates.

That's the best motive I know for a husband to love his wife. His love for her honors Christ. How he treats her is a testimony not only to the wife, but also to the world at large about Christ's love for His people. The husband who understands this sacred mystery will delight to love, purify, protect, and care for his wife.

How is your marriage a demonstration to the world of the truths of Ephesians 5?

What the Bible Says About Parenting, 180

Building a Strong Marriage

Husbands, likewise, dwell with them with understanding, giving honor to the wife.

1 PETER 3:7

Marriage for two Christians is first of all a commitment to Jesus Christ and then to each other. Satan loves to destroy marriages, and the best protection against his attacks is a deep, profound, mutually shared relationship with Jesus Christ and a commitment to obedience of God's Word. In the presence of that kind of commitment, I don't believe a marriage can fail.

But to expand on that, here are two principles that strengthen a marriage. First, concentrate on being who you should be on the inside, not just on what you say, what you have, or even how you look externally. Peter gives this principle to wives in 1 Peter 3:3–4, but it surely applies to husbands as well: "Do not let your adornment be merely outward; arranging the hair, wearing gold, or putting on fine apparel; rather let it be the hidden person of the heart, with the incorruptible beauty of a gentle and quiet spirit, which is very precious in the sight of God."

A second principle is this: concentrate on learning who your spouse is. I have counseled many people whose marriages were faltering simply because they had never taken time to get to know each other. It's important to realize that no person, and no marriage, is perfect. If you're clinging in frustration to an ideal of what you want your spouse to be like, you are hurting your marriage. Abandon your idea of the perfect mate, and begin learning to understand and love the one you have. Live with your partner "with understanding" (1 Peter 3:7).

What can or will you do to be a scholar of your spouse?

What the Bible Says About Parenting, 233–234

Marriage Is a Union

So then, they are no longer two but one flesh. Therefore what God has joined together, let not man separate.

MATTHEW 19:6

Every marriage is consummated in an earthly sense by a *physical* "The two shall become one flesh." Children conceived by that union will literally bear the genetic pattern of two people who have become one flesh. But marriage also involves a *spiritual* union. *God* is the one who joins husband and wife together (Matt. 19:6). Marriage is the union of two souls, so that the marriage union knits the two together in every aspect of life. Their emotions, intellects, personalities, desires, and life goals are inextricably bound together. They share every aspect of life: worship, work, and leisure. That is how God designed marriage to be.

Naturally, then, God also designed marriage to be a *permanent* union, unbroken and uncorrupted. Scripture says, "The LORD God of Israel says that He hates divorce" (Mal. 2:16). The biblical terminology of Ephesians 5:31 stresses the permanence of the marriage union: "A man shall leave his father and mother and be joined to his wife."

Leaving father and mother is an essential part of every marriage. When either the husband or the wife in a new marriage fails to move completely out from under the parents' umbrella both physically and emotionally, it invariably causes problems in the marriage.

The word translated "be joined to" is a Greek term (*proskolla*) that literally speaks of gluing something together. It describes a permanent, unbreakable bond. That is an apt description of God's ideal for marriage. It's a union held together by lasting love that absolutely refuses to let go.

How does society's view of marriage contrast with the biblical view? To which do you adhere?

The Fulfilled Family, 75–77

An Ungodly Example

For it was so, when Solomon was old, that his wives turned his heart after other gods; and his heart was not loyal to the LORD his God, as was the heart of his father David.

1 KINGS 11:4

Sarah had a maidservant, named Hagar, whom she had acquired during their time in Egypt. Sarah apparently reasoned that since she owned Hagar, if Abraham fathered a child by Hagar, it would in effect be Sarah's child.

This was the first recorded case of polygamy in Scripture involving a righteous man. The very first bigamist on biblical record was Lamech (Gen. 4:19). He was an evil descendant of Cain. (He is not to be confused with another Lamech, described in Genesis 5:25–29, who was Noah's father and who descended from the line of Seth.)

Abraham took a concubine, at his wife's urging (Gen. 16:3). This was a sorry precedent for the patriarch of the nation to set. In generations to come, Jacob would be duped by his uncle into marrying both Leah and Rachel (Gen. 29:23–30); David would take concubines (2 Sam. 5:13); and Solomon would carry polygamy to an almost unbelievable extreme, maintaining a harem of more than a thousand women (1 Kings 11:1–3).

But God's design for marriage was monogamy from the beginning (see Matt. 19:4–5). Paul likewise made clear what God's ideal for marriage is: "Let each man have *his own wife*, and let each woman have *her own husband*" (1 Cor. 7:2, emphasis added). Disobedience to that standard has always resulted in evil consequences. David's polygamous heart led to his sin with Bathsheba. Solomon's marital philandering destroyed him and divided his kingdom (1 Kings 11:4). No good has ever come from any violation of the "one-flesh" principle of monogamy. Abraham's union with Hagar is certainly no exception.

How would you explain the value of monogamy to a teen growing up in a society that sees monogamy as passé?

Twelve Extraordinary Women, 39

The Husband as Head of the Home

But I want you to know that the head of every man is Christ, the head of woman is man, and the head of Christ is God.

1 CORINTHIANS 11:3

What is included in the biblical idea of headship? It is a much-disputed idea these days, thanks to evangelical feminism. For the past two decades or so, people seeking an egalitarian understanding of the New Testament have had to grapple with the clear meaning of Ephesians 5:23. They have sought creative ways to strip the concepts of leadership and authority from the notion of headship.

If the husband's role as head in a marriage relationship involves any degree of authority over the wife, the feminist and egalitarian approach to gender relationships is biblically untenable. Evangelical feminists have therefore long insisted that the word *head* in Ephesians 5:23 means nothing more than "source." They suggest that it means the husband is to be a loving protector to the wife, but it does not grant him any particular leadership responsibility over her. Marriage is an absolutely equal partnership, they say, with neither husband nor wife having any kind of authority over the other.

But the headship of Christ is so linked to the headship of the husband in Ephesians 5 that if the husband's role is divested of authority, Christ's authority over the church is likewise diminished. As a matter of fact, in 1 Corinthians 11:3, Paul even links the idea of headship to the relationship of authority and submission between the Father and the Son within the Trinity. So in the same way Christ voluntarily submitted Himself to His Father's will (John 6:38), wives are commanded to submit themselves to their husbands, and the church is to submit to Christ (Eph. 5:24).

How is your marriage a model of the biblical ideal of headship?

The Truth War, 160–161

Different Functions, Same Status

The older men be sober, reverent, temperate, sound in faith, in love, in patience; the older women likewise, that they be reverent in behavior, not slanderers . . . that they admonish the young women to love their husbands, to love their children.

TITUS 2:2–4

Marriage itself is founded on the principle of mutuality. Don't imagine for a moment that the husband's God-ordained headship relegates the wife to some secondary status or destroys the essential oneness of the marriage relationship. Marriage is a partnership, not a private fiefdom for dominant husbands. That truth is woven into everything Scripture teaches about the principles of marriage and the husband's relationship.

In the first place, Scripture makes it perfectly clear that men and women are spiritual equals in the sight of God. They have equal standing in Christ and equal spiritual privileges, because we are all united with Him in the same way. Galatians 3:28 says, "There is neither male nor female; for you are all one in Christ Jesus." There is no second-class spiritual relationship. Men are not superior to women.

It's nonetheless true (and perfectly obvious) that both Scripture and nature assign different roles and different functions to men and women. The Bible is quite clear in assigning headship in every family to the husband, not the wife (Eph. 5:23). The responsibilities of teaching and leading the church are given to men, not women (1 Tim. 2:12). But women are uniquely and exclusively equipped to bear and nurture young children, and the fulfillment of that role assures that they can never be relegated to any second-class status. Remember, however, that while their *roles* are clearly different, the *spiritual standing* of men and women in Christ is perfectly equal.

What challenges or blessings have you experienced as you live out these roles?

The Fulfilled Family, 19–21

Mutual Submission

Wives, submit to your own husbands, as is fitting in the Lord. Husbands, love your wives and do not be bitter toward them.

Colossians 3:18–19

Wives have often borne the brunt of Ephesians 5, as if this passage were all about the wife's subservience and the husband's dominance in the home. I have heard of more than one home where an overzealous, authoritarian husband constantly held verse 22 ("Wives, submit to your own husbands") over the wife's head.

But that kind of attitude is a violation of the whole spirit of the passage. It's interesting to note that in the Greek text, the word for *submit* doesn't even appear in verse 22. The idea is certainly implied, but the Greek expression is elliptical, omitting the word *submission*, and relying on the force of verse 21 to make the meaning clear. In other words, a literal translation of verses 21–22 would read something like this: "Submit to one another in the fear of God. Wives, to your own husbands, as to the Lord."

So keep in mind that Paul's stress was first and foremost on the *mutuality* of submission. Everyone in the church is to submit to everyone else. The command to submit is not for wives only, but for husbands too. And verses 22–24 simply explain *how* wives are to submit to their husbands: with the same kind of respect and devotion they owe to Christ.

This does not mean, of course, that the husband is supposed to abdicate his God-ordained role of leadership and authority in the home. What it *does* mean is that the way he must exercise his leadership is not by lording it over his wife and family, but by serving them and sacrificing himself for them with a Christlike humility.

What does the mutuality of submission look like in your marriage? In the marriages of those around you?

The Fulfilled Family, 15–17

Submission of the Wife

Wives, likewise, be submissive to your own husbands, that even if some do not obey the word, they, without a word, may be won by the conduct of their wives, when they observe your chaste conduct accompanied by fear.

1 PETER 3:1–2

The admonition to wives in Ephesians 5 is simple, covering just three verses (22–24).

Notice that Paul started and ended this section by specifying *whom* wives should submit to: "their own husbands" (v. 24). Women as a group are not made serfs to men in general, and men aren't automatically elevated to a ruling class over all women. But Scripture calls each woman to submit in particular to her own husband's headship.

The command is general and sweeping. It's not limited to wives whose husbands are fulfilling *their* functions. It's categorical and unconditional: *wives*. Anyone who fits that classification is obligated to obey the command of this verse by submitting to her own husband.

Notice also that the word *submit* is not the word *obey*. What it calls for is an active, deliberate, loving, intelligent devotion to the husband's noble aspirations and ambitions. It does *not* demand blind, fawning, slavish kowtowing to every whim. A wife is neither a child nor a slave, waiting on her husband while he sits in an easy chair and issues commands.

How do you make submission a positive trait in your household?

The Fulfilled Family, 30–32

Christianity Values Women

The twelve were with Him, and . . . Mary called Magdalene, out of whom had come seven demons, and Joanna the wife of Chuza, Herod's steward, and Susanna, and many others who provided for Him from their substance.

LUKE 8:1–3

In the social and religious life of Israel and the New Testament church, women were never relegated to the background. They partook with men in all the feasts and public worship of Israel (Deut. 16:14; Neh. 8:2–3). Women were not required to be veiled or silent in the public square, as they are in some Middle Eastern cultures even today (Gen. 12:14; 24:16; 1 Sam. 1:12). Mothers (not merely fathers) shared teaching responsibilities and authority over their children (Prov. 1:8; 6:20). Women could even be landowners in Israel (Num. 27:8; Prov. 31:16). In fact, wives were expected to administer many of the affairs of their own households (Prov. 14:1; 1 Tim. 5:9–10, 14).

All of that stands in sharp contrast to the way other ancient cultures routinely degraded and debased women. Women in pagan societies during biblical times were often treated with little more dignity than animals. Some of the best-known Greek philosophers taught that women are inferior creatures by nature. In the Roman Empire women were usually regarded as personal possessions of their husbands or fathers, with hardly any better standing than household slaves.

Christianity, born in a world where Roman and Hebrew cultures intersected, elevated the status of women to an unprecedented height. Jesus' disciples included several women (Luke 8:1–3), a practice almost unheard-of among the rabbis of His day. Not only that, He *encouraged* their discipleship by portraying it as something more needful than domestic service (Luke 10:38–42). Thus He exalted the position of womanhood itself.

How are women encouraged to serve in your church? In your family?

Twelve Extraordinary Women, xiii–xiv

Christianity Elevates Women

The wise woman builds her house.

Proverbs 14:1

Wherever the gospel has spread, the social, legal, and spiritual status of women has, as a rule, been elevated. When the gospel has been eclipsed (whether by repression, false religion, secularism, humanistic philosophy, or spiritual decay within the church), the status of women has declined accordingly.

When secular movements have arisen claiming to be concerned with women's rights, their efforts have generally been detrimental to the status of women. The feminist movement of our generation, for example, is a case in point. Feminism has devalued and defamed *femininity*. Natural gender distinctions are usually downplayed, dismissed, despised, or denied. Women are encouraged to act and talk like men. Modern feminists heap scorn on women who want family and household to be their first priorities—disparaging the role of motherhood, the one calling that is most uniquely and exclusively feminine. The whole message of feminist egalitarianism is that there is really nothing extraordinary about women.

That is certainly not the message of Scripture. Scripture honors women *as women*, and it encourages them to seek honor in a uniquely feminine way (Prov. 31:10–30).

Scripture never discounts the female intellect, downplays the talents and abilities of women, or discourages the right use of women's spiritual gifts. But whenever the Bible expressly talks about the marks of an excellent woman, the stress is always on feminine *virtue*. The most significant women in Scripture were influential not because of their careers, but because of their *character*. The message these women collectively give is not about "gender equality"; it's about true feminine excellence.

How can you encourage your wife or other women in your life toward true feminine excellence?

Twelve Extraordinary Women, xvi–xvii

True Beauty

Women [should] adorn themselves in modest apparel, with propriety and moderation, not with braided hair or gold or pearls or costly clothing, but, which is proper for women professing godliness, with good works.

1 Timothy 2:9–10

"Do not let your adornment be merely outward—arranging the hair, wearing gold, or putting on fine apparel" (1 Peter 3:3). Peter's words could not be more timely today. Women shaped by contemporary society's values tend to be obsessed with external adornment. That is not where a woman's priorities should be focused, Peter said. Paul said something similar in 1 Timothy 2:9–10.

Don't misunderstand what this means. The apostles were not completely forbidding jewelry, stylish hair, or other feminine adornments; they were simply saying these things are not what is most important. The way a woman looks is not the measure of her true beauty.

Women first of all need to cultivate inner beauty. They should be primarily concerned with "the hidden person of the heart, with the incorruptible beauty of a gentle and quiet spirit, which is very precious in the sight of God" (1 Peter 3:4). It's hard to imagine anything Peter might have said that would be more out of step with twenty-first-century notions of political correctness! He was saying that women ought to be gentle and quiet and submissive, not loud and boisterous and pushy. They ought to be concerned with their own character, and not with the world's fashion. In other words, the real attractiveness of a godly woman—and her true strength—is that she is supportive of her husband and submissive to him, and she shows that submission through gentleness and serene stillness.

What aspects of true beauty have you seen or celebrated recently?

The Fulfilled Family, 36–38

The Wife's Primary Responsibility

Who can find a virtuous wife? For her worth is far above rubies. The heart of her husband safely trusts her; so he will have no lack of gain.

PROVERBS 31:10–11

Notice, by the way, that all the women's biblical priorities are centered in the family and in the home: "to love their husbands, to love their children, to be discreet, chaste, homemakers, good, obedient to their own husbands" (Titus 2:4–5). The starting point is love—the woman's love for her own husband and children. And she expresses that love in her virtue and her self-sacrifice, chiefly in the arena of her own family home.

One expression in Titus 2 deserves special notice. It is the word *homemakers*. The Greek word is *oikourgous*, which literally means "workers at home." *Oikos* is the Greek word for "home," and *ergon* means "work, employment." It suggests that a married woman's first duty is to her own family, in her own household. Managing her own home should be her primary employment, her first task, her most important job, and her true career. I am convinced the Holy Spirit meant for believers to apply this even in the twenty-first century.

Of course I'm aware of all the economic and sociological arguments people have set forth in favor of working mothers. Those arguments are frankly not very persuasive in light of the obvious detrimental effects of so many absentee mothers in today's society. But more important, the Word of God stands squarely against the modern feminist agenda when it comes to the issue of working mothers. According to the Bible, a mother's life belongs in the home. That's where her first, most important, God-given responsibility lies. That is precisely what older women are supposed to teach younger women.

How do you encourage your spouse, or are you yourself encouraged in the role described above?

The Fulfilled Family, 41–43

The Ideal Woman

Give her of the fruit of her hands, and let her own works praise her in the gates.

PROVERBS 31:31

Proverbs 31 portrays the ideal woman for us. She's creative, industrious, intelligent, resourceful, and enterprising. There's nothing drab or monotonous or suffocating about her career as a wife and a mother.

Notice that the passage begins by acknowledging the rarity of such a virtuous woman. Her worth is unsurpassed (v. 10). But in no way is she repressed or enslaved to tedium because of her domestic responsibilities. She is quite literally a homemaker: a positive, constructive force in the home and family.

She is trustworthy. Her husband can trust her with the checkbook (v. 11). She is not only frugal, but she is also devoted for life to her husband's welfare (v. 12).

On top of that, she is industrious and resourceful, working with her own hands (v. 13). This is her hobby. This is her joy. This is what she loves to do. The expression literally means that she derives joy from doing handiwork for her family.

And far from being imprisoned by her domestic duties, "she is like the merchant ships" (v. 14), seeking out bargains wherever they may be found.

She sacrifices a great deal for her family, rising up early to prepare meals for them (v. 15).

Not only that, but she is shrewd in business (v. 16). She is strong (v. 17); she is enterprising (v. 18); she is generous (v. 20); and she is confident (v. 21).

But here's the real prize: "Her children rise up and call her blessed; her husband also, and he praises her" (v. 28). There's no way such a woman would ever feel trapped in a dull and dreary existence.

How is this "ideal woman" a contrast to society's "ideal woman"?

The Fulfilled Family, 46–51

The Love of a Husband

And He sat down, called the twelve, and said to them, "If anyone desires to be first, he shall be last of all and servant of all."

MARK 9:35

Authentic love is incompatible with a despotic or domineering approach to headship. When Paul commanded husbands to love their wives as Christ loved the church, he was in effect forbidding them to exercise severe or abusive authority over their wives. If the model of this love is Christ, who "did not come to be served but to serve, and to give His life as a ransom for many" (Matt. 20:28), then the husband who thinks he exists so his wife and children can serve him couldn't be farther off the mark.

Consider the implications of a *command* to love. This suggests that genuine love is not merely a feeling or an involuntary attraction. It involves a willful choice, and that is why this is in the form of an imperative. Far from being something we "fall into" by happenstance, authentic love involves a deliberate, voluntary commitment to sacrifice whatever we can for the good of the person we love.

When Paul commanded husbands to love their wives, he was calling for all the virtues outlined in 1 Corinthians 13, including patience, kindness, generosity, humility, meekness, thoughtfulness, liberality, gentleness, trust, goodness, truthfulness, and long-suffering. It is significant that all the properties of love stress selflessness and sacrifice. The husband who truly loves his wife simply cannot wield his authority over her like a club. Far from being overlord of the family, the godly husband and father must make himself a servant of all (see also Mark 9:35).

In what ways have you seen this genuine love played out in your family?

The Fulfilled Family, 58–60

June 16

True Leadership in the Home

Let deacons be the husbands of one wife, ruling their children and their own houses well.

1 Timothy 3:12

Notice the primary way Christ maintains the purity of the church: "with the washing of water by the word" (Eph. 5:26). Husbands have a duty to ensure that their wives are regularly exposed to the cleansing and purifying effect of the Word of God. The husband is to be the spiritual leader and priestly guardian of the home. It is his duty to make sure the Word of God is at the center of the home and family. Of course he ought to lead his family in participation in a church where the Word of God is revered and obeyed. But above all, he himself needs to be devoted to the Word of God and proficient enough in handling the Scriptures that he can be the true spiritual head in the marriage (see also 1 Cor. 14:34–35).

That means the husband's priorities must be in order. If a man sits for hours, day after day, month after month, year after year, watching sports on television or otherwise neglecting his family's spiritual needs, he will eventually reap a bitter harvest. Here is where the husband's willingness to sacrifice for the good of his wife becomes intensely practical. If cultivating her sanctification and guarding her purity are not priorities over the evening television lineup, that husband is falling short of loving his wife the way Christ loved the church.

But in the same way Christ lovingly guards the purity of His church, the godly husband will seek his wife's sanctification, purity, and spiritual growth. That is every husband's responsibility.

How do you guard the spiritual growth of your spouse, or how is your spiritual growth guarded by your spouse?

The Fulfilled Family, 65–66

A Caring Husband

So husbands ought to love their own wives as their own bodies; he who loves his wife loves himself.

EPHESIANS 5:28

Genuine love also involves tender care, and Paul expressed that idea this way: "Husbands ought to love their own wives as their own bodies" (Eph. 5:28).

We spend a lot of time and energy taking care of our own bodies. We exercise; we eat; we wear clothes to look nice and stay warm. When we're sick and fatigued, we rest. When our bodies hurt, we seek relief from pain. We're attentive to our own bodies, concerned with their needs, sensitive and responsive to whatever they desire.

That is the kind of love Paul commanded husbands to show their wives. Notice, once again, Scripture is not describing love only as an emotion. This sort of love is active, voluntary, dynamic—something we do, not something we passively "feel."

It's only reasonable that a man would love his wife the way he loves his own body, because in marriage "the two . . . become one flesh" (Eph. 5:31). That is the way that God designed marriage. It applies universally, and it has been true from the beginning (Gen. 2:24). Husbands ought to love their wives with the same care they give their own bodies, because, after all, the two *are* one flesh.

Marriage itself is consummated with the literal bodily union of husband and wife. From that point on, the husband should regard the wife as his own flesh. If she hurts, he ought to feel the pain. If she has needs, he should embrace those needs as his own. He should seek to feel what she feels, desire what she desires, and in effect, give her the same care and consideration he gives his own body.

In what practical ways will you show love to your spouse today?

The Fulfilled Family, 67–68

A Husband's Responsibility

Let the husband render to his wife the affection due her, and likewise also the wife to her husband. The wife does not have authority over her own body, but the husband does. And likewise the husband does not have authority over his own body, but the wife does.

1 Corinthians 7:3–4

First Peter 3:7 reveals a number of truths about the role of the husband.

First, from the husband's perspective, headship is something that carries a greater *responsibility*, not necessarily a higher degree of privilege. Peter recognized that the wife is "the weaker vessel." And yet he saw this as a reason for the husband to sacrifice personal privilege and "[give] honor to the wife."

Second, although the husband's duties clearly include leadership, nothing here indicates that the husband ought to regard the wife as anything other than a joint heir and partner. Husband and wife are "heirs together of the grace of life."

Third, the text suggests three practical ways husbands ought to prefer their wives over themselves.

Consideration. Husbands need to be aware of the concerns their wives express, the goals they have set, the dreams they cherish, the desires that drive them, the things they fear, and the anxieties they carry. That is what every wife needs—and that is what Scripture demands.

Chivalry. A husband honors his wife when he employs his strength to serve her in ways that account for her weakness.

Communion. Husband and wife are joint heirs of the "grace of this life." By that expression, Peter was indicating that marriage itself is the best part of life—like the topping on a sundae. The husband and wife share together in that grace.

How will you honor your spouse this week?

The Fulfilled Family, 68–71

A Hard Decision

For I have come to "set a man against his father, a daughter against her mother, and a daughter-in-law against her mother-in-law."

MATTHEW 10:35

"For I have come to 'set a man against his father'" (Matt. 10:35). Jesus was saying, "I will cut a man off totally from his father, and all these other relatives from each other. I'll fracture families every way possible."

This is the worst rending that can happen. It's not so bad when you're at odds with your neighbor, your boss, your friend, or your society, but when it gets into the family, and your commitment to Jesus Christ means that you are severed from your relatives, that's where it really begins to rub.

Being a Christian and following Jesus Christ may mean you create a division in your own home. But that's the mark of a true disciple. Clinging to Christ often means letting go of family members who reject you because you won't reject the gospel. That's especially true in Jewish families, as well as those in false religions.

This is a hard standard, and many people decide it's too much of a sacrifice. Some wives will not come to Christ for fear of separation from their husbands. Some husbands will not come to Christ for fear of separation from their wives. Children may not come to Christ for fear of their fathers or mothers, and vice versa. People will not take a stand for Christ, because they want to maintain that family harmony. But Jesus said the true disciple will turn from his family, if he is forced to make a choice. This is part of self-denial, accepting gladly the high cost of following Jesus to receive His infinite blessings for time and eternity.

What family challenges have you faced as a result of following Christ?

Hard to Believe, 131–132

He Left Everything!

As Jesus passed on from there, He saw a man named Matthew sitting at the tax office. And He said to him, "Follow Me." So he arose and followed Him.

MATTHEW 9:9

It must have been a stunning reality to Matthew when Jesus chose him. It came out of the blue. By Matthew's own account, Jesus saw him sitting in the tax office and simply said, "Follow Me" (Matt. 9:9).

Matthew instantly and without hesitation "arose and followed Him." He abandoned the tax office. He left his toll booth and walked away from his cursed profession forever.

The decision was irreversible as soon as he made it. There was no shortage of money-grubbing piranha who coveted a tax franchise like Matthew's, and as soon as he stepped away, you can be sure that someone else stepped in and took over. Once Matthew walked away, he could never go back. Nor did he ever regret his decision.

What was it in a man like Matthew that caused him to drop everything at once like that? We might assume that he was a materialist. And at one time he must have been, or he never would have gotten into a position like that in the first place. So why would he walk away from everything and follow Jesus, not knowing what the future held?

The best answer we can deduce is that whatever Matthew's tortured soul may have experienced because of the profession he had chosen to be in, down deep inside he was a Jew who knew and loved the Old Testament. At some point in his life, most likely *after* he had chosen his despicable career, he was smitten with a gnawing spiritual hunger and became a true seeker. Of course, God was seeking and drawing *him*, and the draw was irresistible.

What have you left behind to follow Christ?

Twelve Ordinary Men, 155

Real Righteousness Requires Truth

But to him who does not work but believes on Him who justifies the ungodly, his faith is accounted for righteousness.

ROMANS 4:5

What we believe rather than *what we do* is what secures us a righteous standing before God—because we lay hold of justifying righteousness by faith alone, and not by our works (Rom. 4:5).

Paul says in Romans 9:31–32 that "Israel, pursuing the law of righteousness, has not attained to the law of righteousness. Why? Because they did not seek it by faith, but as it were, by the works of the law." In other words, regardless of how meticulous they may have been in their external observance of God's law, their *unbelief* was sufficient to exclude them from the kingdom. They doubted the truth of Christ, and that proved spiritually fatal in spite of how well they had perfected an external display of piety.

Notice: Paul explicitly says they were pursuing righteousness. But they were looking for it in all the wrong places. Because they clung to wrong *beliefs* about the righteousness God requires and rejected the righteousness that Christ would have provided for them, they were eternally condemned. Their failure was first of all an error about a vital article of faith, not merely a flaw in their practice. Their whole belief system (not merely their behavior) was wrong. Unbelief was enough to condemn them, regardless of how they acted.

Real righteousness simply cannot exist in isolation from belief in the truth.

On what do you base your beliefs?

The Truth War, 33–34

Witnesses to the Truth

Go therefore and make disciples of all the nations, baptizing them in the name of the Father and of the Son and of the Holy Spirit.

MATTHEW 28:19

Every member of the body can and should be a witness. "You shall receive power," said Jesus, "when the Holy Spirit has come upon you; and you shall be witnesses" (Acts 1:8). Jesus also said, "Go therefore and make disciples of all the nations, baptizing them in the name of the Father and of the Son and of the Holy Spirit, teaching them to observe all things that I have commanded you; and lo, I am with you always, even to the end of the age" (Matt. 28:19–20). There is no waiver given, no excuse accepted. "Therefore, if anyone is in Christ, he is a new creation; old things have passed away; behold, all things have become new. Now all things are of God, who has reconciled us to Himself through Jesus Christ, and has given us the ministry of reconciliation" (2 Cor. 5:17–18). Anyone reconciled to Christ has the ministry of telling others about Him.

This doesn't mean that you have to witness by preaching on street corners—though I can tell you from firsthand experience that it's an unforgettable adventure. Your witness may be by example, or something you write one day, or take any number of other forms. But however it happens, don't worry about whether or not you'll do a good job. Just remember that the Holy Spirit empowers us—individually and as a body—to witness: "When the Helper comes, whom I shall send to you from the Father . . . He will testify of Me. And you also will bear witness, because you have been with Me from the beginning" (John 15:26–27).

To whom will you bear witness this week?

Welcome to the Family, 88–89

True Dependence

I am the vine, you are the branches. He who abides in Me, and I in him, bears much fruit; for without Me you can do nothing.

John 15:5

Faithfulness to Christ is impossible without total dependence on Him. The strongest disciple is utterly impotent when he trusts his own resources for courage and strength to endure. "For we do not wrestle against flesh and blood, but against principalities, against powers, against the rulers of the darkness of this age, against spiritual hosts of wickedness in the heavenly places" (Eph. 6:12). Without spiritual armor from the Lord, we expose ourselves to the worst kinds of defeat and shame.

Jesus had told Peter, "Simon, Simon! Indeed, Satan has asked for you, that he may sift you as wheat" (Luke 22:31). The word for "you" in the Greek text is plural, indicating that this warning applied not only to Peter, but to the others as well. Peter replied, "Lord, I am ready to go with You, both to prison and to death" (v. 33), and Jesus forewarned him, "I tell you, Peter, the rooster shall not crow this day before you will deny three times that you know Me" (v. 34).

Peter, wrongly assuming that the plot to take Jesus was merely a flesh-and-blood conflict, was depending on fleshly resources such as his own courage and physical stamina—and his sword (v. 38). But such things are always insufficient weapons in a spiritual battle. "Woe to those who go down to Egypt for help, and rely on horses, who trust in chariots because they are many, and in horsemen because they are very strong, but who do not look to the Holy One of Israel, nor seek the Lord!" (Isa. 31:1).

In a conflict situation, on what resources do you depend?

The Murder of Jesus, 53

No Boasting

Then He brought him outside and said, "Look now toward heaven, and count the stars if you are able to number them. . . . So shall your descendants be."
And he believed in the LORD, and He accounted it to him for righteousness.

GENESIS 15:5–6

If people could earn justification by works, they would indeed have something to boast about. The doctrine of justification by faith is therefore a humbling truth. We do not merit salvation. We cannot be good enough to please God. There is no room in God's redemptive plan for human pride. Even Abraham, the father of the faith, had no reason to glory in himself: "If Abraham was justified by works, he has something to boast about, but not before God. For what does the Scripture say? 'Abraham believed God, and it was accounted to him for righteousness'" (Rom. 4:2–3).

Paul was quoting Genesis 15:6. That single Old Testament verse is one of the clearest statements in all of Scripture about justification. The word *reckoned* shows the forensic nature of justification.

This reckoning was a one-sided transaction. God designated righteousness to Abraham's spiritual account. Abraham *did* nothing to earn it. Even his faith was not meritorious. Faith is never said to be the *ground* for justification, only the channel through which justifying grace is received.

Faith, then, means the end of any attempt to earn God's favor through personal merit. God saves only those who do not trust in themselves—those who trust "Him who justifies the ungodly." Therefore, until a person confesses that he is ungodly, that person cannot be saved, because he still trusts in his own goodness. Those who are saved know they have nothing to boast about.

Have you ever tried to earn God's favor through good works? Why or why not?

The Gospel According to the Apostles, 100–101

How True Change Happens

And daily in the temple, and in every house, they did not cease teaching and preaching Jesus as the Christ.

ACTS 5:42

After Pentecost all eleven disciples were markedly changed men. These same men who deserted their Master out of craven fear became intrepid witnesses for Him. When they were told to stop preaching by the high priest (the same high priest who had them cowering in fear on the eve of Jesus' crucifixion) their response was to keep right on preaching. They told the high priest, "We ought to obey God rather than men" (Acts 5:29). Though beaten, imprisoned, and threatened with death, they kept right on preaching. In fact, when an angel supernaturally released them from prison, rather than going into hiding, they went straight back to the temple and began preaching publicly again, right under the high priest's nose (Acts 5:18–21). Were these the same men who forsook Jesus and fled in the hour of His betrayal?

They were the same men, but now they were filled with the Holy Spirit. They were drawing on a power that was not their own. They had set aside their reckless self-assurance and were depending on the sufficiency of their Lord. That made all the difference in the world. Clearly they had all learned a great lesson from their failure. These same men who all forsook Jesus and fled on the night of His arrest spent the rest of their lives standing up for Him, in the face of every imaginable threat and persecution. They never abandoned their Lord again.

Christ Himself drew them back, forgave them, commissioned them for service, and empowered them to succeed where they once had failed so miserably.

What changes in your life have people noticed since you became a believer?

The Murder of Jesus, 59–60

A Cleansed Conscience

How much more shall the blood of Christ, who through the eternal Spirit offered Himself without spot to God, cleanse your conscience from dead works to serve the living God?

Hebrews 9:14

One aspect of the miracle of salvation is the cleansing and rejuvenating effect the new birth has on the conscience. At salvation, the believer's heart is "sprinkled clean from an evil conscience" (Heb. 10:22 NASB). The means through which the conscience is cleansed is the blood of Christ (Heb. 9:14). That does not mean, of course, that Jesus' actual blood has some mystical or magical potency as a conscience-cleansing agent. What does it mean?

The Old Testament Law required blood sacrifices to atone for sin. But Old Testament sacrifices could do nothing for the conscience. Hebrews 9:9–10 (NASB) says, "Gifts and sacrifices [under the Levitical system] cannot make the worshiper perfect in conscience, since they relate only to food and drink and various washings, regulations for the body imposed until a time of reformation."

Christ's sacrifice on the cross therefore accomplished what the blood of goats and bulls and the ashes of heifers could only symbolize.

Whenever our own conscience would mercilessly condemn us, the blood of Christ cries for forgiveness. We confess our sin so that the Lord can cleanse our conscience and give us joy (1 John 1:9). That is how "the blood of Christ, who through the eternal Spirit offered Himself without spot to God, cleanse[s] your conscience from dead works to serve the living God" (Heb. 9:14). Our faith communicates to our conscience that we are pardoned through the precious blood of Christ.

What a gift it is to be cleansed from a defiled conscience! In the same way that a grieved conscience is a flash of hell, so a pure conscience is a foretaste of glory.

How has this cleansing changed your life?

The Vanishing Conscience, 41–43

True Cleansing

Create in me a clean heart, O God, and renew a steadfast spirit within me.

Psalm 51:10

"Cleanse your hands, you sinners, and purify your hearts, you double-minded" (James 4:8). The expressions "cleanse your hands" and "purify your hearts" both speak of the need for cleansing from guilt.

True cleansing from sin is not something sinners can do for themselves. There is no suggestion in the command "Cleanse your hands . . . and purify your hearts" that sinners have the ability to reform themselves in a way that will gain God's blessing and approval. We have no more power to cleanse ourselves from sin than we have to change our skin color (see Jer. 13:23). Sin is deeply ingrained in our fallen nature; it is a reflection of our depraved moral character. We cannot, by sheer force of will, change our own character.

But cleansing and complete heart-renewal are works *God* does for those who draw near to Him in faith and with genuine repentance. He says, "I will sprinkle clean water on you, and you shall be clean; I will cleanse you from all your filthiness and from all your idols. I will give you a new heart and put a new spirit within you; I will take the heart of stone out of your flesh and give you a heart of flesh" (Ezek. 36:25–26). It is a work God does for us and in us; it is not something we can do for ourselves.

So James underscores the sinner's need for cleansing and urges his readers to seek that cleansing as they draw near to God.

When have you experienced a need for cleansing? What happened as a result?

Can God Bless America? 15–17

Prejudice Can Blind Against the Truth

Then Peter opened his mouth and said: "In truth I perceive that God shows no partiality. But in every nation whoever fears Him and works righteousness is accepted by Him."

ACTS 10:34–35

Prejudice is ugly. Generalizations based on feelings of superiority, not on fact, can be spiritually debilitating. Prejudice cuts a lot of people off from the truth. As a matter of fact, much of the nation of Israel rejected their Messiah because of prejudice. They did not believe their Messiah should come out of Nazareth. It was inconceivable to them that the Messiah and all His apostles would come from Galilee. They mocked the apostles as uneducated Galileans.

They did not like the fact that Jesus spoke against the religious establishment from Jerusalem. And from the religious leaders down to the people sitting in the synagogues, it was to some degree their prejudice that caused them to reject Him. This happened even in Jesus' own hometown. They derided Jesus as Joseph's son (Luke 4:22). He was without honor even in His own country, because He was nothing but a carpenter's son (v. 24). And the entire synagogue in Nazareth—His own synagogue, where He had grown up—were so filled with prejudice against Him that after He preached a single message to them, they tried to take Him to a cliff on the edge of town and throw Him off to kill Him (vv. 28–29).

Prejudice skewed their view of the Messiah. The people of Israel were prejudiced against Him as a Galilean and a Nazarene. And their prejudice against Him shut them off from the gospel. They refused to hear Him because they were cultural and religious bigots.

What offends you about Jesus, or His message, or the people He accepts?

Twelve Ordinary Men, 140–141

Contending for the True Faith

But you, beloved, building yourselves up on your most holy faith, praying in the Holy Spirit, keep yourselves in the love of God, looking for the mercy of our Lord Jesus Christ unto eternal life.

JUDE VV. 20–21

"I found it necessary to write to you exhorting you to contend earnestly for the faith which was once for all delivered to the saints" (Jude v. 3).

Notice what we are supposed to be fighting for. It is not anything petty, personal, mundane, or ego related. This warfare has a very narrow objective. What we are called to defend is no less than "the faith which was once for all delivered to the saints."

Jude is speaking of apostolic doctrine (Acts 2:42)—objective Christian truth—*the* faith, as delivered from Jesus through the agency of the Holy Spirit by the apostles to the church. As Jude says in verse 17: "Remember the words which were spoken before by the apostles of our Lord Jesus Christ."

Notice: no one discovered or invented the Christian faith. It was delivered to us. It was not as if someone mystically ascended into the transcendental realm and drew down an understanding of the truth. We don't need an enlightened guru to open the mysteries of the faith for us (cf. 1 John 2:27). The truth was entrusted by God to the whole church—intact and "once for all." It came by revelation, through the teaching of the apostles as preserved for us in Scripture. Jude speaks of "the faith" as a complete body of truth already delivered—so there is no need to seek any additional revelation or to embellish the substance of "the faith" in any way. Our task is simply to interpret, understand, publish, and defend the truth God has once and for all delivered to the church.

How have you defended the truth of Christ?

The Truth War, 75

Fighting for the Truth Is Unpopular but Essential

Fight the good fight of faith, lay hold on eternal life, to which you were also called and have confessed the good confession in the presence of many witnesses.

1 TIMOTHY 6:12

No idea is more politically incorrect among today's new-style evangelicals than the old fundamentalist notion that *truth* is worth fighting for—including the essential propositions of Christian doctrine. In fact, many believe that arguments over religious beliefs are the most pointless and arrogant of all conflicts. That can be true—and *is* true in cases where human opinions are the only thing at stake. But where God's Word speaks clearly, we have a duty to obey, defend, and proclaim the truth He has given us, and we should do that with an authority that reflects our conviction that God has spoken with clarity and finality. This is particularly crucial in contexts where cardinal doctrines of biblical Christianity are under attack.

Scripture itself clearly teaches that the main battleground where Satan wages his cosmic struggle against God is *ideological*. In other words, the spiritual warfare every Christian is engaged in is first of all a conflict between truth and error, not merely a competition between good and wicked deeds. The chief aim of Satan's strategy is to confuse, deny, and corrupt the truth with as much fallacy as possible, and that means the battle for truth is *very* serious. Being able to distinguish between sound doctrine and error should be one of the highest priorities for every Christian—as should defending the truth against false teaching.

Take such a stand today, however, and you will be scolded by a cacophony of voices telling you that you are out of line and you need to shut up.

How will you take a stand for Christ this week?

The Jesus You Can't Ignore, xxv–xxvi

July

FREEDOM, AMERICA, LEADERSHIP, AND WAR

The War with the Flesh

I say then: Walk in the Spirit, and you shall not fulfill the lust of the flesh. For the flesh lusts against the Spirit, and the Spirit against the flesh; and these are contrary to one another, so that you do not do the things that you wish.

Galatians 5:16–17

Flesh" in such contexts does not refer to the physical body. Nor does it describe a specific part of our being. Paul is not setting up a dualism between the material and the immaterial part of humanity, or between the body and the soul. "Spirit" in those verses refers to the Holy Spirit. "Flesh" refers to the sinfulness that remains in us while we are on this earth. It is a corruption that permeates and influences every aspect of our being—body, mind, emotions, and will. It is what makes us susceptible to sin even after we are made partakers in the divine nature (cf. 2 Peter 1:4). Though sin does not *reign* in us, it nevertheless *remains* in us. It is *dethroned*, but not *destroyed*.

"The flesh," then, is not the body, or the soul, or any other *part* of our beings. It is a *principle* that works in us. It is the source and stimulus of our sin. Though deprived of its dominion, it has not been divested of its potency, passions, or persuasive ability. The flesh wages battle against our godly desires with the fervor of a deposed monarch seeking to regain his throne.

In what area is your flesh battling against the Spirit most strongly?

The Vanishing Conscience, 138

How to Be Free

For this is the will of God, that by doing good you may put to silence the ignorance of foolish men—as free, yet not using liberty as a cloak for vice, but as bondservants of God.

1 Peter 2:15–16

As shocking as it is profound, God's Word teaches that true freedom can only be found through slavery to Christ. Though they think they are free, all unbelievers are in reality slaves to sin—held captive to their lusts and ensnared in their trespasses. In fact, the Bible denotes only two categories of people in this world: those who are slaves to sin and those who are slaves to righteousness. Paul contrasted those two groups in Romans 6:16–18.

There is no such thing as absolute moral independence. Every person is a slave—either to sin or to God.

Slavery to Christ not only means freedom *from* sin, guilt, and condemnation. It also means freedom *to* obey, *to* please God, and *to* live the way our Creator intended us to live—in intimate fellowship with Him. Thus, "having been freed from sin [we have been] enslaved to God" (Rom. 6:22 NASB; cf. 1 Peter 2:16). Slavery to Christ, then, is the only freedom.

Having been redeemed by Christ and empowered by the Holy Spirit, believers have everything they need to gain victory over temptation and sin. The power of sin has been permanently broken. The condemnation of the Law has been forever removed. The freedom of obedience is ours to possess. Now "we serve in newness of the Spirit" (Rom. 7:6). In being Christ's slaves, we are finally and fully liberated; in submitting to Him we experience true emancipation, for His law has forever set us free from the law of sin and death (Rom. 8:2).

What can you do this week to submit more fully to Christ?

Slave, 200–203

How to Free Sinners

But God be thanked that though you were slaves of sin, yet you obeyed from the heart that form of doctrine to which you were delivered.

Romans 6:17

Probably nothing is more true of sinners today than that they think they are free. They see Christianity as some kind of bondage. It is all about rights: "No one is going to infringe on my rights. I can be what I want to be. I'm free to be myself."

Such people are not free. The Bible defines them as prisoners. Sin has indebted them to God, and it's a debt they cannot pay. They are in bondage, and they are awaiting eternal death. According to Hebrews 2:15, Satan wields the power of death and holds captive "those who through fear of death [are] all their lifetime subject to bondage." Ephesians 2:2 calls them "sons of disobedience" who are under the power of, and in bondage to, their own sin. The divine sentence on them is incarceration for eternity in hell, where they will never die.

To lead others to Christ, to save them from this eternal judgment, you have to speak that truth in love; you have to tell them the truth without pulling any punches. Does that seem impossible? Will your audience turn you off? They turned Jesus off. In fact, they hated His message so much, His own neighbors and relatives, in a rage, tried to kill Him for preaching it.

If you suffer for the truth of the gospel, and you will, remember you're in good company. You're following the best example who ever served God; you are on the Lord's side, casting off self-righteousness to walk through the narrow gospel gate that leads to eternal life, and faithfully giving that gospel to others.

How would you explain slavery to sin to an unbeliever?

Hard to Believe, 70–71

The True Blessing of America

If My people who are called by My name will humble themselves, and pray and seek My face, and turn from their wicked ways, then I will hear from heaven, and will forgive their sin and heal their land.

2 Chronicles 7:14

Originally, "God Bless America" was a *prayer* for divine blessing. In its current form it sometimes seems nothing more than a patriotic battle-cry—usually intoned without much serious reflection.

God *has* blessed America throughout history to a remarkable degree. But His blessings are not measured—as most people believe—by material affluence, power, and world dominance. The greatest blessings God has graciously given America have been *spiritual* blessings—knowledge of the good news of salvation in Christ, freedom for the gospel to be propagated, sweeping revivals like those of the Great Awakenings, and growth and spiritual prosperity for the church in our nation.

What do we really mean when we invoke God's blessing on our nation? Do people in America truly long for the spiritual awakening that would be the necessary condition for true divine blessing? Are people in America prepared to embrace God's Son as Lord and Savior, or do they just want God's favor on their own terms?

Scripture is clear that a wholesale spiritual renewal, brought about through the clear and persuasive preaching of the gospel of Jesus Christ, is the sole pathway to divine blessing. What is needed is not merely moral reform, but spiritual regeneration. And unless this occurs on a widespread scale that deeply impacts all of society, we will continue to forfeit the true blessings of God for our nation. Merely reciting the slogan "God Bless America" will do nothing for us, until it becomes a heartfelt prayer for spiritual renewal and regeneration through the gospel.

How can you pray for this kind of blessing?

Can God Bless America? vii–viii

The Way to National Revival

Let every one turn from his evil way and from the violence that is in his hands. . . . Then God saw their works, that they turned from their evil way; and God relented from the disaster that He had said He would bring upon them, and He did not do it.

Jonah 3:8, 10

The revival our nation needs so badly will not occur unless we as *individuals* repent. Authentic repentance involves a change of heart, not merely a change of public policy. And the *first* to repent must be the people of God—Christians who know and love Christ but who have fallen into a state of spiritual lethargy or indifference and have left their first love (cf. Rev. 2:4). We have diverted our efforts and energies and strategies from evangelism. We need to repent of that.

No national revival has ever occurred because of political strategizing or legislative initiatives. Revivals don't occur when the people of God protest and demonstrate against the sins of unbelievers. Revivals aren't the fruit of boycotts or debates about public policy. Revivals occur when the Word of God is proclaimed and people are called to repentance. This was true in Nineveh, when an entire city of pagans responded to the preaching of Jonah by repenting in sackcloth and ashes (Jonah 3:5–10). It was true at Pentecost, when thousands in Jerusalem suddenly repented (Acts 2:41). That is how revivals invariably occur. That is exactly what happened in the Great Awakening, when our nation's forefathers repented under the passionate, relentless preaching of men like Jonathan Edwards and George Whitefield. Study the history of revival, and you will discover that this has always been the case. Revival comes in response to the clear and forceful preaching of God's Word out of hearts filled with love for the lost.

What would a revived nation look like?

Can God Bless America? 26–28

How the Covenant Applies to America

And the Scripture, foreseeing that God would justify the Gentiles by faith, preached the gospel to Abraham beforehand, saying, "In you all the nations shall be blessed."

Galatians 3:8

Unlike ancient Israel, America is not a covenant nation. God has made no promise that guarantees our national status forever.

But for those of us who are Christians, the covenant blessings *do* apply. "If you are Christ's, then you are Abraham's seed, and heirs according to the promise" (Gal. 3:29). All the promises of salvation, mercy, forgiveness for our sins, and spiritual prosperity are ours to claim as long as we remain faithful to God.

That is why the spiritual state of the church in our nation is the key to the blessing of the nation as a whole. If God is going to bless America, it will not be for the sake of the nation itself. He blesses the nation, and has always done so, for the sake of His people. If we who are called by His name are not fulfilling the conditions for divine blessing, there is no hope whatsoever for the rest of the nation.

On the other hand, if the church is fit to receive God's blessing, the whole nation will be the beneficiary of that, because the Word of God will be proclaimed with power, God will add to His church, and spiritual blessings of all kinds will result. And those are the truest blessings of all.

Scripture says, "Judgment must begin at the house of God" (1 Peter 4:17 KJV). It is equally true that blessing begins with the people of God, and it spills over from there. That is the one true hope for real blessing on our nation.

How have you seen God's blessings flow from believers to those around them?

Can God Bless America? 39–41

Christians and Politics

Then the proconsul believed, when he saw what had been done, being astonished at the teaching of the Lord.

ACTS 13:12

Complete noninvolvement in politics would be contrary to what God's Word says about doing good in society: "Therefore, as we have opportunity, let us do good to all, especially to those who are of the household of faith" (Gal. 6:10; see Titus 3:1–2). It would also display a lack of gratitude for whatever amount of religious freedom the government allows us to enjoy. Furthermore, such pious apathy toward government and politics would reveal a lack of appreciation for the many appropriate legal remedies believers in democracies have for maintaining or improving the civil order. A certain amount of healthy and balanced concern with current trends in government and the community is acceptable, as long as we realize that such interest is not vital to our spiritual growth, our righteous testimony, or the advancement of the kingdom of Christ. Above all, the believer's political involvement should never displace the priority of preaching and teaching the gospel.

Believers are certainly not prohibited from being directly involved in government as civil servants, as some notable examples in the Old and New Testaments illustrate. Joseph in Egypt and Daniel in Babylon are two excellent models of servants God used in top governmental positions to further His kingdom. The centurion's servant (Matt. 8:5–13), Zacchaeus the tax collector (Luke 19:1–10), and Cornelius the centurion (Acts 10) all continued in public service even after they experienced the healing or saving power of Christ. (Acts 13:4–12 records that the Roman proconsul Sergius Paulus also remained in office after he was converted.)

The issue again is one of priority. The greatest temporal good we can accomplish through political involvement cannot compare to what the Lord can accomplish through us in the eternal work of His kingdom.

Where can you be more involved in public service that would bless others?

Why Government Can't Save You, 8–9

People of Obedience

And seek the peace of the city where I have caused you to be carried away captive, and pray to the LORD for it; for in its peace you will have peace.

JEREMIAH 29:7

God commands that we be model citizens, law-abiding, obedient, and respectful toward governmental authority. When observing our relationship to those over us, people should never characterize us as rabble-rousers, rebels, or insolent critics. The Lord expects us to speak out against sin, injustice, immorality, and ungodliness with courage and diligence. But we must do so in a law-abiding manner, according to the civil laws that legislative bodies and governing officials have established for us. The church is to be a godly society within the larger ungodly society, living peaceably and exhibiting good works through the transformed lives of its members. Only in those ways will we truly affect society and allow the Holy Spirit to draw unconverted people to the saving power of God.

"Be subject to" in Romans 13:1 is from the familiar Greek New Testament term *hupotasso*, which was primarily a military word that denoted soldiers ranked under and subject to the absolute authority of a superior officer. Paul used the expression in the passive imperative, which makes it a command and indicates that believers should willingly place themselves under all government leaders.

Notice that the apostle, under the inspiration of the Holy Spirit, gives this command without qualification or condition. We are to obey *every* civil authority, no matter how immoral, cruel, ungodly, or incompetent he or she might be.

Civil obedience was also an Old Testament principle. Even while the Jews were held as captives in Babylon, God commanded them to seek peace and pray for the city (Jer. 29:7).

Where have you seen the church's insolence against the government hurt its witness?

Why Government Can't Save You, 21–22

Pray for Our Leaders

And whatever they need . . . let it be given them day by day without fail, that they may offer sacrifices of sweet aroma to the God of heaven, and pray for the life of the king and his sons.

Ezra 6:9–10

We carry out our responsibility toward authority and display a God-honoring desire that everyone respect and obey government when we heed the apostle Paul's instructions to Timothy, "Therefore I exhort first of all that supplications, prayers, intercessions, and giving of thanks be made for all men, for kings and all who are in authority, that we may lead a quiet and peaceable life in all godliness and reverence. For this is good and acceptable in the sight of God our Savior, who desires all men to be saved and to come to the knowledge of the truth" (1 Tim. 2:1–4).

Notice that Paul is not at all commanding us to pray for the removal from office of evil rulers or those who are politically "incompatible" with our views. And it is not merely an exhortation for us to pray that our leaders be wise and just, but that they would eventually repent, believe the gospel, and be saved. While the contemporary church seems to have largely forgotten that the priorities for effecting change in society are faithful prayer, godly living, and diligent evangelism rather than persistent lobbying, self-righteous confrontation, and political organizing, the ancient church had its priorities in good order.

The ancient church, often during periods of the worst persecution against it, prayed for unbelieving and dictatorial rulers. If we truly desire to fulfill our citizenship responsibilities—which include submission to and respect for the authorities—and thereby positively influence our culture as the early believers did theirs, we must follow their example.

For whom among our nation's leadership are you especially praying?

Why Government Can't Save You, 34–35

A Divine Purpose for Government

Therefore submit yourselves to every ordinance of man for the Lord's sake, whether to the king as supreme, or to governors, as to those who are sent by him for the punishment of evildoers and for the praise of those who do good.

1 Peter 2:13–14

One of God's ordained roles for government is for it to restrain evil by placing sufficient fear into the hearts of wrongdoers. Romans 13:3 says, "For rulers are not a terror to good works, but to evil."

The word *terror* in the original comes from the same root that gives us the English term *phobia*. The civil authorities should produce that kind of fear in the lives of those who perpetrate evil. Proper government will not be a terror to those citizens who perform good works, that category of deeds which is inherently good. Rather it will be a source of profound terror for those disobedient, lawbreaking citizens who engage in that category of deeds which is inherently evil. Throughout history, even the most wicked of governments have been a deterrent to major crimes such as murder, rape, and theft. Although it hardly justifies totalitarian systems, the reality is that those regimes often experience lower crime rates than do democratic nations.

The point is, even ungodly, worldly rulers have a basic awareness of morality. Every man and woman who is born has an innate knowledge of right and wrong. That knowledge is the basis of human conscience for both the saved and the unsaved (see Rom. 2:14–15).

Even the poorest form of government is better than no government at all. It's frightening to imagine what would occur in any society in which no one was in charge—anarchy is disastrous. To prevent such a bleak scenario, God established human government to restrain evildoers and lawbreakers.

Where have you seen the consequences of a government that has failed to restrain evil?

Why Government Can't Save You, 42–43

When to Disobey

Shadrach, Meshach, and Abed-Nego answered and said to the king, ". . . Let it be known to you, O king, that we do not serve your gods, nor will we worship the gold image which you have set up."

DANIEL 3:16, 18

There is one exception or limitation to our divinely mandated obligation of civil obedience: whenever an ordinance or official command would require that we disobey God's will or His Word.

The pharaoh in Egypt once ordered the killing of all Israelite male babies by their Jewish midwives. But the two midwives involved, Shiphrah and Puah, knew that murder was wrong and refused to comply with the monarch's decree (Ex. 1:17). Because the two women were faithful to the Lord's teaching, He "dealt well with the midwives, and the people multiplied and grew very mighty" (v. 20).

The book of Daniel records three significant accounts of justifiable civil disobedience. First, when Daniel and his three Jewish countrymen, as exiles in a foreign land, were ordered by the king of Babylon to eat "a daily provision of the king's delicacies and of the wine which he drank" (Dan. 1:5), they politely declined to do so.

A second account of legitimate civil disobedience in the book of Daniel concerns how Daniel's three colleagues (Shadrach, Meshach, and Abed-Nego) refused to engage in the open idolatry that King Nebuchadnezzar's command would have required (Daniel 3).

The third example of righteous civil disobedience is the well-known report of Daniel in the lions' den. He submitted himself to possible death rather than obey King Darius's decree that sought to keep him from worshiping the true God (Dan. 6:7–23).

What could the government command that you would need to disobey in order to obey God?

Why Government Can't Save You, 22–24

Key Truths About Civil Disobedience

If you are reproached for the name of Christ, blessed are you, for the Spirit of glory and of God rests upon you. . . . But let none of you suffer as a murderer, a thief, an evildoer, or as a busybody in other people's matters.

1 Peter 4:14–15

Most of us will seldom face the need to "obey God rather than men." Nearly always it will be God's will that we obey, both from His Word and through human authority. Likewise, our churches ought to obey ordinances and regulations concerning zoning, fire safety, structural standards, building permits, and every other law that does not conflict with Scripture. In all such matters we are to obey local, regional, and national government directives willingly, without grumbling or complaining (see Phil. 2:14–16). Even on those rare occasions when we must follow the exception principle regarding civil obedience, we should do so respectfully, prepared to suffer the consequences or penalties that may result. In those instances, we must heed Peter's instruction that "it is better, if it is the will of God, to suffer for doing good than for doing evil" (1 Peter 3:17). And above all we should never, in any of our dealings with authority (or in any societal relationships), "suffer as a murderer, a thief, an evildoer, or as a busybody in other people's matters" (1 Peter 4:15).

A contemporary and applicable example that relates to 1 Peter 4:15 is the extreme protest strategy of some antiabortion groups, some of which claim to be Christian. Such groups have disregarded police orders not to block entrances to abortion clinics, bombed some clinics, and shot and killed clinic workers and doctors—all in the name of legitimate civil disobedience. It is certainly not honorable as a professed believer to be in such a position—it's disgraceful.

What would it look like to disobey the government respectfully?

Why Government Can't Save You, 25–26

Protection by Government

For if I am an offender, or have committed anything deserving of death, I do not object to dying; but if there is nothing in these things of which these men accuse me, no one can deliver me to them. I appeal to Caesar.

ACTS 25:11

It's entirely appropriate for believers to look to the government at certain times for protection and support. The apostle Paul did that when he used his Roman citizenship to appeal to Caesar for justice (Acts 25:11). Paul also relied on the law's protection during his third missionary journey. In Ephesus, Demetrius the silversmith incited a mob against him, and the town clerk took Paul into protective custody to rescue him from the riotous crowd. The clerk took seriously his responsibility as an advocate of what is good and right when he told the unruly throng, "Therefore, if Demetrius and his fellow craftsmen have a case against anyone, the courts are open and there are proconsuls. Let them bring charges against one another. But if you have any other inquiry to make, it shall be determined in the lawful assembly" (Acts 19:38–39).

By looking out for you and protecting your legitimate rights and interests, any government official is "God's minister" or servant (the Greek word used in Romans 13:4 is *diakonos*, "deacon") on your behalf. Such rulers, whether presidents or prime ministers, senators or members of parliament, high court justices, county commissioners or supervisors, or members of a city council, are due honor and respect as servants of God. Regardless of their personal beliefs about our relationship to God, they represent Him and are doing His work (whether they realize it or not) by promoting peace, justice, and safety among their subjects.

How does it change your perspective on government leaders to know they are God's ministers?

Why Government Can't Save You, 44–45

Living at Peace with Unbelievers

Remind them to be subject to rulers and authorities, to obey, to be ready for every good work, to speak evil of no one, to be peaceable, gentle, showing all humility to all men.

Titus 3:1–2

We have the scriptural duty of not maligning anyone, not even those unbelievers who are most antagonistic toward biblical standards. Titus 3:2 begins with Paul's command "to speak evil of no one," and refers to cursing, slandering, and treating with contempt. In fact the Greek term rendered "speak evil of" is the one from which we derive the English *blasphemy*. We can never use such speech with a righteous motive.

It is sad that many believers today speak scornfully of politicians and other public figures. When they do that, they actually manifest a basic disregard of their responsibility toward authority and hinder God's redemptive plan.

Paul goes on in Titus 3:2 to mention two more Christian duties. First, he reminds us that we must be friendly and peaceful toward the lost, not belligerent and quarrelsome. In the ungodly, postmodern world we live in, it's easy to condemn those who contribute to the culture's demise and write them off as corrupt sinners who will never change. If God's love for the world was so broad and intense that His Son died for a multitude of sinners (John 3:16), how can we who have received that redeeming grace be harsh and unloving toward those who have not yet received it?

Second, Paul reminds us that we must be "gentle," a word in the Greek that means being fair, moderate, and forbearing toward others. Some have translated this term "sweet reasonableness," a definition denoting an attitude that does not hold grudges but gives others the benefit of the doubt.

In what areas can you better follow Paul's instructions in this verse?

Why Government Can't Save You, 133–134

The True Kingdom

"Therefore, as I live," says the Lord GOD, "I will prepare you for blood, and blood shall pursue you; since you have not hated blood, therefore blood shall pursue you."

EZEKIEL 35:6

The cause of Christ has never been advanced by earthly warfare, though many misguided souls have tried. When such tactics are employed, they invariably hurt our Christian witness rather than help it. The kingdom of God cannot be enlarged by physical weapons or worldly strategies. As Jesus told Pilate, "My kingdom is not of this world. If My kingdom were of this world, My servants would fight, so that I should not be delivered to the Jews; but now My kingdom is not from here" (John 18:36).

Jesus severely rebuked Peter: "Put your sword into the sheath" (John 18:11). Matthew says He added, "for all who take the sword will perish by the sword" (Matt. 26:52). The words were an echo of Genesis 9:6: "Whoever sheds man's blood, by man his blood shall be shed." Jesus was signifying that He regarded Peter's deed as no legitimate act of self-defense, but rather an unlawful act of attempted murder, worthy of punishment by death. Even though the arrest of Jesus was an unjust, cowardly act, it was being done by the duly established authorities in Jerusalem and therefore was not to be resisted with unlawful force (cf. Rom. 13:2). Acts of violence or civil disobedience by an individual against duly constituted governments are always wrong, even if the government itself is unjust. (This is a point that needs to be reemphasized in an era when many Christians feel they are justified in breaking the law to protest government-sanctioned wrongs.)

In what ways might you be trying to enlarge the kingdom of God by worldly strategies?

The Murder of Jesus, 93–94

The Head of the Church

Speaking the truth in love, [we] may grow up in all things into Him who is the head—Christ—from whom the whole body . . . causes growth of the body for the edifying of itself in love.

Ephesians 4:15–16

The heroes of church history defended Christ's headship, not on the basis of an arbitrary opinion or out of personal ambition, but because they found that truth unmistakably revealed in the Scriptures. Ephesians 5:23 states that "Christ is head of the church," and Colossians 1:18 (NASB) echoes, "He is also head of the body, the church; and He is the beginning, the firstborn from the dead, so that He Himself will come to have first place in everything." In the first chapter of Ephesians, Paul explained that God the Father "put all things under His [Christ's] feet, and gave Him to be head over all things to the church, which is His body, the fullness of Him who fills all in all" (vv. 22–23). Other New Testament Scriptures speak of growing "up in all things into Him who is the head" (Eph. 4:15) and "holding fast to the head, from whom the entire body . . . grows with a growth which is from God" (Col. 2:19 NASB).

But what does the New Testament mean when it speaks of Christ as the "head of the church"? The Greek word for "head" (*kephalē*) designates "first or superior rank" or "anything *supreme*, *chief*, [or] *prominent*." Its meaning overlaps with the word *kyrios* ("Lord") and "points to Christ's superior rank or status." To say that Christ is the head of the church is to say that He is the Lord and Master over the church.

Where have you seen the church living from a genuine belief that Christ is its head?

Slave, 71–72

How Jesus Shows Lordship

For God is not the author of confusion but of peace,
as in all the churches of the saints.

1 Corinthians 14:33

Two thousand years of accumulated Christian scholarship has been basically consistent on all the major issues: the Bible is the authoritative Word of God, containing every spiritual truth essential to God's glory, our salvation, faith, and eternal life. Scripture tells us that all humanity fell in Adam, and our sin is a perfect bondage from which we cannot extricate ourselves. Jesus is God incarnate, having taken on human flesh to pay the price of sin and redeem believing men and women from sin's bondage. Salvation is by grace through faith, and not a result of any works we do. Christ is the only Savior for the whole world, and apart from faith in Him, there is no hope of redemption for any sinner. So the gospel message needs to be carried to the uttermost parts of the earth. True Christians have always been in full agreement on all those vital points of biblical truth.

The postmodernized notion that everything should be perpetually up for discussion and nothing is ever really sure or settled is a denial of both the perspicuity of Scripture and the unanimous testimony of the people of God.

It also is a denial of Christ's lordship over the church. How could He exercise headship over His church if His own people could never truly know what He meant by what He said? Jesus Himself settled the question of whether His truth is sufficiently clear in John 10:27–28, when He said, "My sheep hear My voice, and I know them, and they follow Me. And I give them eternal life, and they shall never perish; neither shall anyone snatch them out of My hand."

When have you avoided obeying Christ by claiming His commands were unclear?

The Truth War, 157–158

Christ Is Preeminent over All, Especially in the Church

The Father loves the Son, and has given all things into His hand.

John 3:35

Paul underscores Christ's authority as supreme and sovereign Lord over all. He says that God has "seated Him at His right hand in the heavenly places, far above all principality and power and might and dominion, and every name that is named" (Eph. 1:20–21). That authority applies "not only in this age but also in that which is to come" (v. 21). It is absolute supremacy in every sense. Not only are all things put under Christ's feet (v. 22), but He also "fills all in all" (v. 23).

So the church's Head is ordained to be the consummate authority in all the universe by God the Father Himself. This is the ultimate expression of the Father's eternal love for His only begotten Son. He did not give an archangel like Michael or Gabriel to be head of the church. He didn't establish an earthly priesthood to mediate the headship of the church either. But by God the Father's own decree, Christ alone is Head of the church, and all others must fall on their knees before Him.

Colossians 1:18 settles every question about the relationship of Christ's authority as Lord to His headship over the church. There Paul says, "He is the head of the body, the church, who is the beginning, the firstborn from the dead, that in all things He may have the preeminence." First place belongs to Him. Nowhere should that be truer and more clearly evident than in the church, where His people openly submit to Him as Lord. Christ is the *only* proper and legitimate Head of the church. No king, no pope, and no politician has any right to usurp the title or pretend to occupy the office.

When have you been tempted to see another leader as having more authority than Christ in the church?

The Truth War, 162–163

The Truth About Leadership

And let us consider one another in order to stir up love and good works.

Hebrews 10:24

What we learn from the apostle Paul is the same thing Jesus taught: that character—not style, not technique, not methodology, but *character*—is the true biblical test of great leadership. Entrepreneurship is wonderful, but the most skilled entrepreneur in the world without character is no true leader. Strategic planning is important, but if you don't have leaders whom people will follow, your strategic plan will fail. The clarity of a well-drafted purpose statement is crucial, but the true spiritual leader must go beyond merely clarifying people's focus. The real leader is *an example to follow*. And the best example to follow, as Paul knew, is the one who follows Christ.

Therefore Scripture, not the corporate world or the political arena, is the authoritative source we need to turn to in order to learn the truth about spiritual leadership.

Obviously, not everyone is called to be a leader at the same level, or leadership by definition would not exist (cf. 1 Cor. 12:18–29). But every Christian is called to be a leader of sorts, at some level, because all of us are given a mandate to teach and to influence others in the Great Commission (Matt. 28:19–20). The writer of Hebrews rebuked his readers for their spiritual immaturity, saying, "You ought to be teachers" (5:12). Clearly, then, all Christians are called to influence others and teach them the truth about Christ. Therefore, no matter what your status, position, giftedness, or occupation, you are called to be a leader at some level.

Who can you lead by your teaching and Christlike example?

Called to Lead, xi–xii

Leadership in the Church

Therefore, brethren, seek out from among you seven men of good reputation, full of the Holy Spirit and wisdom, whom we may appoint over this business.

ACTS 6:3

If we are to be faithful to the New Testament, we must acknowledge that the Lord has established leaders in His church—pastors and elders.

The qualifications for elders and church leaders are not *just* for them. These qualities are especially mandated for them because they set the pattern for all. "Like people, like priest" (Hosea 4:9). What the pastor and elders are to be is the model for all Christians. And the principles that are true of leaders in the church are also good principles for every Christian in any position of leadership to apply.

Notice that in every list of qualifications the apostle Paul gave for church leaders, the first and most indispensable qualification for men in leadership was that they be "blameless" (1 Tim. 3:2, 10; Titus 1:6–7). Paul employed a Greek word that means "above reproach"—inculpable, unblemished, irreprehensible. Literally, it means "not subject to accusation." The term does not speak of sinlessness, of course, or no one would qualify (1 John 1:8). It does not disqualify people from leadership on the basis of sins they committed before conversion, or Paul himself would have been disqualified (1 Tim. 1:12–16). But it describes a person whose Christian testimony is free from the taint of scandal—someone who is upright, sound in character, and without any serious moral blemish.

The early church held leaders to the highest moral and ethical standards. Nowhere is that more clear in Scripture than Acts 6, where Luke recorded how the first leaders were marked out and chosen by their fellow believers to assist the work of the apostles.

Who are the church leaders you look to as good models of Christ?

Called to Lead, 161–163

True Care of the Flock

But when I saw that they were not straightforward about the truth of the gospel, I said to Peter before them all, "If you, being a Jew, live in the manner of Gentiles and not as the Jews, why do you compel Gentiles to live as Jews?"

Galatians 2:14

Indiscriminate congeniality, the quest for spiritual common ground, and peace at any price all naturally have great appeal, especially in an intellectual climate where practically the worst gaffe any thoughtful person could make is claiming to know what's true when so many other people think something else is true.

Besides, dialogue does sound nicer than debate. Who but a fool wouldn't prefer a calm conversation instead of conflict and confrontation?

Generally speaking, avoiding conflicts is a good idea. Warmth and congeniality are normally preferable to cold harshness. Civility, compassion, and good manners are in short supply these days, and we ought to have more of them. Gentleness, a soft answer, and a kind word usually go further than an argument or a rebuke. That which edifies is more helpful and more fruitful in the long run than criticism. Cultivating friends is more pleasant and more profitable than crusading against enemies. And it's ordinarily better to be tender and mild rather than curt or combative—especially to the victims of false teaching.

But those qualifying words are vital: *usually, ordinarily, generally*. Avoiding conflict is not always the right thing. Sometimes it is downright sinful. Particularly in times like these, when almost no error is deemed too serious to be excluded from the evangelical conversation, and while the Lord's flock is being infiltrated by wolves dressed like prophets.

Even the kindest, gentlest shepherd sometimes needs to throw rocks at the wolves who come in sheep's clothing.

When have you seen a group carry out poor ideas because its members avoided debate?

The Jesus You Can't Ignore, 18–19

Jesus Chose Sinners to Be Disciples

For you see your calling, brethren, that not many wise according to the flesh, not many mighty, not many noble, are called. But God has chosen the foolish things of the world to put to shame the wise.

1 Corinthians 1:26–27

It wasn't that the self-righteous religious leaders did not believe in Jesus' miracles. Nowhere on the pages of the Gospel record did anyone ever deny the *reality* of Jesus' miracles. Who could deny them? There were too many, and they had been done too publicly to be dismissed by even the most skeptical gainsayers. Of course, some desperately tried to attribute Jesus' miracles to the power of Satan (Matt. 12:24). No one, however, ever denied that the miracles were *real*. Anyone could see that He had the power to cast out demons and do miracles at will. No one could honestly question whether He truly had power over the supernatural world.

But what irritated the religious leaders was not the miracles. They could have lived with the fact that He could walk on water or that He could make food to feed thousands of people. What they could *not* tolerate was being called sinners. They would not acknowledge themselves as poor, prisoners, blind, and oppressed (Luke 4:18). They were too smugly self-righteous. So when Jesus came (as John the Baptist had come before Him) preaching repentance and saying they were sinners, wretched, poor, blind, lost people under the bondage of their own iniquity, needing forgiveness and cleansing—they could not and would not tolerate that. Therefore it was ultimately because of His *message* that they hated Him, vilified Him, and finally executed Him.

That is precisely why when it came time for Him to appoint apostles, He chose lowly, ordinary men. These were men who were not reluctant to acknowledge their own sinfulness.

Who are the godly believers around you who may be overlooked because they are not leaders?

Twelve Ordinary Men, 150–151

Group Leadership

Where there is no counsel, the people fall; but in the multitude of counselors there is safety.

Proverbs 11:14

The clear New Testament pattern for church government is a plurality of God-ordained men who lead the people of God together. The church is not to be led by dictators, autocrats, or solitary rulers. From the beginning, oversight was shared by twelve apostles, and we see here that when they appointed subordinate leaders, those men also functioned as a team.

When Paul and Barnabas founded churches in Asia Minor, Luke said they "appointed elders in every church" (Acts 14:23). Paul likewise instructed Titus to "appoint elders in every city as I commanded you" (Titus 1:5). At the end of Paul's third missionary journey, "he sent to Ephesus and called for the elders of the church" (Acts 20:17). Virtually every time elders are spoken of in Scripture in connection with a church, the noun is plural, clearly indicating that the standard practice in the New Testament was for multiple elders to oversee each church.

Every ministry described in the New Testament was a team effort. Jesus called twelve disciples. When they began to take the gospel to "all Judea and Samaria, and to the end of the earth" (Acts 1:8), they did so in teams (Acts 15:22–27; Gal. 2:9).

A comprehensive list of all of Paul's various companions and fellow ministers would fill a page or more.

In other words, ministry as depicted in the New Testament was never a one-man show. That does not preclude the role of a dominant leader on each team. Within the framework of plurality, there will invariably be those who have more influence.

Where have you seen a team of ministers succeed because of their diverse gifts and insights?

Called to Lead, 167–169

True Success

Only Luke is with me. Get Mark and bring him with you, for he is useful to me for ministry. And Tychicus I have sent to Ephesus . . . Greet Prisca and Aquila, and the household of Onesiphorus.

2 TIMOTHY 4:11–12, 19

If we judged success by worldly standards, some might be inclined to assess Paul's leadership career as an abject failure and a bitter disappointment. In the closing days of his life, when Paul wrote 2 Timothy, Luke was virtually his only contact with the outside world (4:11). Paul was confined in a Roman dungeon, dreading the savage cold of coming winter (vv. 13, 21), and without any hope of deliverance from the death sentence that had been imposed on him.

Actually, the apostle Paul was not a failure as a leader by any measure. His influence continues worldwide even today. By contrast, Nero, the corrupt but powerful Roman emperor who ordered Paul's death, is one of history's most despised figures. This is yet another reminder that *influence* is the true test of a person's leadership, not power or position per se.

In the closing section of 2 Timothy, as Paul finished the last chapter of his final epistle what filled the heart and mind of this great leader were the people he ministered to and worked alongside. They were the most visible and immediate legacy of his leadership. Although he was left virtually friendless in prison, although he had been forsaken at his defense before a Roman tribunal, he was clearly *not* alone in life.

In fact, the true character of Paul's leadership is seen in this brief list of people he had poured his life into. This catalog of individuals is therefore instructive in assessing why Paul's leadership was not a failure. This is why his influence continues to be an example to millions of Christians even today.

How have you been measuring success?

Called to Lead, 181–185

Leadership Is About Character

A bishop then must be blameless, the husband of one wife, temperate, sober-minded, of good behavior, hospitable, able to teach; not given to wine, not violent, not greedy for money, but gentle, not quarrelsome, not covetous.

1 TIMOTHY 3:2–3

Lasting leadership is grounded in character. Character produces respect. Respect produces trust. And trust motivates followers.

True leadership is properly associated with character qualities like integrity, trustworthiness, respectability, unselfishness, humility, self-discipline, self-control, and courage. Such virtues reflect the image of God in man. Although the divine image is severely tarnished in fallen humanity, even pagans recognize those qualities as desirable virtues, important requirements for true leadership.

Christ Himself is the epitome of what a true leader ought to be like. He is the embodiment of all the truest, purest, highest, and noblest qualities of leadership.

Obviously, in *spiritual* leadership, the great goal and objective is to bring people to Christlikeness. That is why the leader himself must manifest Christlike character. The apostle Paul summarized the spirit of the true leader when he wrote, "Imitate me, just as I also imitate Christ" (1 Cor. 11:1).

Peter might just as well have written the same thing. His character was molded and shaped after the example he had witnessed in Christ. He had the raw material for becoming a leader, and that was important. His life experiences helped hone and sharpen his natural leadership abilities, and that was also vital. But the real key to everything—the essential foundation upon which true leadership always rises or falls—is character. It was the character qualities Peter developed through his intimate association with Christ that ultimately made him the great leader he became.

What character traits do you need to develop most to inspire trust?

Twelve Ordinary Men, 47

True Leaders Look Out for Others

You know that those who are considered rulers over the Gentiles lord it over them, and their great ones exercise authority over them. Yet it shall not be so among you; but whoever desires to become great among you shall be your servant.

MARK 10:42–43

A leader is not someone who is consumed with his own success and his own best interests. A *true* leader is someone who demonstrates to everyone around him that their interests are what most occupy his heart. A real leader will work hard to make everyone around him successful. His passion is to help make the people under his leadership flourish. That is *why* a true leader must have the heart of a servant.

A person cannot be a true leader and operate only for personal fulfillment or personal gain. People whose motives are selfish end up leading nobody, because everyone abandons them. They cannot be trusted. A person in a position of leadership will succeed only as long as people trust him with their futures, with their money, or even with their lives. Nothing can take the place of trust. Nothing. A leader you can't trust is no true leader at all. He may be a man in power who can force people to do what he wants, but he is no example of true leadership.

Here's how you can easily recognize genuine leaders: they are the ones surrounded by gifted, capable, diligent, effective people who are devoted to their leader. That devotion reflects *trust*. And trust stems from the selfless way the godly leader uses his own energies and his own abilities in a sacrificial, selfless way. If you can show people you truly have *their* best interests at heart, they'll follow you.

Whose success can you begin to promote?

Called to Lead, 12–13

Leaders Must Declare God's Word

For you know what commandments we gave you through the Lord Jesus.

1 THESSALONIANS 4:2

You wouldn't hear Jesus say, "I'd like to share something with you. I have a thought that might be worth your consideration." He amazed people by the way He spoke with authority. Of course, He had inherent authority, because He was God incarnate. But His manner of speaking contrasted starkly with that of the scribes and Pharisees. Matthew said, "The people were astonished at His teaching, for He taught them as one having authority, and not as the scribes" (7:28–29). The scribes were accustomed to quoting rabbinical opinions as their source of authority. They treated truth as theory, often quoting many different possible interpretations of the Law and rarely speaking definitively about anything. Ultimately, they substituted human opinion and human tradition for the authoritative truth of Scripture (Matt. 15:6).

Jesus came on the scene and, by contrast, He quoted no one's opinion. He said things like, "You have heard that it was said . . . But I say to you . . ." (Matt. 5:21–22, 27–28, 31–32, 33–34, 43–44). He spoke with divine authority. He had the truth of God. And He said so plainly.

The wise spiritual leader stands on the very same authority. For us, it's not, "*I* say to you . . ."; it's, "Thus saith *the Lord*." But it is the very same authority. And when you do that correctly and accurately, you lift up others and ennoble them.

How does it change your perspective on preaching to know it comes with Christ's authority?

Called to Lead, 36–37

The Truth War

"Is not My word like a fire?" says the LORD, "and like a hammer that breaks the rock in pieces?"

JEREMIAH 23:29

The Bible says categorically that the Truth War is a completely different kind of war, fought with entirely different weaponry and with totally different objectives in view. "We do not wrestle against flesh and blood" (Eph. 6:12). "We do not war according to the flesh. For the weapons of our warfare are not carnal" (2 Cor. 10:3–4). Every mention of spiritual weaponry in the New Testament makes this point perfectly clear. The tools of our warfare are not the kind that could be forged on any earthly anvil. Our only offensive weapons are "the word of truth [and] the power of God"; and our only defensive armor is "the armor of righteousness" (2 Cor. 6:7).

The people of God corporately have a different—and far more important—kind of warfare to wage. The Truth War is not a carnal war. It is not about territory and nations. It is not a battle for land and cities. It is not a clan war or a personality conflict between individuals. It is not a fight for clout between religious denominations. It is not a skirmish over material possessions. It is a battle for the truth. It is about ideas. It is a fight for the mind. It is a battle against false doctrines, evil ideologies, and wrong beliefs. It is a war for *truth*. The battlefield is the mind; the goal is the absolute triumph of truth; the priceless spoils of conquest are souls won out of the bondage of sin; the outcome is our willing submission to Christ; the highest prize is the honor given to Him as Lord; and the ultimate victory is completely His.

When have you been tempted to use worldly weapons in the war for truth?

The Truth War, 31–32

A History of the Truth War

And the angels who did not keep their proper domain, but left their own abode, He has reserved in everlasting chains under darkness for the judgment of the great day.

JUDE V. 6

Jude's epistle has a very broad sweep. That fact stands out starkly because the epistle is so short. Jude takes a condensed, fish-eye view of all history, starting from the beginning of time. He shows that the Truth War has been a perpetual reality ever since sin first entered the universe. It has been a long, protracted, uninterrupted state of siege—and we are still in the thick of the battle.

Jude mentions, for example, the fall of Satan and the angels who followed him (v. 6). He refers to Adam by name (v. 14). He speaks of the error of Cain (v. 11). He alludes to the central themes of the preaching of Enoch, and hence the apostasy of that generation (vv. 14–15). He recounts the immorality of Sodom and Gomorrah (v. 7), the false teaching of Balaam (v. 11), and the rebellion of Korah (v. 11).

The big-picture perspective is deliberately designed to help us understand the sweeping saga of what God is doing. The point is that we are still embroiled in that conflict today, and we cannot afford to lay down our arms. There is a good and valid reason that the church on earth has always been known as "the church militant." Our generation has by no means been granted an exemption from the necessary conflict. As a matter of fact, Christianity in our time is besieged with spiritual pretenders, and their lies are as subtle and as dangerous as ever. Some of them are even the same old lies simply recycled for a new generation.

What can you do to encourage believers to persevere in this conflict?

The Truth War, 116

The Truth War Is Continual

Guard what was committed to your trust, avoiding the profane and idle babblings and contradictions of what is falsely called knowledge—by professing it some have strayed concerning the faith.

1 Timothy 6:20–21

Battles over the truth were raging inside the Christian community even in apostolic times, when the church was just beginning. In fact, the record of Scripture indicates that false teachers in the church immediately became a significant and widespread problem wherever the gospel went. Virtually all the major epistles in the New Testament address the problem in one way or another. The apostle Paul was constantly engaged in battle against the lies of "false apostles [and] deceitful workers [who transformed] themselves into apostles of Christ" (2 Cor. 11:13). Paul said that was to be expected. It is, after all, one of the favorite strategies of the evil one: "No wonder! For Satan himself transforms himself into an angel of light. Therefore it is no great thing if his ministers also transform themselves into ministers of righteousness" (vv. 14–15).

It takes a willful naïveté to deny that such a thing could happen in our time. As a matter of fact, it is happening on a massive scale. Now is not a good time for Christians to flirt with the spirit of the age. We cannot afford to be apathetic about the truth God has put in our trust. It is our duty to guard, proclaim, and pass that truth on to the next generation (1 Tim. 6:20–21). We who love Christ and believe the truth embodied in His teaching must awaken to the reality of the battle that is raging all around us. We must do our part in the ages-old Truth War. We are under a sacred obligation to join the battle and contend for the faith.

What can you do to pass the truth on to the next generation?

The Truth War, 23

The Real Battle

But let us who are of the day be sober, putting on the breastplate of faith and love, and as a helmet the hope of salvation.

1 THESSALONIANS 5:8

Paul knew the real battle was not merely against the human false teachers who had confused the Corinthians. It was nothing less than full-scale war against the kingdom of darkness. "We do not wrestle against flesh and blood, but against principalities, against powers, against the rulers of the darkness of this age, against spiritual hosts of wickedness in the heavenly places" (Eph. 6:12). We are fighting for the preservation and proclamation of the *truth*. We are fighting for the honor of Jesus Christ. We are fighting for the salvation of sinners, and we are fighting for the virtue of saints.

In fact, for every good and noble effort of Christian leaders in business, politics, education, the military, or any other legitimate pursuit, there is inevitable engagement with the kingdom of darkness. Since all Christians, in whatever they do, are supposed to be engaged in the advance of Christ's kingdom, they face opposition from the powers of evil.

Paul used the language of warfare all the time. He began and ended 1 Timothy by urging Timothy to fight the battle well: "Wage the good warfare" (1:18); "Fight the good fight of faith" (6:12). He said, "Be sober, putting on the breastplate of faith and love, and as a helmet the hope of salvation" (1 Thess. 5:8). In 2 Timothy 2:3 he said, "Endure hardship as a good soldier of Jesus Christ." As Paul neared the end of his own life, he wrote, "I have fought the good fight" (2 Tim. 4:7). His whole life was a spiritual war against anything and everything that opposed the truth.

Where are you facing conflict with the kingdom of darkness?

Called to Lead, 137

August

THE END-TIMES AND OTHER IMPORTANT DOCTRINES

Two Dangers to Avoid

But avoid foolish disputes, genealogies, contentions, and strivings about the law; for they are unprofitable and useless.

TITUS 3:9

Overzealousness is clearly a danger we need to guard against carefully. There are indeed some full-time critics operating today, always looking for a fight, taking fleshly delight in controversy merely for controversy's sake, and making judgments that may be too harsh or too hasty. Don't fall into the trap of assuming that the most censorious and nitpicking opinions are automatically the most "discerning" ones. Watch out for the person who shows no caution or restraint about making severe judgments and yet claims to be a "discernment" expert.

As a matter of fact, Scripture says that those who are merely pugnacious or quarrelsome are unfit for spiritual leadership (1 Tim. 3:3). When Paul laid out the qualifications for church leaders, he was emphatic about this. "A servant of the Lord must not quarrel but be gentle to all, able to teach, patient, in humility correcting those who are in opposition, if God perhaps will grant them repentance, so that they may know the truth" (2 Tim. 2:24–25). That is the spirit we must cultivate. Contending earnestly for the faith does not require us to become brawlers. Let's acknowledge that as plainly as possible and never lose sight of it.

But by far the greater danger facing the church today is utter apathy toward the truth and indifference about false teaching. We tend not to see truth the way Scripture presents it—as a sacred treasure committed to our trust (1 Tim. 6:20–21). Too many have decided it is easier and seems so much "nicer" to pretend that every doctrinal deviation is ultimately insignificant.

Which of these traps is more of a danger to you?

The Truth War, 135

Truth Worth Dying For

Yes, and all who desire to live godly in Christ Jesus will suffer persecution.

2 TIMOTHY 3:12

History is filled with accounts of people who chose to accept torture or death rather than deny the truth. They were valiant warriors for the truth. They were not terrorists or violent people, of course. But they "fought" for the truth by proclaiming it in the face of fierce opposition, by living lives that gave testimony to the power and goodness of truth, and by refusing to renounce or forsake the truth no matter what threats were made.

In every generation across the history of the church, countless martyrs have similarly died rather than deny the truth. Were such people just fools, making too much of their own convictions? Was their absolute confidence in what they believed actually misguided zeal? Did they die needlessly?

Faithfulness to the truth is *always* costly in some way or another (2 Tim. 3:12), and that is precisely why Jesus insisted that anyone who wants to be His disciple must be willing to take up a cross (Luke 9:23–26).

Christians, of all people, ought to be *most* willing to live and die for the truth. Remember, we know the truth, and the truth has set us free (John 8:32). We should not be ashamed to say so boldly (Ps. 107:2). And if called upon to sacrifice for truth's sake, we need to be willing and prepared to give our lives. Again, that is exactly what Jesus was speaking about when He called His disciples to take up a cross (Matt. 16:24). Cowardice and authentic faith are antithetical.

What has given you courage to stand up for the truth?

The Truth War, xii–xiv

Believe the Truth!

The time is fulfilled, and the kingdom of God is at hand.
Repent, and believe in the gospel.

Mark 1:15

One of the central themes of the Bible is the importance of believing the truth about God. Statement after statement in Scripture emphatically declares that our view of God is the most fundamental spiritual issue of all: "Without faith it is impossible to please Him, for he who comes to God must believe that He is, and that He is a rewarder of those who diligently seek Him" (Heb. 11:6). "He who does not believe is condemned already, because he has not believed in the name of the only begotten Son of God" (John 3:18). "We are of God. He who knows God hears us; he who is not of God does not hear us. By this we know the spirit of truth and the spirit of error" (1 John 4:6).

In biblical terms, the difference between true faith and false belief (or unbelief) *is* the difference between life and death, heaven and hell. "Brethren, if anyone among you wanders from the truth, and someone turns him back, let him know that he who turns a sinner from the error of his way will save a soul from death and cover a multitude of sins" (James 5:19–20; cf. 2 Tim. 2:15–26). Paul told the Thessalonians he was thankful to God for them, because "God from the beginning chose you for salvation through sanctification by the Spirit and *belief in the truth*, to which He called you by our gospel, for the obtaining of the glory of our Lord Jesus Christ" (2 Thess. 2:13–14, emphasis added).

When have you been tempted to see truth as unimportant?

The Jesus You Can't Ignore, xx

A True Israelite

For he is not a Jew who is one outwardly, nor is circumcision that which is outward in the flesh; but he is a Jew who is one inwardly; and circumcision is that of the heart, in the Spirit, not in the letter; whose praise is not from men but from God.

Romans 2:28–29

Jesus saw Nathanael coming toward Him and said of him, "Behold, an Israelite indeed, in whom is no deceit!" (John 1:47).

Can you imagine a more wonderful thing than to have words of approval like that come out of the mouth of Jesus? It would be one thing to hear that at the end of your life, along with, "Well done, good and faithful servant; you have been faithful over a few things, I will make you ruler over many things. Enter into the joy of your lord" (cf. Matt. 25:21, 23).We often hear eulogies at funerals that extol the virtues of the deceased. But how would you like Jesus to say that about you from the very start?

This speaks volumes about Nathanael's character. He was pure-hearted from the beginning. Certainly, he was human. He had sinful faults. His mind was tainted by a degree of prejudice. But His heart was not poisoned by deceit. He was no hypocrite. His love for God, and His desire to see the Messiah, were genuine. His heart was sincere and without guile.

Here was an authentic Jew, one of the true spiritual offspring of Abraham. Here was one who worshiped the true and living God without deceit and without hypocrisy. Nathanael was the authentic item. Jesus would later say, in John 8:31, "If you abide in My word, you are My disciples indeed." The Greek word is the same—*alethos*.

Nathanael was a true disciple from the start. There was no hypocrisy in him. He was a truly righteous man—flawed by sin as we all are—but justified before God through a true and living faith.

Where do you most need to grow in purity of heart?

Twelve Ordinary Men, 142–144

Truth Is Absolute and Fixed

Jesus Christ is the same yesterday, today, and forever.

Hebrews 13:8

Clearly, the existence of absolute truth and its inseparable relationship to the person of God is the most essential tenet of all truly biblical Christianity. Speaking plainly: if you are one of those who questions whether truth is really important, please don't call your belief system "Christianity," because that is not what it is.

A biblical perspective of truth also necessarily entails the recognition that ultimate truth is an objective reality. Truth exists outside of us and remains the same regardless of how we may perceive it. Truth by definition is as fixed and constant as God is immutable. That is because real truth (what Francis Schaeffer called "true truth") is the unchanged and unchanging expression of who God is; it is not our own personal and arbitrary interpretation of reality.

Amazingly, Christians in our generation need to be reminded of these things. Truth is never determined by looking at God's Word and asking, "What does this mean to me?" Whenever I hear someone talk like that, I'm inclined to ask, "What did the Bible mean before you existed? What does *God* mean by what He says?" Those are the proper questions to be asking. Truth and meaning are not determined by our intuition, experience, or desire. The true meaning of Scripture—or anything else, for that matter—has already been determined and fixed by the mind of God. The task of an interpreter is to discern *that* meaning. And proper interpretation must precede application.

How can you respond to someone who thinks of truth as subjective?

The Truth War, xx–xxi

The Heavenly Truth

And the ransomed of the Lord shall return, and come to Zion with singing, with everlasting joy on their heads. They shall obtain joy and gladness, and sorrow and sighing shall flee away.

Isaiah 35:10

Through the years, many people have asked me what I believe heaven is going to be like. I tell them it's going to be just as the Bible describes it. One word describes our future life in heaven: *perfection*.

Most of us understand the general concept of perfection, but we have a very difficult time envisioning anything that is truly perfect. Everything in our earthly experience is flawed or imperfect in some way. All of creation is presently agonizing under the cruel effects of sin's curse, waiting for the consummation of all things when the curse is finally removed. At that time, everything will be perfect. Pain, sorrow, and the groaning of creation will end. We will know joy and gladness. Sorrow and sighing will be no more (Isa. 35:10; Rom 8:22).

For our loved ones in heaven, including our little ones, that day of perfection has already come. They live as whole persons—whole in body and soul, completely new and flawless. The apostle John wrote, "Beloved, now we are children of God; and it has not yet been revealed what we shall be, but we know that when He is revealed, we shall be like Him, for we shall see Him as He is" (1 John 3:2). Everything we can envision as the wholeness and perfection of Christ is the wholeness and perfection being experienced by our loved ones who dwell with Him in eternity.

How does the hope of heaven's perfection change your outlook on your everyday life?

Safe in the Arms of God, 113

True Fellowship

Then we who are alive and remain shall be caught up together with them in the clouds to meet the Lord in the air. And thus we shall always be with the Lord.

1 Thessalonians 4:17

Without a doubt, the most marvelous aspect of heaven will be unbroken fellowship with God our heavenly Father! This is heaven's supreme delight.

Our fellowship with God the Father will be perfect, unhindered and unclouded by any sin or darkness.

This is such an incredibly profound concept that there's no way our finite minds can begin to appreciate it. We will be like Christ. We will be *with* Christ. We will enjoy unbroken and unfettered fellowship with God the Father. What glory that will be!

In heaven, we will see the Lord face-to-face. We will be able to see God's glory unveiled in its fullness. That will be a more pleasing, spectacular sight than anything we have known or could ever imagine on earth. No earthly pleasure can even begin to compare to the privilege and ecstasy of an unhindered view of His divine glory. Jesus said very clearly, "Blessed are the pure in heart, for they shall see God" (Matt. 5:8).

This close fellowship with the Lord has always been the deepest longing of the redeemed soul. The psalmist said, "As the deer pants for the water brooks, so pants my soul for You, O God. My soul thirsts for God, for the living God" (Ps. 42:1–2).

As those redeemed by the Lord, our highest satisfaction will be standing before God the Father and His Son, Jesus Christ, in perfect uprightness. We will have an undiminished, unwearied sight of His infinite glory and beauty, and that alone will bring us infinite and eternal delight.

What can you do to remember this truth more often?

Safe in the Arms of God, 125–126

What Are People Like in Heaven?

Beloved, now we are children of God; and it has not yet been revealed what we shall be, but we know that when He is revealed, we shall be like Him, for we shall see Him as He is.

1 JOHN 3:2

People often wonder what age people are in heaven or if physical limitations remain.

Whatever a person's imperfections, limitations, or immaturity here on earth, they are not present in heaven. In heaven, we will be conformed to Christ's image (Rom. 8:29). We will be like Jesus (1 John 3:2).

All the redeemed, of all ages and from all centuries, will be occupied doing one particular activity in heaven: "After these things I looked, and behold, a great multitude which no one could number, of all nations, tribes, peoples, and tongues, standing before the throne and before the Lamb, clothed with white robes, with palm branches in their hands, and crying out with a loud voice, saying, 'Salvation belongs to our God who sits on the throne, and to the Lamb!'" (Rev. 7:9–10).

The redeemed will join the angels and elders and living creatures as they fall on their faces before the throne of God and worship Him (see Rev. 5:13; 7:12).

The largest number of this group may very well be the unborn and the young children saved through the ages by God's sovereign grace. They will come from every nation, tongue, tribe, and people. They are all capable of praising and worshiping God. They must possess, therefore, enough maturity to voice this praise and to understand the significance of their praise.

At no point do we read in Scripture that there are any in heaven who are incapable of worship, incapable of voicing praise, or incapable of falling prostrate in their worship before the throne of God.

What will it be like to worship God forever?

Safe in the Arms of God, 118–119

Our Glorified Bodies in Heaven

And as we have borne the image of the man of dust, we shall also bear the image of the heavenly Man.

1 CORINTHIANS 15:49

Heaven is not a "state of mind"—it is a real place where the redeemed have real bodies in the likeness of the body Jesus Christ had after the resurrection.

God made mankind with body and soul, an inner and outer man (Gen. 2:7). Therefore, ultimate perfection demands that body and soul be renewed.

Death results, of course, in separation of the body and soul. Our bodies go to the grave, and our spirits go to the Lord. The separation continues until the resurrection (John 5:28–29).

Our resurrection body is our earthly body, glorified. The body we receive in the resurrection will have the same qualities as the glorified resurrection body of Christ (1 John 3:2).

Christ's resurrection body was not a wholly different body but rather, the same body He had before His crucifixion. It was in a glorified state, however. The wounds of His crucifixion were still visible. He could be touched and handled; He looked human in every regard. Jesus conversed a long time with the disciples on the road to Emmaus and they never once questioned His humanity (Luke 24:13–18). He ate real, earthly food with His disciples on another occasion (vv. 41–43). Even so, His body had unique otherworldly properties that allowed Him to pass through solid walls (John 20:19) or appear seemingly out of nowhere (Luke 24:51; Acts 1:9). Our bodies will be like His. They will be real, physical, genuinely human bodies, yet wholly perfected and glorified.

How can you answer someone who believes we will be disembodied souls in heaven?

Safe in the Arms of God, 120–121

Future Judgment

And now, little children, abide in Him, that when He appears, we may have confidence and not be ashamed before Him at His coming.

1 John 2:28

The Scripture teaches that all believers from every generation of human history will appear before Christ. Knowing this, the apostle Paul made it his goal, in all of life, "to be pleasing to Him. For we must all appear before the judgment seat of Christ, so that each one may be recompensed for his deeds in the body, according to what he has done, whether good or bad" (2 Cor. 5:9–10 NASB). Elsewhere, he told the Christians in Rome, "We shall all stand before the judgment seat of Christ" (Rom. 14:10).

Whether by death or by rapture, every believer will one day report to the heavenly Master for evaluation and reward. Once again, the obedient slave has nothing to fear from facing the Master.

On the other hand, those believers who spend their lives in temporal and worthless pursuits should expect minimal reward from Christ. The sins of every believer are, of course, forever forgiven through the cross; salvation cannot be forfeited. Yet those who squander their God-given opportunities for spiritual service will one day discover that their works consist of little more than wood, hay, and stubble. Lacking any eternal value, such works will not stand up under the fire of God's scrutiny (see 1 Cor. 3:12–15). The fear of His displeasure, counterbalanced by the promise of His reward, is a powerful motivation for enduring faithfulness. In the same way that first-century slaves were accountable to their human masters, Christ's slaves are ultimately accountable to Him.

In light of the future judgment, how are you spending your time?

Slave, 183–185

Judgment Day

And the dead were judged according to their works, by the things which were written in the books . . . And anyone not found written in the Book of Life was cast into the lake of fire.

REVELATION 20:12, 15

One day, the truth of your faith or the evil of your deception will be revealed. The Chief Winnower is going to come to separate the wheat from the chaff. He's going to blow the wind of judgment, and those who have built their lives on the rock will stand. Revelation 20:12–15 specifically describes how it's going to happen. This is the Great White Throne judgment, where God finally and forever separates the true from the false. And I believe that is a day when there will be echoing through the corridors of that judgment hall, "Lord! Lord!" And echoing back will come the reverberation of His reply, "Depart from Me, I never knew you!"

You may be respectful of Christ; you may be fervent and active in private devotion; you may be busy with public proclamation and spiritual activity; you may be building a religious life in the same community with true believers; and your little religious house may look exactly like theirs. But when the judgment comes, your house will be devastated if it's built on the sand of your own way rather than the rock of obedience to His Word. Make sure you have built your spiritual foundation on Christ and the solid rock of obedience to His Word.

Every presentation of the gospel must end with a warning of doom to the one who rejects it. Mere saying and hearing are no proof that a person's faith is authentic; real faith is visible in the one who *does*.

What can you do to build your life on obedience to Christ?

Hard to Believe, 116–117

August 12

Citizens of Heaven

If then you were raised with Christ, seek those things which are above, where Christ is, sitting at the right hand of God.

Colossians 3:1

We are citizens of heaven, both by emancipation and by birth, and all by grace. As such, we enjoy infinite privilege as well as great responsibility. We possess all of the innumerable advantages of knowing God, walking in His ways, worshipping Him, and relating to Him as both our King and our Father. Heaven's law is our law; heaven's interests are our interests; and heaven's citizens are our fellow citizens.

There is an incredible responsibility that comes with being part of Christ's kingdom. As His subjects, we must properly represent Him. Accordingly, we are commanded to "walk in a manner worthy of God who calls you into His own kingdom and glory" (1 Thess. 2:12).

Our life is synonymous with our citizenship. Our priorities, passions, and pursuits have all been changed because our very identity has been transformed (Phil. 1:21). Like the saints of old, we no longer chase after the passing pleasures of this world (Heb. 11:16, 26; 1 John 2:16–17). Instead, our eyes are fixed on heaven, our true home, the place where Christ is (Heb. 12:22–24; Col. 3:1). Whether we go to Him in death or He comes to us in rapture, we will soon be together with Him forever (2 Cor. 5:8; 1 Thess. 4:17). One day we will stand in His presence, as slaves before the Master. One day we will bow before Him, as subjects before the King. As both slaves and citizens, we will serve Him and reign with Him for all eternity.

What does it look like to seek the things that are above?

Slave, 192–194

All Christians Will Sin, but All Christians Will Obey

But now having been set free from sin, and having become slaves of God, you have your fruit to holiness, and the end, everlasting life.

Romans 6:22

Christians sin. They disobey. They fail. We *all* fall far short of perfection in this life (Phil. 3:12–15). "We all stumble in many things" (James 3:2). Even the most mature and godly Christians "see in a mirror dimly" (1 Cor. 13:12). Our minds need constant renewing (Rom. 12:2). But that doesn't invalidate the truth that salvation in some real sense makes us practically righteous. The same epistle that describes the Christian's hatred of and battle with sin (Rom. 7:8–24) first says that believers are free from sin and slaves of righteousness (Rom. 6:18). The same apostle who wrote, "If we say that we have no sin, we deceive ourselves" (1 John 1:8) later wrote, "No one who abides in Him sins" (1 John 3:6 NASB). In one place he says, "If we say that we have not sinned, we make Him a liar, and His word is not in us" (1 John 1:10), and in another, "No one who is born of God practices sin, because His seed abides in Him" (1 John 3:9 NASB).

There's a true paradox—not an inconsistency—in those truths. All Christians sin (1 John 1:8), but all Christians also obey: "By this we know that we know Him, if we keep His commandments" (1 John 2:3). Sin and carnality are still present with all believers (Rom. 7:21), but they cannot be the hallmark of one's character (Rom. 6:22).

"Beloved, do not imitate what is evil, but what is good. The one who does good is of God; the one who does evil has not seen God" (3 John 11 NASB). That speaks of *direction*, not *perfection*. But it clearly makes behavior a test of faith's reality.

Where do you see evidence of faith in your life?

The Gospel According to the Apostles, 31

True Assurance

For all the promises of God in Him are Yes, and in Him Amen, to the glory of God through us.

2 CORINTHIANS 1:20

Is it possible to have full assurance of one's salvation? Can Christians rest in the firm and settled confidence that they are redeemed and bound for eternal heaven?

Scripture categorically answers yes. Not only does the Bible teach that assurance is *possible* for Christians in this life, but the apostle Peter also gave this command: "Be . . . diligent to make certain about His calling and choosing you" (2 Peter 1:10 NASB). Assurance is not only a privilege; it is the birthright and sacred trust of every true child of God. We are commanded to *cultivate* assurance, not take it for granted.

True assurance is a taste of heaven on earth. Fanny Crosby expressed that truth in a well-known hymn:

Blessed assurance, Jesus is mine! O what a foretaste of glory divine!

The Bible suggests that a well-grounded assurance has both objective and subjective support. The objective ground is *the finished work of Christ on our behalf*, including the promises of Scripture, which have their yea and amen in Him (2 Cor. 1:20). The subjective ground is *the ongoing work of the Holy Spirit in our lives*, including His convicting and sanctifying ministries. Romans 15:4 (NASB) mentions both aspects of assurance: "Whatever was written in earlier times was written for our instruction, that through *perseverance* [subjective] *and the encouragement of the Scriptures* [objective] we might have hope."

Both the objective and subjective grounds for our assurance are applied to us by the Holy Spirit, who "bears witness with our spirit that we are children of God" (Rom. 8:16).

What would you say to a believer who is lacking assurance?

The Gospel According to the Apostles, 157–164

A Living Hope

Blessed be the God and Father of our Lord Jesus Christ, who according to His abundant mercy has begotten us again to a living hope through the resurrection of Jesus Christ from the dead.

1 PETER 1:3

According to 1 Peter 1:3–4, every Christian is born again to a *living hope*—that is, a hope that is perpetually alive, a hope that cannot die. Peter seems to be making a contrast to mere human hope, which is always a dying or a dead hope. Human hopes and dreams inevitably fade and ultimately disappoint. That's why Paul told the Corinthians, "If we have hoped in Christ in this life only, we are of all men most to be pitied" (1 Cor. 15:19 NASB). This living hope in Christ cannot die. God guarantees that it will finally come to a complete and total, glorious eternal fulfillment. "This hope we have as an anchor of the soul, a hope both sure and steadfast" (Heb. 6:19).

Also, we are guaranteed "an inheritance which is imperishable and undefiled and will not fade away, reserved in heaven" (1 Peter 1:4 NASB). Unlike everything in this life, which may be corrupted, decay, grow old, rust, corrode, be stolen, or lose its value, our heavenly inheritance is reserved for us where it remains incorruptible, undefiled, and unfading. Our full inheritance will one day be the culmination of our living hope. It is "reserved in heaven."

Did you realize that we have already received part of that inheritance? According to Ephesians 1:13–14, when a person first believes, the Holy Spirit Himself moves into that person's heart. He is the security deposit on our eternal salvation. He is an advance on the Christian's inheritance. He is the guarantee that God will finish the work He has started.

How does it change your perspective to have this living hope of an incorruptible inheritance?

The Gospel According to the Apostles, 184

The Two Roads

Enter by the narrow gate; for wide is the gate and broad is the way that leads to destruction, and there are many who go in by it.

MATTHEW 7:13

I've heard preachers say the narrow way is the way of Christianity that people choose when they want to go to heaven, and the broad way is the way people choose who are content to go to hell. But they are misinformed or confused. It is not a contrast between godliness and Christianity on one hand and irreligious, lewd, lascivious pagan masses headed merrily for hell on the other. It is a contrast between two kinds of religions, both roads marked "This Way to Heaven." Satan doesn't put up a sign that says, "Hell—Exit Here." That's not his style. People on the broad road think that road goes to heaven.

The choice we all make is this: either we're good enough on our own, through our belief system and morality, to make it to heaven; or we're not, and we have to cast ourselves on the mercy of God through Christ to get there. Those are the only two systems of religion in the world. One is a religion of human merit; the other recognizes that we find true merit in Christ alone, and it comes to the sinner only by grace. There may be a thousand different religious names and terms, but only two religions really exist. There is the truth of divine accomplishment, which says God has done it all in Christ, and there is the lie of human achievement, which says we have some sort of hand in saving ourselves. One is the religion of grace, the other the religion of works. One offers salvation by faith alone; the other offers salvation by the flesh.

How are you tempted to enter through the gate of human merit?

Hard to Believe, 78–79

Never Compromise the Absolutes

For a bishop must be blameless . . . holding fast the faithful word as he has been taught, that he may be able, by sound doctrine, both to exhort and convict those who contradict.

TITUS 1:7, 9

When God has spoken, there can be no compromise. It's one thing to compromise on matters of preference. It's entirely different to compromise on matters of principle.

Compromise is good and necessary in most human relationships. In marriage, for example, couples often have to compromise to handle disagreements on matters of preference and opinion. In secular government, compromise is sometimes necessary to break executive and legislative logjams. In business, compromise is often a vital part of closing a deal. The person who refuses to compromise under any and every circumstance is obstinate, unreasonable, and selfish. That sort of strong-willed inflexibility is sinful and has been the ruin of many relationships and organizations.

But when it comes to matters of *principle*—moral and ethical foundations, biblical absolutes, the axioms of God's Word, God's clear commands, and the truthfulness of God Himself—it is *never* right to compromise. The true leader understands that.

For the *spiritual* leader, the absolutes are established by the Word of God. A leader who applies all the other principles of leadership can perhaps achieve a measure of pragmatic effectiveness. But *this* principle will test your true mettle as a leader. No one can be a truly effective spiritual leader unless he understands the essential truth of Scripture and refuses to compromise its absolute authority. This principle applies, I am convinced, not just to pastors and church leaders, but to Christians in any walk of life who desire to be good leaders.

What consequences have you seen when spiritual leaders have compromised the truth?

Called to Lead, 51–52

Justification

But of Him you are in Christ Jesus, who became for us wisdom from God—and righteousness and sanctification and redemption.

1 CORINTHIANS 1:30

In its theological sense, justification is a forensic, or purely legal, term. It describes what God *declares* about the believer, not what He *does to change* the believer. In fact, justification effects no actual change whatsoever in the sinner's nature or character. Justification is a divine judicial edict. It changes our status only, but it carries ramifications that guarantee other changes will follow. Forensic decrees like this are fairly common in everyday life.

When a jury foreman reads the verdict, the defendant is no longer "the accused." Legally and officially he instantly becomes either guilty or innocent—depending on the verdict. Nothing in his actual nature changes, but if he is found not guilty he will walk out of court a free man in the eyes of the law, fully justified.

In biblical terms, justification is a divine verdict of "not guilty—fully righteous." It is the reversal of God's attitude toward the sinner. Whereas He formerly condemned, He now vindicates. Although the sinner once lived under God's wrath, as a believer he or she is now under God's blessing. Justification is more than simple pardon; pardon alone would still leave the sinner without merit before God. So when God justifies He imputes divine righteousness to the sinner (Rom. 4:22–25). Christ's own infinite merit thus becomes the ground on which the believer stands before God (Rom. 5:19; 1 Cor. 1:30; Phil. 3:9). So justification elevates the believer to a realm of full acceptance and divine privilege in Jesus Christ.

What effects does being justified have on your everyday life?

The Gospel According to the Apostles, 89–90

Justification and Sanctification Are Different

For just as you presented your members as slaves of uncleanness, and of lawlessness leading to more lawlessness, so now present your members as slaves of righteousness for holiness.

ROMANS 6:19

Justification is distinct from sanctification because in justification God does not *make* the sinner righteous; He *declares* that person righteous (Rom. 3:28; Gal. 2:16). Justification *imputes* Christ's righteousness to the sinner's account (Rom. 4:11); sanctification *imparts* righteousness to the sinner personally and practically (Rom. 6:1–7; 8:11–14). Justification takes place outside sinners and changes their standing (Rom. 5:1–2); sanctification is internal and changes the believer's state (Rom. 6:19). Justification is an event, sanctification a process. The two must be distinguished but can never be separated. God does not justify whom He does not sanctify, and He does not sanctify whom He does not justify. Both are essential elements of salvation.

The corruption of the doctrine of justification results in serious theological errors. If sanctification is included in justification, then justification is a process, not an event. That makes justification progressive, not complete. One's standing before God is then based on subjective experience, not secured by an objective declaration. Justification can therefore be experienced and then lost. Assurance of salvation in this life becomes practically impossible because security can't be guaranteed. The ground of justification ultimately is the sinner's own continuing present virtue, not Christ's perfect righteousness and His atoning work. Clearly, that idea runs contrary to biblical teaching.

Where have you seen the consequences of confusing sanctification for justification?

The Gospel According to the Apostles, 90–91

The Nature of Sanctification

But you were washed, but you were sanctified, but you were justified in the name of the Lord Jesus and by the Spirit of our God.

1 CORINTHIANS 6:11

Note this crucial distinction: At justification we surrender the *principle* of sin and self-rule. In sanctification we relinquish the *practice* of specific sins as we mature in Christ. Total surrender to Christ's lordship does not mean that we make all of life's decisions as a prerequisite to conversion. It does not demand that we give up all our sins before we can be justified. It means that when we trust Christ for salvation we settle the issue of who is in charge. At salvation we surrender to Christ in principle, but as Christians we will surrender in practice again and again. This practical outworking of His lordship is the process of sanctification.

There *is* an immediate aspect of sanctification that is simultaneous with justification: "Such were some of you; but you were washed, but you were sanctified, but you were justified in the name of the Lord Jesus Christ and by the Spirit of our God" (1 Cor. 6:11). This once-for-all aspect of sanctification is undoubtedly what the apostle had in view when he addressed the Corinthians as "those who *have been* sanctified" (1 Cor. 1:2 NASB).

But sanctification, unlike justification, is not a onetime, legal declaration. It is an experiential separation from sin that begins at salvation and continues in increasing degrees of practical holiness in one's life and behavior. Sanctification may be observable in greater or lesser degrees from believer to believer. But it is not optional, nor is it separable from the other aspects of our salvation.

In what ways have you been progressing in sanctification this month?

The Gospel According to the Apostles, 109–110

True Faith Seeks God

But from there you will seek the LORD your God, and you will find Him if you seek Him with all your heart and with all your soul.

DEUTERONOMY 4:29

It is not enough just to believe that the God of the Bible exists. It is not enough to know about His promises or even intellectually believe the truth of the gospel. In order to please Him it is also necessary to "believe . . . that He is a rewarder of those who diligently seek Him" (Heb. 11:6). That phrase brings together assent and trust to make the picture of faith complete. *Assent* goes beyond a dispassionate observation of who God is. The assenting heart affirms the goodness of His character as "a rewarder." *Trust* applies this knowledge personally and practically by turning to God in sincere faith as a seeker of *Him*.

It is not enough merely to postulate a supreme being. It is not enough even to accept the *right* God. Real faith is not just knowing *about* God: it is *seeking* God. In fact, "seeking God" is often used in Scripture as a synonym for faith. Isaiah 55:6 is a call to faith: "Seek the LORD while He may be found, call upon Him while He is near." God Himself told Israel, "You will seek Me and find Me, when you search for Me with all your heart" (Jer. 29:13). "For thus says the LORD to the house of Israel, 'Seek Me that you may live'" (Amos 5:4 NASB). "But seek first the kingdom of God and His righteousness, and all these things shall be added to you" (Matt. 6:33).

Faith, then, is seeking and finding God in Christ, desiring Him, and ultimately being fulfilled with Him.

What are you doing to seek God?

The Gospel According to the Apostles, 47–48

What Is Repentance?

I was not disobedient to the heavenly vision, but declared first to those in Damascus and in Jerusalem, and throughout all the region of Judea, and then to the Gentiles, that they should repent, turn to God, and do works befitting repentance.

Acts 26:19–20

It is not merely a positive "decision for Christ." We cannot simply add Christ to a sin-laden life, then go on loving sin, as if giving lip-service to Him somehow sanctifies all our wickedness. Repentance means turning from our love of sin, and turning to Jesus Christ for salvation: "Repent therefore and be converted" (Acts 3:19).

Specifically, repentance means "turn[ing] away from all your transgressions" (Ezek. 18:30). It means confessing and forsaking your iniquities (Prov. 28:13). It means abhorring your sin, being full of indignation against it (2 Cor. 7:11).

Repentance certainly does not mean you must do works of penance or correct your behavior *before* you can turn to Christ. Turn to the Savior *now*, and in turning to Him, you will turn your heart from all that dishonors Him (cf. 1 Thess. 1:9). *He* will begin a good work in you that He Himself will see through to completion (Phil. 1:6). "Repent and turn to God," and you will discover that changed behavior is the inevitable fruit (Acts 26:20; Luke 3:8; Matt. 7:20).

Repentance means you turn now and follow Jesus.

But you cannot follow Him halfheartedly. The full invitation is this: "If anyone desires to come after Me, let him *deny himself, and take up his cross daily*, and follow Me" (Luke 9:23, emphasis added). "If anyone comes to Me, and does not hate his own father and mother and wife and children and brothers and sisters, yes, and even his own life, he cannot be My disciple" (Luke 14:26 NASB).

How would you express the need for repentance to an unbeliever?

The Vanishing Conscience, 121–122

True Happiness

Blessed are the undefiled in the way, who walk in the law of the LORD!

PSALM 119:1

True happiness in life results from the transformation of your thinking processes. Colossians 1:16 says that "all things were created through Him and for Him." This includes you. Since you were made for God, you won't know true happiness until you know what pleases Him. But you won't know that until you know what His manual for living—the Bible—says. As you study His Word and learn to live by His principles, you'll begin to experience great satisfaction and happiness. The prophet Jeremiah realized that when he said, "Your words were found, and I ate them, and Your word was to me the joy and rejoicing of my heart" (Jer. 15:16).

When you understand what God wants out of your life and all the promises He has prepared for you, it will bring you joy beyond imagining. Maybe you're having problems in a relationship. Perhaps your home isn't all it ought to be. Maybe you don't have the money to buy something you desperately need. You might be struggling in school or on the job. Even though nothing seems to be working for your good now, I can promise you everything will work out in the end. How can I make a reckless promise like that? Because God's promises in Christ will be fulfilled in you. The Bible says so. And that gives every Christian a reason to rejoice.

How has living by God's principles brought you true happiness?

Welcome to the Family, 26–27

Two Types of People

Through these [promises] you may be partakers of the divine nature, having escaped the corruption that is in the world through lust.

2 PETER 1:4

Life in the Spirit is markedly different from the life of the unbeliever. *All* true Christians are "in the Spirit." They "do not walk according to the flesh, but according to the Spirit." Those who walk according to the flesh are unbelievers, and Paul is quite definite in making that clear: "If anyone does not have the Spirit of Christ, he does not belong to Him" (Rom. 8:9 NASB). Later he adds, "For all who are being led by the Spirit of God, these are sons of God" (v. 14 NASB).

That means there are only two kinds of people in the world—those who are in accord with the flesh, and those who are in accord with the Spirit. Of course, there are in-the-Spirit people at many different levels of spiritual maturity. In-the-flesh people also come in varying degrees of wickedness. But everyone is either "in the flesh" (v. 8) or "in the Spirit" (v. 9). There is no category called "in between."

What Paul is suggesting is that the Holy Spirit changes our basic disposition when we are born again. He brings us into accord with Himself. He actually indwells us (vv. 9, 11). We become partakers of the divine nature (2 Peter 1:4). Our orientation to God changes. Central to all of this is the reality that our whole mind-set is new. Whereas the mind set on the flesh meant death, the mind set on the things of the Spirit results in life and peace (Rom. 8:6).

How has your disposition toward God changed since you became a believer?

The Vanishing Conscience, 151

Finding Truth in Parables

Another parable He put forth to them, saying: "The kingdom of heaven is like a mustard seed, which a man took and sowed in his field."

Matthew 13:31

A good rule for interpreting any parable is to keep focused on the central lesson. It's not a good idea to try to milk meaning out of every incidental detail in a parable. Medieval theologians were notorious for that. They might expound for hours on the minute particulars of every parable, trying to find very detailed, symbolic, spiritual meanings in every feature of the story—sometimes while virtually ignoring the real point of the parable. That's a dangerous way to handle any Scripture. But it is an especially easy mistake to fall into when it comes to interpreting the various figures of speech in the Bible. Parables are plainly and purposely figurative, but they are not *allegories*, in which every detail carries some kind of symbolism. A parable is a simple metaphor or simile conveyed in story form. It is first and foremost a *comparison*. "The kingdom of heaven is *like* [this thing or that]" (see, for example, Matt. 13:31, 33, 44–45, 52; 20:1; 22:2).

The word *parable* is transliterated from a Greek word that literally speaks of something placed alongside of something else for the purpose of pointing out the likeness or making an important association between the two things. It's a basic literary form with a very specific purpose: to make a focused analogy through an interesting word picture or story. Interpreters of the parables will always do well to bear that in mind and avoid looking for complex symbolism, multiple layers of meaning, or abstruse lessons in the peripheral details of the parables.

How have you seen parables interpreted allegorically?

A *Tale of Two Sons*, xiii–xiv

Stories Have a True Interpretation

No prophecy of Scripture is of any private interpretation.

2 Peter 1:20

Do a simple survey and you'll notice that when Jesus explained His own parables to the disciples, He always did so by giving definite, objective meanings for the symbols He used: "The seed is the word of God" (Luke 8:11). "The field is the world" (Matt. 13:38). Sometimes His symbolism is perfectly obvious without any explanation, such as the shepherd in Luke 15:4–7 (who is a figure of Christ Himself). Other times the meaning takes a little more careful thought and exegesis, but the true meaning can still be understood and explained clearly.

Whether the true meaning of this or that symbol is patently obvious or one that requires a little detective work, the point is still the same: Jesus' parables were all *illustrative* of gospel facts. The stories were not creative alternatives to propositional truth statements, designed to supplant certainty. They were not dreamy fantasies told merely to evoke a feeling. And they certainly weren't mind games contrived to make everything vague. Much less was Jesus employing fictional forms in order to displace truth itself with mythology.

He was not inviting His hearers to interpret the stories any way they liked and thus let each one's own personal opinions be the final arbiter of what is true for that person. The conviction that the Bible itself is the final rule of faith (and the corresponding belief that Scripture itself should govern how we interpret Scripture) is a longstanding canon of biblical Christianity. Deny it, and you have in effect denied the authority of Scripture.

How would you reply to people who interpret the parables by their personal opinions?

A *Tale of Two Sons*, 200

Stories and Truth Are Not Incompatible

And He said to them, "Do you not understand this parable? How then will you understand all the parables?"

MARK 4:13

Jesus was a master storyteller, but He never told a story merely for the story's sake. His parables weren't word games or do-it-yourself mysteries where each hearer was invited to provide his or her own meaning. Each of His parables had an important lesson to convey, originating with Christ Himself and built into the fabric of the parable by Him.

That is a crucial fact to keep in mind, because it explains how *truth* is compatible with storytelling. Even pure fiction is not altogether incompatible with our conventional ideas of truth—because every well-told story ultimately makes a point. And the point of a good story is supposed to be true (or at least true to life on *some* level), even when the story itself paints a totally imaginary scenario.

Parables highlight one important truth—just like the moral of a well-told story.

That explains why the vital truth contained in a parable is fixed and objective—not a metaphysical glob of modeling clay we can bend and shape however we like. Remember that when Jesus got alone with the disciples, He carefully explained the parable of the sower to them (Matt. 13:18–23). It had a clear, simple, single, straightforward, *objective* meaning, and as Jesus explained it to them, He indicated that all the parables could be understood through a similar method (see Mark 4:13). Thus there is absolutely no reason to surmise that Jesus' use of parables is somehow an indication that truth itself is so entangled in mystery as to be utterly unknowable.

When has the meaning of a parable clarified a spiritual truth for you?

A *Tale of Two Sons*, 204–205

Jesus' Stories Reveal Truth

All these things Jesus spoke to the multitude in parables . . . that it might be fulfilled which was spoken by the prophet, saying: "I will open My mouth in parables; I will utter things kept secret from the foundation of the world."

Matthew 13:34–35

Jesus' stories were remarkable for both their simplicity and their sheer abundance. In Matthew and Luke, multiple parables are sometimes given in rapid-fire fashion, one after another, with little or no interpretive or elaborative material interspersed between them. Extended discourses containing virtually nothing but parables sometimes fill chapter-length portions of Matthew and Luke. (See, for example, Matt. 13; 24:32–25:30; and, of course, Luke 15:4–16:13.)

Jesus clearly *liked* to teach by telling stories rather than by giving a list of raw facts for rote memorization or by outlining information in a neatly catalogued, systematic layout. He was never stiff and pedantic when He taught, but always informal and conversational. The parables contained familiar figures, and sometimes they stirred raw emotions. These things were what made Jesus' preaching most memorable, rather than tidy lists or clever alliteration.

But the fact that Jesus showed such a preference for narrative forms *still* doesn't nullify either the didactic purpose of the parables or the unchanging truth they were meant to convey.

Matthew 13:34–35 sums up the proper perspective on the parables and their truth-value in very simple terms. He was quoting Psalm 78:2–4, which describes the primary purpose of the parables as a means of *revelation*.

Which parables have been especially effective for teaching you truth?

A Tale of Two Sons, 206–207

The Truth Is Clear and Not Changing

Let the words of my mouth and the meditation of my heart be acceptable in Your sight, O Lord, my strength and my redeemer.

Psalm 19:14

The meaning of God's Word is neither as obscure nor as difficult to grasp as people today often pretend. Admittedly, some things in the Bible *are* hard to understand (2 Peter 3:16), but its central, essential truth is plain enough that no one need be confused by it. "Whoever walks the road, although a fool, shall not go astray" (Isa. 35:8).

Moreover, our individual perception of truth certainly can and does change. Of course we gain better understanding as we grow. We all begin by being nourished on the milk of the Word. As we gain the ability to chew and digest harder truths, we are supposed to be strengthened by the meat of the Word (1 Cor. 3:2; Heb. 5:12). That is, we move from a merely childlike knowledge to a more mature grasp of truth in all its richness and relationship to other truth.

But truth itself does not change just because our point of view does. As we mature in our ability to perceive truth, truth itself remains fixed. Our duty is to conform all our thoughts to the truth (Ps. 19:14); we are not entitled to redefine "truth" to fit our own personal viewpoints, preferences, or desires. We must not ignore or discard selected truths just because we might find them hard to receive or difficult to fathom. Above all, we can't get apathetic or lazy about the truth when the price of understanding or defending the truth turns out to be demanding or costly. Such a self-willed approach to the truth is tantamount to usurping God (Ps. 12:4). People who take that route guarantee their own destruction (Rom. 2:8–9).

When has the truth corrected your preferences?

The Truth War, xxi

Christianity Is Not Irrational

"Come now, and let us reason together," says the Lord, "though your sins are like scarlet, they shall be as white as snow; though they are red like crimson, they shall be as wool."

Isaiah 1:18

Postmodernism is largely a reaction against the unbridled rationalism of modernity. But many postmodernists' response to rationalism is a serious overreaction. Lots of postmodernists seem to entertain the notion that *ir*rationality is superior to rationalism.

Actually, both ways of thinking are dead wrong and equally hostile to authentic truth and biblical Christianity. One extreme is as deadly as the other. *Rationalism* needs to be rejected without abandoning *rationality*.

Rationality (the right use of sanctified reason through sound logic) is never condemned in Scripture. Faith is not irrational. Authentic biblical truth demands that we employ logic and clear, sensible thinking. Truth can always be analyzed and examined and compared under the bright light of other truth, and it does not melt into absurdity. Truth by definition is never self-contradictory or nonsensical. And contrary to popular thinking, it is not rationalism to insist that coherence is a necessary quality of all truth. Christ is truth incarnate, and He cannot deny Himself (2 Tim. 2:13). Self-denying truth is an absolute contradiction in terms. "No lie is of the truth" (1 John 2:21).

Nor is logic a uniquely "Greek" category that is somehow hostile to the Hebrew context of Scripture. Scripture frequently employs logical devices, such as antithesis, if-then arguments, syllogisms, and propositions. These are all standard logical forms, and Scripture is full of them. (See, e.g., Paul's long string of deductive arguments about the importance of the resurrection in 1 Corinthians 15:12–19.)

Do you tend to fall into rationalism or irrationalism?

The Truth War, 13–14

Orthodoxy and Orthopraxy Go Together

You ran well. Who hindered you from obeying the truth?

GALATIANS 5:7

Scripture is clear: "As the body without the spirit is dead, so faith without works is dead also" (James 2:26). A high view of orthodoxy cannot nullify or undermine the importance of orthopraxy. That might *seem* to be the case if you start with the presupposition that certainty and strong convictions are always wrong and arguments about the truth value of propositions are always arrogant. But surely from a biblical perspective we can recognize the truth of James 2 without automatically discounting sound doctrine and assurance altogether.

Biblical orthodoxy encompasses orthopraxy. Both right doctrine and right living are absolutely essential and totally inseparable for the true child of God. That is the consistent teaching of Christ Himself. "If you abide in My word, you are My disciples indeed. And you shall know the truth, and the truth shall make you free" (John 8:31–32).

Furthermore, Scripture does clearly and consistently teach the primacy of right belief as the foundation of right behavior. In other words, righteous living is properly seen as a fruit of authentic faith, and never the other way around. Pious actions devoid of any real love for the truth do not even constitute genuine orthopraxy by any measure. On the contrary, that is the worst kind of self-righteous hypocrisy.

So truth is worth fighting over. It is the one thing in this world the church is supposed to fight for. Lose that fight and all else is lost.

How have you seen righteous living come from knowing the truth?

The Truth War, 37

September

WORK

Why We're Still Here

How then shall they call on Him in whom they have not believed? And how shall they believe in Him of whom they have not heard? And how shall they hear without a preacher?

ROMANS 10:14

I believe every true Christian would agree that the gospel is the heart of Christianity, that we find it only in the Scripture, and that it must be preached to the ends of the earth. The heart of the Christian faith is the gospel as found in the New Testament, whose foundations are in the Old Testament. And if it is going to save people, we must preach it throughout the world.

That is essentially the Christian mission, which the church has traditionally affirmed. Jesus said, "Go therefore and make disciples of all the nations, baptizing them in the name of the Father and of the Son and of the Holy Spirit, teaching them to observe all things that I have commanded you" (Matt. 28:19–20). He also said it another way: "Go into all the world and preach the gospel to every creature" (Mark 16:15).

True Christians have always believed that if people don't hear the gospel, they can't be saved, and that they will consequently spend eternity in hell under the judgment of God. So it's absolutely critical not only that the world hears the gospel of Jesus Christ, but that people understand it accurately and believe it absolutely. Compelled by this clear biblical mandate, Christians through the centuries have taken the saving message of the gospel to the ends of the earth. It's the only reason we're still here. True Christians are already saved and sealed for eternity. There's no reason to leave us on earth, except for this responsibility of evangelism.

In what ways is evangelism a priority in your life?

Hard to Believe, 183–184

God Is at Work

Now a certain woman named Lydia heard us. She was a seller of purple from the city of Thyatira, who worshiped God. The Lord opened her heart to heed the things spoken by Paul.

Acts 16:14

God calls all Christians to proclaim the message of Christ. Most do it by word and deed, as a part of daily living. Some make evangelism their lives' work.

If you looked at the world and judged God's power by the responses of men, you would give up trying to share the Word of God. I have gone places and poured out my heart, and nothing happened. But that's all right, because all that the Father gives to Christ are going to come home. That's what Jesus said: "All that the Father gives Me will come to Me" (John 6:37).

I'm not responsible for who gets saved, and neither are you. I refuse that responsibility. Then who is responsible? "No one can come to Me," Jesus said, "unless the Father who sent Me draws him" (John 6:44). God has that responsibility, not us. Therefore, I can look over the multitude and say, as Jesus said, "Most of you won't believe." But some *will* believe, brought to faith through reading the Bible, talking with a friend, or hearing a preacher on the street. Then, instead of being unbelievable and foolish, these words that are so hard to believe become the only balm that soothes a sinful heart; the only guide through the narrow gate that leads to eternal life; the only truth rich, complete, and holy enough to save a soul from eternal fire.

Those hard words become precious and welcome and treasured. "All that the Father gives to Christ, they will come."

They will come. Our calling is to reach them with the truth.

How does it change your perspective on evangelism to know that God is the One who converts people?

Hard to Believe, 214–215

The Work of Prayer

Then He spoke a parable to them, that men always ought to pray and not lose heart.

LUKE 18:1

We're not inclined to think of prayer as work. We tend to think of prayer as inactivity. But it is not. Good praying is hard work, and prayer is the first and most important work of all ministry.

Prayer itself is an implicit recognition of the sovereignty of God. We know that we cannot change people's hearts, so we pray for God to do it. We know that it is the Lord who adds to His church, so we pray to Him as Lord of the harvest. We know that "unless the LORD builds the house, they labor in vain who build it; unless the LORD guards the city, the watchman stays awake in vain" (Ps. 127:1).

Good praying *is* hard labor—make no mistake about it. It is hard to stay focused. It is no easy task to intercede for others. Nothing, no matter how vital it may seem, is more urgent. And therefore we must not let anything else crowd prayer off our already-busy agendas.

My advice is to start each day with a specific time of prayer. Don't let interruptions or appointments distract you from your first business. Go to the Lord when your mind is fresh. Prayer is hard enough work without putting it off until your mind is fatigued. Don't squander your brightest hours doing less important things.

But don't limit your praying to mornings. "[Pray] always with all prayer and supplication in the Spirit, being watchful to this end with all perseverance and supplication for all the saints" (Eph. 6:18).

What can you do to grow in your habit of prayer?

Called to Lead, 173–174

Praying in Jesus' Name

Ask, and it will be given to you; seek, and you will find;
knock, and it will be opened to you.

MATTHEW 7:7

Jesus' statement on the night He was betrayed carries this incredible promise: "Whatever you ask in My name, that I will do, that the Father may be glorified in the Son. If you ask anything in My name, I will do it" (John 14:13–14). Jesus will do *anything you ask* if you ask according to His will!

This is not a carte blanche for every whim of the flesh. There's a qualifying statement repeated twice for emphasis. He doesn't say, "I'll give you *absolutely anything* you ask for," but "I'll do what you ask *in My name*." The name of Jesus stands for all that He is. Throughout Scripture, God's names are the same as His attributes. When Isaiah prophesied that Messiah would be called "Wonderful, Counselor, Mighty God, Everlasting Father, Prince of Peace" (9:6), he was not giving Him actual names, but rather an overview of Messiah's character. "I AM WHO I AM," the name revealed to Moses in Exodus 3:14, is as much an affirmation of God's eternal nature as it is a name by which He is to be called.

Therefore, praying in the name of Jesus is more than merely mentioning His name at the end of your prayers. If you truly pray in Jesus' name, you can pray only for that which is consistent with His perfect character, and for that which will bring glory to Him. It implies acknowledgment of all that He has done and submission to His will.

How can you evaluate whether your prayers are in Jesus' name?

Welcome to the Family, 53–54

The Failure to Pray

You lust and do not have. You murder and covet and cannot obtain. You fight and war. Yet you do not have because you do not ask.

JAMES 4:2

Why did Peter deny Jesus? It is important to see that his failure did not occur spontaneously. Peter himself took the wrong steps that put him on the pathway to failure.

One reason for Peter's failure was that he neglected prayer. When Christ entered Gethsemane that night, He deliberately took Peter, James, and John deep into the garden with Him, and said, "Stay here and watch with Me" (Matt. 26:38). He desired them to pray with Him. Repeatedly He awakened them and urged them to pray with Him. It was for their sakes. They needed fortification and renewal of their strength far more than He did. But they did not sense their own need.

Prayer was the one thing that could have strengthened Peter to face the temptation the Lord had forewarned him about. But having already scorned Jesus' warning about his imminent failure, Peter had no sense of his desperate need to pray for God to strengthen him.

I'm convinced that most of the problems and failures Christians face are directly related to prayerlessness (see James 4:2). Perhaps Peter's failure could have been averted if he had been obedient to the Lord and spent that time in the garden praying that the Lord would grant him grace to endure.

But Peter and the other disciples were so physically exhausted after a long and difficult day that they may not have even realized how much their spiritual strength was depleted. They certainly felt their need for physical rest more than they sensed their need for spiritual refreshment. That is why instead of renewing their spirits through prayer, they sought rest and renewal of their bodies through sleep.

What have you been neglecting to pray for?

The Murder of Jesus, 123–124, 126–127

Failure and Forgiveness

So when they had eaten breakfast, Jesus said to Simon Peter, "Simon, son of Jonah, do you love Me more than these?" He said to Him, "Yes, Lord; You know that I love You." He said to him, "Feed My lambs."

JOHN 21:15

The story of Peter's denial is a lesson about the security of God's saving grace. In fact, what is emphasized most in Scripture is not Peter's *failure*, but the Lord's *forgiveness*. The reason the episode is recounted for us in such detail in Scripture is not merely to remind us of our human frailty, but more important to reassure us of the wonderful security we have in Christ.

From the very beginning, when Christ first told Peter and the other disciples that Satan desired to sift them like wheat, He subtly assured them of the inevitable victory they would experience in the long term. He told them, "I have prayed for you, that your faith should not fail; and when you have returned to Me, strengthen your brethren" (Luke 22:32). Clearly, the disciples' temporary failure was just one more element in Jesus' perfect plan, and therefore He would ultimately use even this for good.

Because of the grace shown to them in the midst of their failure, the disciples were uniquely equipped to strengthen their brethren against similar failure. When waves of Roman persecution came against the early church in later years, many believers would be strongly tempted to deny or forsake Christ to save their own lives the same way the disciples had. The disciples, having all drunk deeply of the bitterness and sorrow that come from such defection, knew better than anyone how to encourage weak and fearful believers to remain faithful. Peter himself was used mightily by the Holy Spirit for that very purpose (1 Peter 3:14–17).

Where have you failed and not yet experienced the grace Christ is offering?

The Murder of Jesus, 122–123

True Confession

Furthermore, we have had human fathers who corrected us, and we paid them respect. Shall we not much more readily be in subjection to the Father of spirits and live?

Hebrews 12:9

True confession of sin is not just admitting you did something wrong, but acknowledging that your sin was against God and in defiance of Him personally. Therefore the primary feature of confession is agreeing with God that you are helplessly guilty. In fact, the Greek word for confession literally means "say the same." To confess your sins is to say the same thing God says about them, acknowledging that God's perspective of your transgressions is correct.

For that reason, true confession also involves repentance—turning away from the evil thought or action. You have not honestly confessed your sins until you have expressed the desire to turn from them. Real confession includes a brokenness that inevitably leads to a change of behavior. In Isaiah 66:2 the Lord says, "On this one will I look: on him who is poor and of a contrite spirit, and who trembles at My word." When you pray, go to God trembling at breaking His Word, longing for victory over your weaknesses and failures.

Confessing your sin, however, does not eliminate God's chastening (disciplining) work in your life. Though you repent, God will often chasten you to correct your behavior in the future.

When God chastens us as His children, it is for our benefit. Hebrews 12:5–11 says He chastens us as sons so that we might be better sons. Confession allows us to view chastening from God's perspective. Only then can you see how God, through painful results, is shaping you by drawing you away from sin to righteousness.

What do you need to confess?

Welcome to the Family, 46–47

Children Teaching the Truth

Yes, all of you be submissive to one another, and be clothed with humility, for "God resists the proud, but gives grace to the humble."

1 Peter 5:5

One day Jesus called a little child to Himself, set that child in the midst of His disciples, and then said, "Assuredly, I say to you, unless you are converted and become as little children, you will by no means enter the kingdom of heaven. Therefore whoever humbles himself as this little child is the greatest in the kingdom of heaven. Whoever receives one little child like this in My name receives Me" (Matt. 18:3–5).

Jesus had great regard for the status of the child. He saw in a child the model of dependency and trust, the mind of innocence and humility. He saw a person eager to please and give thanks, quick to express love, and quick to receive and obey what was commanded and taught. So He used a child for that purpose of analogy—to teach His disciples dependency, trust, humility, affection, and obedience.

"But," you may say, "Jesus was only using the children as an analogy for the way adults are converted and become part of the kingdom of God." Let me quickly point out to you that an analogy only works if it is rooted in truth! If children are not readily and fully received into the kingdom of heaven, the analogy of spiritual conversion would be a very poor one. As it is, the analogy is a great one! Children are readily accepted into the kingdom, and because of that, we are wise to become like children in our spiritual dependency upon the Lord so that we, too, might be readily accepted.

What can you do to develop a childlike spirit?

Safe in the Arms of God, 57, 59

The Importance of Hard Work

And whatever you do, do it heartily, as to the Lord and not to men, knowing that from the Lord you will receive the reward of the inheritance; for you serve the Lord Christ.

COLOSSIANS 3:23–24

The Bible decries laziness; it is scandalous and sinful. Proverbs has much to say about this (6:9–11; 10:5; 19:15; 21:25; 24:30–34), including the contrasting of the lazy with the diligent. "The hand of the diligent will rule, but the lazy man will be put to forced labor" (12:24). "The soul of the sluggard craves and gets nothing, but the soul of the diligent is made fat" (13:4 NASB; cf. 14:23). If you're diligent, you're likely to make money; if you're lazy, you probably won't.

The apostle Paul taught similar principles in the New Testament. He exhorted the believers in Thessalonica: "If anyone is not willing to work, then he is not to eat, either" (2 Thess. 3:10 NASB). He told Timothy to instruct church members on their work obligations: "If anyone does not provide for his own, and especially for those of his household, he has denied the faith and is worse than an unbeliever" (1 Tim. 5:8). If you do not work conscientiously and diligently to provide for your family, you're behaving worse than an unbeliever, because most non-Christians will at least work hard to care for their families.

We should be motivated to shun laziness because work is a noble endeavor, which should be performed to please the Lord (Col. 3:22–24). That we are to work "not by way of eyeservice, as men-pleasers, but as slaves of Christ, doing the will of God from the heart" (Eph. 6:6 NASB) should be our elevating motivation.

What can you do to improve your work habits?

Whose Money Is It Anyway? 41–42

The True Path to Prosperity

He who sows sparingly will also reap sparingly, and he who sows bountifully will also reap bountifully.

2 Corinthians 9:6

The "Prosperity Gospel" says God wants His followers to be rich and have all the best from life—large, elaborate homes; expensive luxury cars; the most ostentatious wardrobes, and so on. That greed-driven heresy is popular because it declares that God's primary function is to dole out material goods to His people. The movement claims to be able to teach people (for *lots* of remuneration) how to plug in to the right spiritual wavelength so that God will deliver all the money and goods imaginable to please every personal indulgence.

The secular culture also makes false appeals for how to be prosperous by working hard, earning as much money as possible, then hoarding, saving, and investing your money as shrewdly as possible. It claims that is the only way to increase your net worth and guarantee a prosperous retirement.

Neither of those get-rich philosophies, however, can match God's true path to prosperity. The Lord is concerned about your material needs, and He really does have a plan for your financial prosperity that promises to meet your every need. He does not disregard hard work, saving, or wise investing, but He does reject aberrations like the prosperity gospel and man-centered methods based on accumulation and hoarding. God's plan for the believer's genuine prosperity, as outlined in His Word, is simply this: *You and I must give away what we have*.

Second Corinthians 9:6–15 elucidates God's path to prosperity as well as any passage in Scripture. The generous Christian never needs to fear not having enough. That's because the more you give, the more God gives in return.

What keeps you from giving more?

Whose Money Is It Anyway? 137–138

How to Make Friends

They glorify God for the obedience of your confession to the gospel of Christ, and for your liberal sharing with them and all men, and by their prayer for you, who long for you because of the exceeding grace of God in you.

2 CORINTHIANS 9:13–14

Those who receive your gifts recognize that God is at work in your life, long for fellowship with you, and pray for you. In short, when you give in obedience to God's plan, one of the benefits He returns to you is the blessing of new friends.

We should all desire that friends, old and new, would be praying for us. When we reach out with our giving and meet others' needs, something profound and precious occurs—they become friends who pray for us, because that's how love works in the body of Christ.

In the parable of the unjust steward (Luke 16:1–9), the manager (steward) was using money to make friends of his master's debtors by discounting their debts. He wanted them to be obligated to him so that he might be able to stay in their homes, if need be, after being fired by the master.

Jesus, while not condoning the manager's dishonesty to his master, indicated that the unjust manager was smarter than most believers, because he knew how to get the long-term benefit from this world's wealth. We should learn from the manager's example and invest the Lord's money in ways that advance His kingdom, bring sinners to salvation, and assist fellow believers in need. Such generosity leads us to make new friends on earth whom we will forever fellowship with later in heaven—and all will be part of the benefits of God's gracious harvest to those of us who give away our resources with eternity in view.

Where can you invest your money to advance God's kingdom?

Whose Money Is It Anyway? 146–147

Our True Identity

And having been set free from sin, you became slaves of righteousness.

Romans 6:18

The New Testament commands believers to submit to Christ completely, and not just as hired servants or spiritual employees—but as those who belong wholly to Him. Jesus Christ is our Master—a fact we acknowledge every time we call Him "Lord." We are His slaves, called to humbly and wholeheartedly obey and honor Him.

We don't hear about that concept much in churches today. In contemporary Christianity the language is anything but slave terminology. It is about success, health, wealth, prosperity, and the pursuit of happiness. We often hear that God loves people unconditionally and wants them to be all *they* want to be. He wants to fulfill every desire, hope, and dream. *Personal* ambition, *personal* fulfillment, *personal* gratification—these have all become part of the language of evangelical Christianity—and part of what it means to have a "personal relationship with Jesus Christ." Instead of teaching the New Testament gospel—where sinners are called to submit to Christ—the contemporary message is exactly the opposite: Jesus is here to fulfill all *your* wishes. Likening Him to a personal assistant or a personal trainer, many churchgoers speak of a *personal* Savior who is eager to do their bidding and help them in their quest for self-satisfaction or individual accomplishment.

The New Testament understanding of the believer's relationship to Christ could not be more opposite. He is the Master and Owner. We are His possession. He is the King, the Lord, and the Son of God. We are His subjects and His subordinates.

In a word, we are His *slaves*.

In what ways have you been living for your own fulfillment rather than for Christ?

Slave, 14–15

The Truth About Slavery

But none of these things move me; nor do I count my life dear to myself, so that I may finish my race with joy, and the ministry which I received from the Lord Jesus, to testify to the gospel of the grace of God.

ACTS 20:24

When the apostles used slave imagery, they were fully aware of what it meant in terms of both Jewish history and Roman culture. From the standpoint of Israel's history, to be a slave of God was to identify oneself with those who stood at Mount Sinai and with noble intentions proclaimed, "All the words which the LORD has said we will do!" (Ex. 24:3). Moreover, it was to be aligned with notable men of faith, such as Abraham, Moses, David, and the prophets—spiritual leaders who exemplified wholehearted submission to the will and word of God. From the standpoint of first-century culture, slavery served as an apt picture of the believer's relationship to Christ—one of complete submission and subjugation to the master. In both cases, to be a slave was to be under the complete authority of someone else. It meant rejecting personal autonomy and embracing the will of another. The concept required no great explanation because slavery was commonplace and had been for many centuries.

When the apostle Paul referred to himself as a "slave of Christ" and a "slave of God," his readers knew exactly what he meant. Of course, this did not make the claim any less shocking. In a Greco-Roman context, such as the cities to which Paul wrote, personal freedom was prized, slavery was denigrated, and self-imposed slavery was scorned and despised. But for Paul, whose sole ambition was to be pleasing to Christ, there could not have been a more fitting self-designation. His life revolved around the Master. Nothing else—including his own personal agenda—mattered.

What do you need to let go of to serve God more faithfully?

Slave, 35–36

Slaves Obey Completely

But in a great house there are . . . some [vessels] for honor and some for dishonor. Therefore if anyone cleanses himself from the latter, he will be a vessel for honor, sanctified and useful for the Master, prepared for every good work.

2 TIMOTHY 2:20–21

Being a slave not only meant belonging to someone else; it also meant being always available to obey that person in every way. The slave's sole duty was to carry out the master's wishes, and the faithful slave was eager to do so without hesitation or complaint.

As His slaves, we are expected to obey Jesus Christ (1 Peter 1:2), "to present [our] bodies a living and holy sacrifice, acceptable to God, which is [our] spiritual service of worship" (Rom. 12:1 NASB), and to "keep His commandments and do the things that are pleasing in His sight" (1 John 3:22). "You were bought at a price," Paul told the Corinthians, "therefore glorify God in your body" (1 Cor. 6:20).

Those who claim to belong to Christ but persist in patterns of disobedience betray the reality of that profession. The apostle John explained: "If we say that we have fellowship with Him, and walk in darkness, we lie and do not practice the truth" (1 John 1:6). Such is especially true of false teachers, whom the New Testament describes as "slaves of corruption" (2 Peter 2:19) and as "slaves, not of our Lord Christ but of their own appetites" (Rom. 16:18 NASB). They are "ungodly persons who turn the grace of our God into licentiousness and deny our only Master and Lord, Jesus Christ" (Jude v. 4 NASB; cf. 2 Peter 2:1). The true man of God, by contrast, is "the Lord's slave" making himself "useful to the Master, prepared for every good work" (2 Tim. 2:24, 21 HCSB).

What sinful behavior do you need to end so you can be set apart for Christ's work?

Slave, 46–47

Slaves Are Totally Dependent

And God is able to make all grace abound toward you, that you, always having all sufficiency in all things, may have an abundance for every good work.

2 CORINTHIANS 9:8

As part of the master's household, slaves were completely dependent on their owners for the basic necessities of life, including food and shelter. Unlike free persons, slaves did not have to worry about finding something to eat or somewhere to sleep. Because their needs were met, they could focus entirely on serving the master.

Again, the parallels to the Christian life are striking. As believers, we can focus on the things God has called us to do, trusting Him to meet our needs. "Do not worry then, saying, 'What will we eat?' or 'What will we drink?' or 'What will we wear for clothing?'" Jesus told His followers. "Your heavenly Father knows that you need all these things. But seek first His kingdom and His righteousness, and all these things will be added to you" (Matt. 6:31–33 NASB). Those who make pleasing God their highest priority can be confident that He will take care of them.

No one understood this principle better than the apostle Paul. "Be anxious for nothing," he wrote to the Philippians, "but in everything by prayer and supplication . . . let your requests be made known to God" (4:6). Later in that chapter, he explained that he had learned the secret of being content, no matter his circumstances. Consequently, he could exclaim, "I can do all things through Christ who strengthens me" (v. 13). Paul's contentment came both from relying on Christ completely and also from rightly assessing his needs.

What would it look like to trust God to meet your needs?

Slave, 48–50

Slaves of a Wonderful Master

The LORD is my shepherd; I shall not want.

PSALM 23:1

To be a slave of Jesus Christ is the greatest benediction imaginable. Not only is He a kind and gracious Lord, but He is also the God of the universe. His character is perfect; His love is infinite; His power, matchless; His wisdom, unsearchable; and His goodness, beyond compare.

In Roman times, one's experience as a slave was almost entirely dependent on the nature of one's master. The slave of a good, benevolent master could expect to be well cared for, enjoying a secure and peaceful life.

In the same way that wicked owners often made life unbearable for their slaves, a gracious master could make the situation pleasant and even desirable for those in his household. Such a master would evoke the loyalty and love of his slaves, as they served him out of devotion and not just duty.

Because the Lord is our Master, we can trust Him to take care of us in every situation and stage of life. Even in the most difficult of circumstances, He will provide all that we need in order to be faithful to Him. We can be "anxious for nothing" (Phil. 4:6) because "we know that God causes all things to work together for good to those who love God, to those who are called according to His purpose" (Rom. 8:28 NASB). We are right to trust Him completely, for He is sovereign not only over our lives, but also over everything that exists. "For He Himself has said, 'I will never leave you nor forsake you.' So we boldly say: 'The Lord is my helper: I will not fear. What can man do to me?'" (Heb. 13:5–6).

How have you seen God provide what you needed to serve Him?

Slave, 93–94

How God Chooses Us

You did not choose Me, but I chose you and appointed you that you should go and bear fruit, and that your fruit should remain, that whatever you ask the Father in My name He may give you.

JOHN 15:16

In the Roman slave market, decisions regarding the slave's future rested solely in the hands of the purchaser, not the one being sold. Similarly, the Bible teaches that God has chosen His slaves by His own sovereign, independent, electing choice.

But unlike the Roman slave market—where slaves were selected based on their positive qualities, like strength, health, and physical appearance—God chose His slaves with the full knowledge of their weaknesses and failures. We were "not many wise according to the flesh, not many mighty, not many noble . . . but God has chosen the foolish things of the world to put to shame the wise, and God has chosen the weak things of the world to put to shame the things which are mighty" (1 Cor. 1:26–27). Indeed, He mercifully elected us to salvation in spite of ourselves, saving us not because of any inherent goodness in us, but according to His own eternal purposes and for the sake of His glory.

The New Testament is replete with examples of God's electing and initiating work in salvation. (For example, see John 15:16; Acts 13:48; 16:14.) In each instance, it was God who did the work of choosing, calling, appointing, and opening the heart. Such is still the case whenever a soul is saved, for the new birth always comes not by "the will of the flesh, nor of the will of man, but of God" (John 1:13).

God's will in salvation is singular, dependent on nothing other than His uninfluenced, free, electing choice.

How does it change your perspective to know that God chose you in spite of your failures?

Slave, 132–134

Christ's Call to Serve All

If I then, your Lord and Teacher, have washed your feet, you also ought to wash one another's feet.

John 13:14

When believers realize that they are all *slaves*, called to model the humility of the ultimate slave (Phil. 2:5–7), it becomes obvious how they ought to treat others: "Do nothing from selfishness or empty conceit, but with humility of mind regard one another as more important than yourselves" (v. 3 NASB). As our Lord told His disciples, "Whoever of you desires to be first shall be slave of all. For even the Son of Man did not come to be served, but to serve, and to give His life a ransom for many" (Mark 10:44–45). Sacrificial service and love for one another ought to characterize the followers of Christ. After all, every one of us is a slave, called to imitate the selfless example of our Master Himself.

As the gospel went forth from Israel to Samaria and then to the Gentiles, it broke down previous prejudices between different social classes and racial groups. Jews and Gentiles, men and women, slaves and freemen—all were welcomed into the church, where they enjoyed equal spiritual standing before God as citizens of heaven and fellow slaves of Christ. The gospel had put an end to all prior prejudices. As Paul told the Colossians, "[You have] put on the new self who is being renewed to a true knowledge according to the image of the One who created him—a renewal in which there is no distinction between Greek and Jew, circumcised and uncircumcised, barbarian, Scythian, slave and freeman, but Christ is all, and in all" (3:10–11 NASB).

What types of people do you not normally think about serving?

Slave, 203–204

Faith Works

But someone will say, "You have faith, and I have works." Show me your faith without your works, and I will show you my faith by my works.

James 2:18

The works described in Hebrews 11 are *faith works*. These are not fleshly efforts to earn God's favor. The works described here are in no sense meritorious. They are the pure expression of believing hearts.

Meritorious works have nothing to do with faith. But faith works have everything to do with it. Faith that does not produce works is dead faith, inefficacious faith. Faith that remains idle is no better than the faith the demons display (James 2:19).

Here we must make a clear and careful distinction. Faith works are a consequence of faith, not a component of faith. Faith is an entirely inward response and therefore is complete before it produces its first work. At the moment of salvation, faith does nothing but receive the provision of Christ. The believer himself contributes nothing meritorious to the saving process. As J. Gresham Machen stated, "Faith is the acceptance of a gift at the hands of Christ." Better yet, faith lays hold of Christ Himself. In no sense is this an issue of works or merit.

But true faith never remains passive. From the moment of regeneration, faith goes to work. It doesn't work for divine favor. It doesn't work against God's grace, but in accord with grace. As we "work out [our] salvation with fear and trembling" (Phil. 2:12), we discover that "it is God who works in [us], both to will and to do for His good pleasure" (v. 13). True faith keeps our eyes fixed on Jesus, the author and perfecter of all genuine faith (Heb. 12:2).

What difference have you experienced between working to earn God's favor and working from faith?

The Gospel According to the Apostles, 52–54

Why We Obey

I delight to do Your will, O my God, and Your law is within my heart.

PSALM 40:8

To an outsider—and to many new Christians if we're honest with ourselves—obedience to the will of God can seem incredibly hard and unpleasant, if not impossible. Deny yourself? Take up a cross? You can't be serious! But in 1 John 5:2–3 the apostle reminds us of a startling and reassuring truth: "By this we know that we love the children of God, when we love God and keep His commandments. For this is the love of God, that we keep His commandments. And His commandments are not burdensome." As Jesus Himself said, "My yoke is easy and My burden is light" (Matt. 11:30).

A slave's primary duty is obedience—to do whatever the master tells him to do. But Paul then applied that simple illustration to the crucial phrase "obeyed from the heart" (Rom. 6:16–18). Heart obedience ought to be the overriding attitude and desire in your life. You should obey because you *want* to, not because anyone is forcing you to. It means obedience is a fundamental, inner trait of your new life, and you become so singularly obedient to God's Word that you are called a slave of righteousness.

You delight to obey God's law because you love Him. Yes, loving is a duty—it is an act of the will—but it is not oppressive. Why is it so delightful to obey Him? Because God's law is a reflection of Himself and the way we love Him. Obedience to His law pleases both Him and Christians who love Him and seek His pleasure.

When have you delighted to obey God's law?

Welcome to the Family, 15–16

God's Work in Us

For we are His workmanship, created in Christ Jesus for good works, which God prepared beforehand that we should walk in them.

EPHESIANS 2:10

It cannot be overemphasized that works play no role in *gaining* salvation. But good works have everything to do with *living out* salvation. No good works can *earn* salvation, but many good works *result* from genuine salvation. Good works are not necessary to *become* a disciple, but good works are the necessary *marks* of all true disciples. God has, after all, ordained that we should walk in them.

Note that before we can do any good work for the Lord, He does His good work in us. By God's grace we become "*His* workmanship, created in Christ Jesus for good works." The same grace that made us alive with Christ and raised us up with Him enables us to do the good works unto which He has saved us.

Note also that it is God who "prepared" these good works. We get no credit for them. Even *our* good works are works of *His* grace. It would be appropriate to call them "grace works." They are the corroborating evidence of true salvation. These works, like every other aspect of divine salvation, are the product of God's sovereign grace.

Good deeds and righteous attitudes are intrinsic to who we are as Christians. They proceed from the very nature of one who lives in the realm of the heavenlies. Just as the unsaved are sinners by nature, the redeemed are righteous by nature.

How does it change your perspective to know that God prepared good works for you to do?

The Gospel According to the Apostles, 70

Our Highest Priority

But the hour is coming, and now is, when the true worshipers will worship the Father in spirit and truth; for the Father is seeking such to worship Him.

JOHN 4:23

Nothing, including even service rendered to Christ, is more important than listening to Him and honoring Him with our hearts. Remember what Jesus told the Samaritan woman at the well: God is seeking true worshipers (John 4:23). Christ had found one in Mary. He would not affirm Martha's reprimand of her, because it was Mary, not Martha, who properly understood that worship is a higher duty to Christ than service rendered on His behalf.

It is a danger, even for people who love Christ, that we become so concerned with *doing things for Him* that we begin to neglect *hearing Him* and *remembering what He has done for us*. We must never allow our service for Christ to crowd out our worship of Him. The moment our works become more important to us than our worship, we have turned the true spiritual priorities on their heads.

Whenever you elevate good deeds over sound doctrine and true worship, you ruin the works too. Doing good works for the works' sake has a tendency to exalt self and depreciate the work of Christ. Good deeds, human charity, and acts of kindness are crucial expressions of real faith, but they must flow from a true reliance on *God's* redemption and *His* righteousness. After all, our own good works can never be a means of earning God's favor; that's why in Scripture the focus of faith is always on what God has done for us, and never on what we do for Him (Rom. 10:2–4).

What can you do to remember what Christ has done for you when you see yourself focusing on your works?

Twelve Extraordinary Women, 167

Not Ashamed of the Gospel

For I am not ashamed of the gospel of Christ, for it is the power of God to salvation for everyone who believes, for the Jew first and also for the Greek.

Romans 1:16

Paul made a remarkable statement in Romans 1:16. Now why would Paul say, "I'm not ashamed of the gospel"? Who would ever be ashamed of such good news? Would someone who had found the cure for AIDS have to overcome immense shame to proclaim it? Would a person who had discovered a cure for cancer have to get over terrible shame to be able to open his mouth? Why is the cross so hard to mention?

At some point or other in our Christian lives, we have all been ashamed and kept our mouths closed when we should have opened them. If you have never felt shame in proclaiming the gospel, it's probably because you haven't proclaimed the gospel clearly, in its entirety, the way Jesus proclaimed it.

Why can't the Christian business executive witness to his board of directors? Why can't the Christian university professor stand up before the whole faculty and proclaim the gospel? We all want to be accepted—yet we know, as Paul discovered so many times, that we have a message the world will reject, and the stronger we hold to that message, the more hostile the world becomes. So we begin to feel the shame. Paul rose above that by the grace of God and the power of the Spirit, and he said, "I'm not ashamed." It's a striking example for us, because he knew the price of fidelity to the truth: public rejection, imprisonment, and ultimately, execution.

When have you felt ashamed to speak the gospel?

Hard to Believe, 23–24

It's What You Believe, Not What You Do

One thing I have desired of the Lord, that will I seek: that I may dwell in the house of the Lord all the days of my life, to behold the beauty of the Lord, and to inquire in His temple.

Psalm 27:4

What we *believe* is ultimately more crucial than what we *do*. Martha's "much serving" was a distraction (Luke 10:40) from the "one thing" (v. 42) that was really needed—listening to and learning from Jesus. Religious works often have a sinister tendency to eclipse faith itself. Proper good works always flow from faith and are the fruit of it. What we do is vital, because that is the evidence that our faith is living and real (James 2:14–26). But faith must come first and is the only viable foundation for true and lasting good works.

Martha seems to have forgotten these things momentarily. She was acting as if Christ needed her work for Him more than she needed His work on her behalf. Rather than humbly fixing her faith on the vital importance of Christ's work for sinners, she was thinking too much in terms of what she could do for Him.

Human instinct seems to tell us that what we *do* is more important than what we *believe*. But that is a false instinct, the product of our fallen self-righteousness. It is a totally wrong way of thinking—*sinfully* wrong. We must never think more highly of our works for Christ than we do of His works on our behalf.

Of course, such a thought would never consciously enter Martha's mind. She loved Christ. She genuinely trusted Him, although her faith had moments of weakness. Still, on this occasion, she allowed her anxiety about what she must do for Christ to overwhelm her gratitude over what He would do for her.

Have you made serving Christ or listening to Him primary lately?

Twelve Extraordinary Women, 168–169

Human Wisdom Does Not Lead to God

At that time Jesus answered and said, "I thank You, Father, Lord of heaven and earth, that You have hidden these things from the wise and prudent and have revealed them to babes."

MATTHEW 11:25

Paul's quotation of Isaiah 29:14 in 1 Corinthians 1:19, "I will destroy the wisdom of the wise," had to be an offensive statement to his audience. He was basically saying, "I'll trash all you philosophers and all your philosophy." Nothing was subtle about Paul, nothing vague or ambiguous. But the message wasn't Paul's, as he reminded us when he affirmed, "It is written"—literally, "It stands written"—it stands as divinely revealed truth that the gospel of the cross makes no concession to human wisdom. Paul was just God's mouthpiece. Human intellect plays no role in redemption.

First Corinthians 2:14 reads, "But the natural man does not receive the things of the Spirit of God, for they are foolishness to him; nor can he know them, because they are spiritually discerned." This is the problem. An unconverted person may have great reasoning power and intellect, but when it comes to spiritual reality and the life of God and eternity, he makes no contribution. Whether it's Athens or Rome, whether it's Cambridge, Oxford, Harvard, Stanford, Yale, or Princeton, or wherever else, all the collected wisdom that is outside the Scripture adds up to nothing but foolishness.

God wisely established that no one could ever come to know Him by human wisdom. The only way anyone will come to know God is by divine revelation and through the Holy Spirit. The final word on human wisdom is that it's all nonsense. Man, by wisdom, cannot know God.

In what ways have you been relying on your intellect to know God?

Hard to Believe, 31

True Greatness

You know that the rulers of the Gentiles lord it over them, and those who are great exercise authority over them. Yet it shall not be so among you; but whoever desires to become great among you, let him be your servant.

MATTHEW 20:25–26

Again and again, Christ had emphasized this truth: if you want to be great in the kingdom, you must become the servant of all.

It is astonishing how little this truth penetrated the disciples' consciousness, even after three years with Jesus. But on the final night of His earthly ministry, not one of them had the humility to pick up the towel and washbasin and perform the task of a servant (John 13:1–17). So Jesus did it Himself.

The apostle John *did* eventually learn the balance between ambition and humility. In fact, humility is one of the great virtues that comes through in his writings.

Throughout John's Gospel, for instance, he never once mentions his own name. Rather than write his name, which might focus attention on him, he refers to himself as "the disciple whom Jesus loved" (John 13:23; 20:2; 21:7, 20), giving glory to Jesus for having loved such a man. In fact, he seems utterly in awe of the marvel that Christ loved him.

John's humility also comes through in the gentle way he appeals to his readers in every one of his epistles. He calls them "little children," "beloved"—and he includes himself as a brother and fellow child of God (cf. 1 John 3:2). His last contribution to the canon was the book of Revelation, where he describes himself as "your brother and companion in the tribulation and kingdom and patience of Jesus Christ" (Rev. 1:9). Even though he was the last remaining apostle and the patriarch of the church, we never find him lording it over anyone.

In what situations do you avoid the role of a servant?

Twelve Ordinary Men, 110–111

True Glory Comes with Suffering

In this you greatly rejoice, though now for a little while, if need be, you have been grieved by various trials, that the genuineness of your faith . . . may be found to praise, honor, and glory at the revelation of Jesus Christ.

1 PETER 1:6–7

Suffering is the price of glory. We are "heirs of God and joint heirs with Christ, if indeed we suffer with Him, that we may also be glorified together" (Rom. 8:17). Jesus taught this principle again and again. "If anyone desires to come after Me, let him deny himself, and take up his cross, and follow Me. For whoever desires to save his life will lose it, but whoever loses his life for My sake will find it" (Matt. 16:24–25). "Unless a grain of wheat falls into the ground and dies, it remains alone; but if it dies, it produces much grain. He who loves his life will lose it, and he who hates his life in this world will keep it for eternal life" (John 12:24–25).

Suffering is the prelude to glory. Our suffering as believers is the assurance of the glory that is yet to come (1 Peter 1:6–7). And "the sufferings of this present time are not worthy to be compared with the glory which shall be revealed in us" (Rom. 8:18). Meanwhile, those who thirst for glory must balance that desire with a willingness to suffer.

Jesus said there is a price for seats in glory. Not only are those seats reserved for the humble, but those who sit in those seats will first be prepared for the place of honor by enduring the humility of suffering. That is why Jesus told James and John that before they would receive any throne at all, they would be required to "drink the cup that I drink, and be baptized with the baptism that I am baptized with" (Mark 10:38).

What can you do to face suffering as a prelude to glory?

Twelve Ordinary Men, 112–113

What Are Our Affections?

If you know that He is righteous, you know that everyone who practices righteousness is born of Him.

1 JOHN 2:29

"No one who abides in Him sins; no one who sins has seen Him or knows Him. Little children, make sure no one deceives you; . . . the one who practices sin is of the devil; for the devil has sinned from the beginning. The Son of God appeared for this purpose, to destroy the works of the devil. No one who is born of God practices sin, because His seed abides in him; and he cannot sin, because he is born of God" (1 John 3:6–9 NASB).

Those verses have tripped many people up. The key to their meaning is the definition of sin in 3:4: "Sin is lawlessness." The Greek word for "lawlessness" is *anomia*. It literally means "without law," and it describes those who live immoral, ungodly, unrighteous lives as a matter of continuous practice. They hate God's righteousness and perpetually live as if they were sovereign over God's law. This cannot be true of a genuine Christian.

The apostle is clearly *not* making sinless perfection a test of salvation (see 1 John 1:8).

Nor is he making an issue about the frequency, duration, or magnitude of one's sins. The issue John is raising here has to do with our attitude toward sin and righteousness, our heart's response when we *do* sin, and the overall direction of our walk.

The test is this: What is the object of your affections—sin or righteousness? If your chief love is sin, then you are "of the devil" (1 John 3:8, 10). If you love righteousness and practice righteousness, you are born of God (1 John 2:29). What is the direction of your affection?

What evidence have you seen to indicate your affection's direction?

The Gospel According to the Apostles, 170–171

We Need a Substitute

For by one offering He has perfected forever those who are being sanctified.

Hebrews 10:14

Now it should be obvious to anyone that "it is not possible that the blood of bulls and goats could take away sins" (Heb. 10:4; cf. Mic. 6:6–8). Everyone who ever seriously thought about the sacrificial system and weighed the real cost of sin had to face this truth eventually: animal sacrifices simply could not provide a full and final atonement for sin. Something more needed to be done to make a full atonement.

There were basically two possible answers to the dilemma. One approach was to adopt a system of merit such as the Pharisees' religion, in which the sinner himself tried to embellish or supplement the atoning significance of the animal sacrifices with several more layers of good works.

The other approach was the one followed by every truly faithful person from the beginning of time until the coming of Christ. They acknowledged their own inability to atone for sin, embraced God's promise of forgiveness, and trusted Him to send a Redeemer who would provide a full and final atonement (Isa. 59:20). From the day when Adam and Eve ate the forbidden fruit and their race was cursed, faithful believers had looked for the promised offspring of the woman who would finally crush the serpent's head and thus put sin and guilt away forever (Gen. 3:15). Despite some very strong hints (including Dan. 9:24 and Isa. 53:10), the actual means by which redemption would finally be accomplished remained shrouded in mystery, until Jesus Himself explained it after His resurrection to some disciples on the road to Emmaus (Luke 24:27).

When have you felt your inability to atone for your sin?

A *Tale of Two Sons*, 121–122

Whom God Uses

Now when they saw the boldness of Peter and John, and perceived that they were uneducated and untrained men, they marveled. And they realized that they had been with Jesus.

Acts 4:13

Many Christians become discouraged and disheartened when their spiritual life and witness suffer because of sin or failure. We tend to think we're worthless nobodies—and left to ourselves, that would be true! But worthless nobodies are just the kind of people God uses, because that is all He has to work with.

Satan may even attempt to convince us that our shortcomings render us useless to God and to His church. But Christ's choice of the apostles testifies to the fact that God can use the unworthy and the unqualified. He can use nobodies. They turned the world upside down, these twelve (Acts 17:6). It was not because they had extraordinary talents, unusual intellectual abilities, powerful political influence, or some special social status. They turned the world upside down because God worked in them to do it.

God chooses the humble, the lowly, the meek, and the weak so that there's never any question about the source of power when their lives change the world. It's not the man; it's the truth of God and the power of God *in* the man. (We need to remind some preachers today of this. It's not their cleverness or their personality. The power is in the Word—the truth that we preach—not in us.) And apart from one Person—one extraordinary human being who was God incarnate, the Lord Jesus Christ—the history of God's work on earth is the story of His using the unworthy and molding them for His use the same careful way a potter fashions clay.

When have you seen God work through people in spite of their weaknesses?

Twelve Ordinary Men, 11–12

OCTOBER

SIN, EVIL, AND TEMPTATION

True Kingdom Building

This is the word of the LORD to Zerubbabel: "Not by might nor by power, but by My Spirit," says the LORD of hosts.

Zechariah 4:6

Some might imagine that if Christ had wanted His message to have maximum impact, He could have played off His popularity more effectively. Modern conventional wisdom would suggest that Jesus ought to have done everything possible to exploit His fame, tone down the controversies that arose out of His teaching, and employ whatever strategies He could use to maximize the crowds around Him. But He did not do that. In fact, He did precisely the opposite. Instead of taking the populist route and exploiting His fame, He began to emphasize the very things that made His message so controversial. At about the time the crowds reached their peak, He preached a message so offensive in its content that the multitude melted away, leaving only the most devoted few (John 6:66–67).

Among those who stayed with Christ were the Twelve. They were twelve perfectly ordinary, unexceptional men. But Christ's strategy for advancing His kingdom hinged on those twelve men rather than on the clamoring multitudes. He chose to work through the instrumentality of those few fallible individuals rather than advance His agenda through mob force, military might, personal popularity, or a public-relations campaign. From a human perspective, the future of the church and the long-term success of the gospel depended entirely on the faithfulness of that handful of disciples. There was no plan B if they failed.

A dozen men under the power of the Holy Spirit are a more potent force than the teeming masses whose initial enthusiasm for Jesus was apparently provoked by little more than sheer curiosity.

The strategy Jesus chose typified the character of the kingdom itself (see Zech. 4:6).

What misconceptions, if any, do you have about the kingdom of God?

Twelve Ordinary Men, 2–3

Truth in Propositions

The word which God sent to the children of Israel, preaching peace through Jesus Christ—He is Lord of all.

Acts 10:36

Propositions are the building blocks of logic. A proposition is nothing more than an assertion that either affirms or denies something. "Jesus Christ is Lord of all" (cf. Acts 10:36) is a classic biblical proposition that expresses one of the foundational truths of all Christian doctrine. Another is "There is no salvation in any other" (cf. Acts 4:12). The first example is an affirmation of Jesus' supremacy and exclusivity; the second is a denial of the converse.

The truth-value of every proposition is binary: it can only be either true or false. There is no middle value.

Since the form of a proposition demands either an affirmation or a denial, and postmodern thinking prefers obscurity and vagueness rather than clarity, it is no wonder that the very notion of propositional truth has fallen out of favor in these postmodern times.

It is more and more common these days to hear people express the belief that the brand of truth embodied in stories is somehow of an altogether different nature from the kind of truth that we can express in propositions. What they generally are arguing for is a fluid, subjective, ambiguous concept of truth itself.

To embrace that perspective is in effect to make mincemeat of the very notion of truth. Truth cannot be verbally expressed or formally affirmed at all—even in story form—without recourse to propositions. So the postmodern attempt to divorce truth from propositions is nothing more than a way of talking about truth, toying with the idea of truth, and giving lip service to the existence of truth—without actually needing to affirm anything as true or deny anything as false.

How would you answer someone who believes that truth is relative?

A *Tale of Two Sons*, 208–209

The Devil's Attack on the Truth

For such are false apostles, deceitful workers, transforming themselves into apostles of Christ. And no wonder! For Satan himself transforms himself into an angel of light.

2 Corinthians 11:13–14

Ever since that day in the garden when the serpent tempted Eve, he has relentlessly attacked the truth with lies, using the same strategies over and over to sow doubt and disbelief in the human mind. "We are not ignorant of his devices" (2 Cor. 2:11).

The form of his evil dialectic rarely changes. He *questions* the truth God has revealed ("Has God indeed said, 'You shall not eat of every tree of the garden'?" [Gen. 3:1]). Then he *contradicts* what God has said ("You will not surely die" [v. 4]). Finally, he *concocts an alternative version of "truth"* ("God knows that in the day you eat of it your eyes will be opened, and you will be like God, knowing good and evil" [v. 5]). The devil's alternative credo often has a few carefully chosen elements of truth in the mix—but always diluted and thoroughly blended with falsehoods, contradictions, misrepresentations, distortions, and every other imaginable perversion of reality. Add it all up and the bottom line is a big lie.

Furthermore, in the promotion of his dishonesty, Satan employs every agent he can dupe into being a shill for him—demons, unbelievers, and (most effectively) people who are in some way actually associated with the truth, or (even worse) who merely *pretend* to be agents of the truth and angels of light. That is one of Satan's favorite and time-tested strategies (2 Cor. 11:13–15).

What is your strategy for discerning the truth of a matter?

The Truth War, 40

Resist the Devil

Be sober, be vigilant; because your adversary the devil walks about like a roaring lion, seeking whom he may devour. Resist him, steadfast in the faith.

1 Peter 5:8–9

Resist the devil" (James 4:7). Unfortunately, modern American society, by and large, is characterized by *resistance* to God's standards and *tolerance* of the devil's.

In fact, most of our society's values in recent years have been shaped by the devil's agenda. The problem is becoming worse every year as our culture becomes more and more brazen in rejecting the God of Scripture and embracing a devilish worldview.

People who truly desire God's blessing must resist the devil and his schemes. That means before we have a right to expect God to bless us, we must turn away from the evil that hinders that blessing. For many Americans—Christians included—that calls for major changes in lifestyle and interests.

The devil and his influence are more prevalent in American culture than most people realize. Scripture says those who practice sin are "of the devil" (1 John 3:8). Jesus told even the religious scribes and Pharisees, "You are of your father the devil, and the desires of your father you want to do" (John 8:44). All who resist God are, in effect, in league with the devil, whether they realize it or not.

But resisting the devil doesn't mean we should declare war on unbelievers. It simply means we ourselves must forsake evil, say no to temptation, and refuse everything that would advance the program of the evil one. Above all, we should be alert to the wiles of the devil and fortify ourselves against his deceit and his cunning (Eph. 6:11) by resisting the father of lies with God's truth.

How can you be proactive in turning "away from the evil that hinders"?

Can God Bless America? 10–13

The Nature of Temptation

So when the woman saw that the tree was good for food, that it was pleasant to the eyes, and a tree desirable to make one wise, she took of its fruit and ate.

GENESIS 3:6

Eve saw three features of the forbidden fruit that seduced her. First, "the tree was good for food." We have no idea what kind of fruit it was. The specific variety of fruit is not important. What is important is that Eve was seduced by her *physical appetite*. This was not a legitimate hunger. It was an illicit appetite. It was a fleshly lust provoked by a selfish discontent and a distrust in God—as if He were keeping something good from her.

Second, she saw "that it was pleasant to the eyes." This seduction appealed to her *emotional appetite*. The fruit excited her sense of beauty and other passions. As covetousness grew in her heart, the forbidden fruit looked better and better.

Third, she saw "a tree desirable to make one wise." This was an appeal to her *intellectual appetite*. Incipient pride caused her to fancy the "wisdom" that would come with knowing good and evil.

Temptation always comes in one or more of these three categories. When Satan tempted Christ, he urged Him to turn stones to bread (Matt. 4:3). That was an appeal to the lust of the flesh. The devil also showed Him all the kingdoms of the world and their glory, promising Him authority over them (vv. 8–9). That was an appeal to the lust of the eyes. And he set Him on the pinnacle of the temple (v. 5), appealing to the pride of life. That's why Hebrews 4:15 says, "[He] was in all points tempted as we are, yet without sin."

What does temptation look like in your life?

The Battle for the Beginning, 208–209

Temptation Can Be Overcome

No temptation has overtaken you except such as is common to man; but God is faithful, who will not allow you to be tempted beyond what you are able, but with the temptation will also make the way of escape, that you may be able to bear it.

1 Corinthians 10:13

We who are Christians are besieged with constant temptation. It seems overwhelming at times. We might pose the question—is it really possible to overcome temptation in any meaningful sense? How can we be triumphant? With Satan, the world, and our own flesh against us, is there any hope for us to overcome sin's pull? Our enemies are so subtle and their strategies so sophisticated, how can we fight them? Aren't we sometimes confronted with temptations that are so effective that we frankly have no hope of defeating them? Isn't Satan so wily that we cannot possibly overcome some of his schemes? And isn't our own heart so deceitful and desperately wicked that it leaves us without a proper defense? Isn't it really folly for us to dream of victory over our sin?

Scripture clearly answers that question. In fact, it answers all those questions in one verse: "No temptation has overtaken you except such as is common to man; and God is faithful, who will not allow you to be tempted beyond what you are able, but with the temptation will also make the way of escape, that you may be able to bear it" (1 Cor. 10:13).

That verse is surely one of the most welcome and comforting promises in all of Scripture. No temptation can be so overpowering that we are left helpless to resist. Satan is not so powerful; demons are not so effective; the evil conspiracy is not so cleverly devised; the flesh is not so weak; the human heart is not so deceitful—that we are left helpless to be victimized by temptation.

How is 1 Corinthians 10:13 an encouragement to you?

The Vanishing Conscience, 170–172

Escape from Temptation

And do not lead us into temptation, but deliver us from the evil one.

MATTHEW 6:13

When God allows us to be tested, He always provides a way out. There is always a path to victory. There is always an escape hatch. *Ekbasis* is the Greek word for "escape" in 1 Corinthians 10:13. It literally means "an exit."

Here is a truth you may never have noticed in this verse—Paul tells us exactly what the way of escape is: God "with the temptation will provide the way of escape also, that you may be able to endure it." *The way out is through*. The way out of the temptation is to endure it as a trial and never let it become a solicitation to evil. You have been wronged. You have been falsely accused. You have been maligned or treated unkindly or dealt with unjustly. So what? Accept it. Endure it with joy (James 1:2); that is the way of escape. Usually we look for a quick and easy escape route. God's plan for us is different. He wants us to count it all joy, "and let endurance have its perfect result, that [we] may be perfect and complete, lacking in nothing" (v. 4 NASB). God is using our trials to bring us to maturity.

How can we endure? There are several practical answers. I will mention only a few.

First, *meditate on the Word*: "Your word I have hidden in my heart, that I might not sin against You" (Ps. 119:11). Second, *pray*: "Do not lead us into temptation, but deliver us from evil" (Matt. 6:13). Third, *resist Satan and yield to God*: "Therefore submit to God. Resist the devil and he will flee from you" (James 4:7).

What is your escape route through temptation?

The Vanishing Conscience, 177–178

Sin Starts in the Mind

Jesus said to him, "'You shall love the LORD your God with all your heart, with all your soul, and with all your mind.'"

MATTHEW 22:37

By engaging the inner faculties—mind, emotions, desire, memory, and imagination—thought-sins work directly on the soul to bias it toward evil. Sow a thought, reap an act. Sow an act, reap a habit. Sow a habit, reap a character. Sow a character, reap a destiny. Evil thoughts thus underlie and lay the groundwork for all other sins.

No one ever "falls" into adultery. The adulterer's heart is always shaped and prepared by lustful thoughts before the actual deed occurs. Likewise, the heart of the thief is bent by covetousness. And murder is the product of anger and hatred. All sin is first incubated in the mind.

Jesus taught this truth to His disciples: "The things that proceed out of the mouth *come from the heart*, and those defile the man. For *out of the heart* come evil thoughts, murders, adulteries, fornications, thefts, false witness, slanders. *These are the things which defile the man*; but to eat with unwashed hands does not defile the man" (Matt. 15:18–19 NASB, emphasis added).

Defilement, Jesus suggested, is not primarily a ceremonial or external problem; what is truly defiling in the spiritual sense is the wickedness that emanates from the heart.

The Pharisees' teaching had so inculcated this notion into people that it was commonly believed evil thoughts were not really sinful, as long as they did not become acts. That is precisely why our Lord targeted sins of the heart in His Sermon on the Mount (see Matt. 5:21–22, 27–28).

What *should* take place in our minds and hearts? What *should* be the deepest secret of our souls? Worship to God.

How do your actions show your worship of God?

The Vanishing Conscience, 182–184

Twenty-First-Century Idolatry

You shall have no other gods before Me. You shall not make for yourself a carved image—any likeness of anything that is in heaven above, or that is in the earth beneath, or that is in the water under the earth.

Exodus 20:3–4

People are by nature inclined to turn from the glory of God to idols, to "[exchange] the truth of God for the lie, and [worship and serve] the creature rather than the Creator" (Rom. 1:25). That is why the first commandment addresses idolatry (Ex. 20:3–5). But even while Moses was receiving that commandment from the Lord, Aaron and the Israelites were making a golden calf to worship (Ex. 32:1–6).

Is our society any different from the Romans 1 description? Certainly not. People in modern culture tend to have materialistic idols—money, prestige, success, philosophy, health, pleasure, sports, entertainment, possessions, and other such things. Those things become idols when we give them the love and dedication we owe to God. The problem is the same—worshiping the creation rather than the Creator.

But don't get the idea that the idolatry in our society is somehow more sophisticated than the idolatry of primitive paganism. Consider the changes that have taken place in religion in America in the past fifty years or so. The New Age movement has popularized Hinduism. Astrology, spiritism, and other occult religions have enjoyed unprecedented popularity. Native American religions, Voodoo, Santeria, Druidism, Wicca (witchcraft), and other ancient pagan beliefs have been revived. Satan worship, a thing unheard-of in our nation two generations ago, is one of the fastest-growing cults in the nation.

Now people in our culture are worshiping the elements, spotted owls, or dolphins and whales. Earth- and creature-worship seem at their apex in this society, which has no place for the Creator God. Mother Earth is preferred to Father God.

What tempts you toward idolatry?

The Vanishing Conscience, 65

God's Wrath at Work in Society

And even as they did not like to retain God in their knowledge, God gave them over to a debased mind, to do those things which are not fitting.

Romans 1:28

The apostle Paul describes God's wrath in Romans 1, and he is very specific: "Therefore God also gave them up to uncleanness, in the lusts of their hearts, to dishonor their bodies among themselves, who exchanged the truth of God for the lie, and worshiped and served the creature rather than the Creator." He repeats the same idea in verse 26: "God gave them up to vile passions." And again he says it in verse 28: "God gave them over to a debased mind."

What is the most fearful expression of divine wrath a society can face? It is this: God gives them over to their own sin. He abandons them to whatever they love. They love uncleanness? God abandons them to that. They love vile passions? God gives them up to homosexuality and perversions of all kinds (vv. 26–27).

But there's another step in the declension, described in verse 28: "God gave them over to a debased mind." The Greek word translated "debased" is *adokimos*. It speaks of something useless, spurned, and reprobate. The mind becomes spiritually useless—morally incapable of making a right judgment. And when a society has gone that far, there is no way back. You know society is reaching that point when people will not tolerate anyone making moral judgments.

Scripture says when a society descends to that point, they give approval to sin even though they know such sins are destructive to society and damning to the individual. All sense of guilt is finally eradicated.

When have you noted God's wrath in action?

Can God Bless America? 48–52

Demon Possession

Then His fame went throughout all Syria; and they brought to Him all sick people who were afflicted with various diseases and torments, and those who were demon-possessed, epileptics, and paralytics; and He healed them.

Matthew 4:24

The symptoms of demonic possession in the New Testament were varied. Demoniacs were sometimes insane, as in the case of the two demon-possessed men who lived in a graveyard and behaved so fiercely that no one dared approach them (Matt. 8:28–34; Mark 5:1–5). More frequently, demonic possession was manifest in physical infirmities.

Don't imagine (as many do) that the biblical descriptions of demon possession were actually manifestations of epilepsy, dementia, or other purely psychological and physiological afflictions. Scripture *does* make a clear distinction between demon possession and diseases, including epilepsy and paralysis (Matt. 4:24). Demon possession involves bondage to an evil spirit that indwells the afflicted individual. Scripture describes how evil spirits spoke through the lips of those whom they tormented (Mark 1:23–24; Luke 4:33–35). Jesus sometimes forced the demonic personality to reveal itself in that way, perhaps to give clear proof of His power over evil spirits (Mark 5:8–14).

In every case, however, demon possession is portrayed as an affliction, not a sin, per se. Lawlessness, superstition, and idolatry undoubtedly have a major role in opening a person's heart to demonic possession, but none of the demonized individuals in the New Testament is explicitly associated with immoral behavior. They are always portrayed as tormented people, not willful malefactors.

What erroneous views of demon possession have you seen portrayed in society?

Twelve Extraordinary Women, 174

Mary Magdalene

Now when He rose early on the first day of the week, He appeared first to Mary Magdalene, out of whom He had cast seven demons.

MARK 16:9

While Mary Magdalene is currently being talked about more than ever, much of the discussion is mere hype and hyperbole borrowed from ancient cults. What Scripture actually says about her is extraordinary enough without any false embellishment.

Luke introduced her as "Mary called Magdalene, out of whom had come seven demons" (Luke 8:2). It's the only detail we have been given about Mary Magdalene's past.

Satan tormented her with seven demons. There was nothing any mere man or woman could do for her. She was a veritable prisoner of demonic afflictions. These undoubtedly included depression, anxiety, unhappiness, loneliness, self-loathing, shame, fear, and a host of other similar miseries. In all probability, she suffered even *worse* torments, too, such as blindness, deafness, insanity, or any of the other disorders commonly associated with victims of demonic possession described in the New Testament. Whatever her condition, she would have been in perpetual agony—at least seven kinds of agony. Demoniacs in Scripture were always friendless, except in rare cases when devoted family members cared for them. They were perpetually restless because of their inability to escape the constant torments of their demonic captors. They were continually joyless because all of life had become darkness and misery for them. And they were hopeless because there was no earthly remedy for their spiritual afflictions.

That is all that can be said with certainty about the past of Mary Magdalene. Luke and Mark seem to mention her former demonization only for the purpose of celebrating Christ's goodness and grace toward her.

When have you witnessed God's release of someone in bondage?

Twelve Extraordinary Women, 173–175

The Truth About Other Religions

You cannot drink the cup of the Lord and the cup of demons; you cannot partake of the Lord's table and of the table of demons.

1 CORINTHIANS 10:21

In 1 Corinthians 10:20, Paul said that an idol itself wasn't really anything: "Rather, that the things which the Gentiles sacrifice they sacrifice to demons and not to God, and I do not want you to have fellowship with demons." Nothing the whole heathen world sacrifices to their supposed stone, silver, and gold idols is engaging the true God; it is engaging the forces of hell. They are linked with Satan and demons.

You might say, "Oh, those poor well-intentioned pagans! They're working their way toward God the best way they know how." No, they're working their way toward hell. They're connecting with demonic forces impersonating idols that don't exist. There are no other gods than the true God. People believe there are, because demons impersonate the gods they worship and do enough tricks to keep those people connected to their false deities.

It's not just a case of "Too bad they're ignorant." Natural reason seeking God ends up ignorant, idolatrous, and demonic. Demons are behind all false religions. They are behind all philosophical and religious systems. They are behind every lofty thing lifted up against the knowledge of God. Any unbiblical, anti-God idea is demonic.

People have asked me, "Is there a lot of satanic religion in our society?" Yes. Everything but true Christianity is satanic, to one degree or another, and in one manifestation or another. It's not that everybody worships Satan directly, though some do. But anybody who doesn't worship the true and living God through Jesus Christ, in effect, worships Satan.

What can you do to help someone who is trapped in a false belief about God?

Hard to Believe, 209–210

Religion Is an Ordinary Tool of Satan

For certain men have crept in unnoticed, who long ago were marked out for this condemnation, ungodly men, who turn the grace of our God into lewdness and deny the only Lord God and our Lord Jesus Christ.

Jude v. 4

Men and women who lack a biblical worldview tend to think of religion as the noblest expression of the human character. Popular opinion in the world at large has generally regarded religion as something inherently admirable, honorable, and beneficial.

In reality, no other field of the humanities—philosophy, literature, the arts, or whatever—holds quite as much potential for mischief as religion. Nothing is more thoroughly evil than *false* religion, and the more false teachers try to cloak themselves in the robes of biblical truth, the more truly satanic they are.

Nevertheless, benign-looking, suavely religious emissaries of Satan are ordinary, not extraordinary. Redemptive history is full of them, and the Bible continually warns about such "false apostles, deceitful workers, transforming themselves into apostles of Christ. And no wonder! For Satan himself transforms himself into an angel of light. Therefore it is no great thing if his ministers also transform themselves into ministers of righteousness" (2 Cor. 11:13–15).

Delivering his farewell speech at Ephesus, the apostle Paul told the elders of that young but already beleaguered church that false teachers would arise not only from within the church, but that they would creep unnoticed into the *leadership* of the church (see Acts 20:29–30; cf. Jude v. 4). It has happened again and again in every phase of church history. False teachers want people to believe that they represent God, that they know God, that they have special insight into divine truth and wisdom, even though they are emissaries of hell itself.

What is your strategy for discerning whether a teaching is true or false?

The Jesus You Can't Ignore, 11–12

Satan's Power in the World

The prince of the kingdom of Persia withstood me twenty-one days; and behold, Michael, one of the chief princes, came to help me, for I had been left alone there with the kings of Persia.

Daniel 10:13

Within the context of His total authority, God has permitted Satan great but not unlimited power over the people and affairs of this world. Satan did not directly cause mankind's fall into sin, but his sinister and evil temptation hastened Adam and Eve's disobedience of God, which was the first sin and a characteristic passed on to all their posterity. Ever since that tragic episode in the Garden, the devil has waged a relentless, multifaceted campaign to get men and women to yield to their naturally sinful impulses and defy God.

Consequently, "the whole world lies under the sway of the wicked one" (1 John 5:19), who is now "the ruler of this world" (John 12:31; see also 14:30; 16:11). When Satan tempted Jesus, our Lord did not dispute his claim to "all the kingdoms of the world" or his ability to give Him "all this authority . . . and their glory; for this has been delivered to me [Satan], and I give it to whomever I wish" (Luke 4:5–6).

In both Isaiah 14:12–17 and Ezekiel 28:12–16, Satan is closely identified with the kings of the nations involved. Thus a clear pattern emerges from Scripture. God instituted government to fulfill His plan for maintaining civil and social order. However, He has allowed many, if not most, regimes throughout history to be strongly influenced by Satan and become the vehicles for promoting satanic activity.

The evil, ruthless, totalitarian governments of Nazi Germany, Imperial Japan, the Soviet Union, and Communist China illustrate that point, as do the ancient autocratic empires of Egypt, Assyria, Babylon, and Rome.

Knowing that Satan is behind many ruthless regimes, how will this affect the direction of your prayer life?

Why Government Can't Save You, 28–29

The Truth About Morality

So Jesus said to him, "Why do you call Me good? No one is good but One, that is, God."

MARK 10:18

Degenerate people can sometimes become more moral. The scoundrel turns over a new leaf. Political organizations can sometimes achieve a degree of "moral rearmament" in society. People who have failed miserably can, to some degree, reorder their lives. The delinquent youth can decide to live a better life to impress a girlfriend. But when such changes are nothing but fleshly willpower divorced from faith in Christ, they are ultimately all for naught.

The biblical message is not that humanity is divided between the moral and the immoral. The clear message of the Bible is that "all have sinned and fall short of the glory of God" (Rom. 3:23). There is no division between *good* people and *bad* people; all are sinners, and all deserve condemnation. The moral unbeliever may actually be in a *worse* state than the profligate sinner, because the moral person does not understand his own need.

Whatever level of external morality a person might attain, he or she is a condemned sinner apart from Christ. You might be the most moral Pharisee in Israel; you might be the most generous philanthropist in your town; you might be the most clean-living student in the college dorm; you might be the kindest and most active parent in the PTA; or you might be the most devoted follower of the latest spiritual fad. But without Christ, you're going to hell with the dope dealers and prostitutes. Unless you've been reconciled to God through His Son Jesus Christ, all the morality in the world will not help you.

Are you ever tempted to use categories like "good" and "bad" in regard to people? Why or why not?

Can God Bless America? 72–73

Two Types of Sinners

Two men went up to the temple to pray, one a Pharisee and the other a tax collector. . . . Everyone who exalts himself will be humbled, and he who humbles himself will be exalted.

Luke 18:10, 14

Sinners come in two basic varieties. Some are straightforward and intrepid in their evildoing, and they don't really care who sees what they do. Invariably, their besetting sin is pride—the kind of pride that is seen in an undue love for oneself and uncontrollable lusts for self-indulgent pleasures.

At the other end of the spectrum are secretive sinners, who prefer to sin when they think no one else is looking. They try to mask their more obvious sins in various ways—often with the pretense of religion. Their besetting sin is also pride, but it's the kind of pride that manifests itself in hypocrisy.

There are varying degrees and mixtures of those two types of sinners, of course, and the two obviously have a lot in common—like two brothers whose personalities make them seem very different, even though genetically they might be nearly identical.

Of the two types of sinners, the wanton sinner is much more likely than the sanctimonious sinner to face the reality of his own fallenness, repent, and seek salvation. His sin is already uncovered. It is undeniable. He *has* to face up to it. Not so with the Pharisee. He will try as long as possible to camouflage his immorality, deny his guilt, disavow his need for redemption, and declare his own righteousness. That's why Jesus repeatedly said things like, "Those who are well have no need of a physician, but those who are sick" (Matt. 9:12).

Both stand under the judgment of God unless they repent and turn to Christ.

When, if ever, have you been tempted to deny your guilt?

A *Tale of Two Sons*, 147–148

What Is Total Depravity?

But the natural man does not receive the things of the Spirit of God, for they are foolishness to him; nor can he know them, because they are spiritually discerned.

1 Corinthians 2:14

Scripture teaches from beginning to end that all humanity is totally depraved. Total depravity does not mean that unbelieving sinners are always as bad as they could be (cf. Luke 6:33; Rom. 2:14). It does not mean that the expression of sinful human nature is always lived out to the fullest. It does not mean that unbelievers are incapable of acts of kindness, benevolence, goodwill, or human altruism. It certainly does not mean that non-Christians cannot appreciate goodness, beauty, honesty, decency, or excellence. It *does* mean that none of this has any merit with God.

Depravity also means that evil has contaminated every aspect of our humanity—our heart, mind, personality, emotions, conscience, motives, and will (cf. Jer. 17:9; John 8:44). Unredeemed sinners are therefore incapable of doing anything to please God (Isa. 64:6). They are incapable of truly loving the God who reveals Himself in Scripture. They are incapable of obedience from the heart, with righteous motives. They are incapable of understanding spiritual truth. They are incapable of genuine faith. And that means they are incapable of pleasing God or truly seeking Him (Rom. 3:11).

Total depravity means sinners have no ability to do spiritual good or work for their own salvation from sin. They are so completely disinclined to love righteousness, so thoroughly dead in sin, that they are not able to save themselves or even to fit themselves for God's salvation. Unbelieving humanity has no capacity to desire, understand, believe, or apply spiritual truth (see 1 Cor. 2:14).

When have you seen evidence of the depravity of humanity?

The Vanishing Conscience, 87–88

The True Effects of Sin

Cast him into outer darkness; there will be weeping and gnashing of teeth.

Matthew 22:13

Sin never truly satisfies. There are momentary pleasures in sin (cf. Heb. 11:25), but they invariably give way to sorrow and misery and pain. In a moment of pleasure seeking motivated by his love of money, Judas had bartered away any opportunity of real joy or satisfaction forever. Paul wrote, "The love of money is a root of all kinds of evil, for which some have strayed from the faith in their greediness, and pierced themselves through with many sorrows" (1 Tim. 6:10). Judas is the prototype of what Paul was describing. No one ever pierced himself through with more sorrow—and all for the foolish love of money.

Judas would receive no sympathy or support from his fellow conspirators. Their response to his confession was in effect sheer mockery: "And they said, 'What is that to us? You see to it!'" (Matt. 27:4).

Judas, utterly friendless, hopeless, and disconsolate under the weight of his own guilt, then sealed his self-destruction forever with an act of suicide.

Perhaps Judas thought by killing himself he could finally get relief from his guilt. The opposite is true. By killing himself he bound himself to his guilt forever. Judas of all people ought to have known this, for he had repeatedly heard Jesus teach about hell—how it is a place of eternal torment, unquenchable fire, and weeping and gnashing of teeth that goes on day and night forever (Matt. 8:12; 13:42, 50; 22:13; 24:51; 25:30; Mark 9:43–48; Luke 13:28). In hell the pain of guilt and conscience pangs are eternally intensified.

What argument would you use to convince someone of the reality of hell?

The Murder of Jesus, 152–153

Sin's Mastery

To the pure all things are pure, but to those who are defiled and unbelieving nothing is pure; but even their mind and conscience are defiled.

Titus 1:15

Sin corrupts the entire person—infecting the soul, polluting the mind, defiling the conscience, contaminating the affections, and poisoning the will. It is the life-destroying, soul-condemning cancer that festers and grows in every unredeemed human heart like an incurable gangrene.

Unbelievers are not just infected by sin; they are enslaved by it. Jesus told His listeners in John 8:34 (NASB), "Truly, truly I say to you, everyone who commits sin is the slave of sin." The apostle Peter likewise described false teachers as "slaves of corruption; for by what a man is overcome, by this he is enslaved" (2 Peter 2:19 NASB). Every human being, until the moment of redemption, is under the domain of darkness and the dominion of sin.

Not surprisingly, the very notion of such absolute enslavement (a doctrine known as "total depravity" or "total inability") is repugnant to the fallen human heart. Though the doctrine of total depravity is often the most attacked and minimized of the doctrines of grace, it is the most distinctly Christian doctrine because it is foundational to a right understanding of the gospel (in which God initiates everything and receives all the glory). Scripture is clear: unless the Spirit of God gives spiritual life, all sinners are completely unable to change their fallen nature or to rescue themselves from sin and divine judgment. Contrast that with every other religious system, in which people are told that through their own efforts they *can* achieve some level of righteousness, thereby contributing to their salvation. Nothing could be further from the truth.

What will you do to aid someone who is enslaved to sin?

Slave, 120–122

The True Solution to Our Guilt

He who covers his sins will not prosper, but whoever confesses and forsakes them will have mercy.

PROVERBS 28:13

What is evident is that people in our culture are becoming very good at blame-shifting—making scapegoats of parents, childhood disappointments, and other dysfunctions beyond their control. No matter what problem you suffer from—whether you are a cannibalizing serial murderer or just someone struggling with emotional distress—you can easily find someone who will explain to you why your failing is not your fault.

This can be spiritually destructive. It fails to address the real problem of human sinfulness. It feeds the worst tendencies of human nature. It engenders the most catastrophic form of denial—denial of one's own guilt. It adds more guilt for blaming someone who isn't really to blame at all.

Disavowing our personal culpability can never free us from a sense of guilt. On the contrary, those who refuse to acknowledge their sinfulness actually place themselves in bondage to their own guilt. "If we say that we have no sin, we are deceiving ourselves and the truth is not in us. [But] if we confess our sins, He is faithful and righteous to forgive us our sins and to cleanse us from all unrighteousness" (1 John 1:8–9 NASB).

Jesus Christ came into the world to save sinners! Jesus specifically said He had *not* come to save those who want to exonerate themselves (Mark 2:17). Where there is no recognition of sin and guilt, when the conscience has been abused into silence, there can be no salvation, no sanctification, and therefore no real emancipation from sin's ruthless power.

When are you most tempted to blame-shift? Based on today's reading, what will you do instead?

The Vanishing Conscience, 33–34

How to Reach a Pagan Society

Walk in wisdom toward those who are outside, redeeming the time.

COLOSSIANS 4:5

How can we live in a pagan society in a God-honoring manner, in such a way that we do not alienate the very people God wants us to reach with the gospel? We must remember to be engaged in good works, which Scripture says will result from our salvation. Paul summarizes the final reminder well in Titus 3:8: "This is a faithful saying, and these things I want you to affirm constantly, that those who have believed in God should be careful to maintain good works. These things are good and profitable to men." We simply need to understand and obey all the instructions the apostle, through the Holy Spirit, gives us concerning what the body of Christ is and how it ought to function while still on earth.

It is not your primary calling to change your culture, to reform the outward moral behavior and professed political convictions of those around you, or to remake society superficially, according to some kind of "evangelical Christian blueprint." Instead, you must constantly remember that the Lord has called you to be His witness before the lost and condemned world in which you now live. Such a mission is far more "good and profitable to men" than any amount of social and political activism. Such endeavors may renovate people's outward lives, but they cannot transform their hearts and bring them to a saving relationship with Jesus Christ. That ultimate transformation will happen only as you and other faithful believers cheerfully perform your Christian duties, remember your previous lost condition and your current saved one, and then diligently "maintain good works."

What will you do this week to "maintain good works"?

Why Government Can't Save You, 144–145

Our Hope and Challenge in a Sinful World

And for their sakes I sanctify Myself, that they also may be sanctified by the truth.

JOHN 17:19

I am convinced that we are living in a post-Christian society—a civilization that exists under God's judgment.

If that sounds the least bit pessimistic or cynical to you, it isn't. Scripture predicted times exactly like these (see 2 Tim. 3:1–5, 13).

But God's purposes are being fulfilled, no matter how vainly people strive against Him. Titus 2:11–12 assures us that God's grace appears, bringing salvation in the midst of the lowest human depravity, teaching us to live "soberly, righteously, and godly in the present age" (v. 12).

There is great hope, even in the midst of a wicked and perverse generation, for those who love God. Remember, He will build His church and "the gates of Hades shall not prevail against it" (Matt. 16:18). He also is able to make all things work together for the good of His elect (Rom. 8:28). Christ Himself intercedes for His chosen ones, people who are not of this world, even as He is not of this world (John 17:14). What is His prayer? "I do not pray that You should take them out of the world, but that You should keep them from the evil one. . . . Sanctify them by Your truth. Your word is truth" (vv. 15, 17).

As believers, then, our duty with regard to sin is not to try to purge all society's ills, but to apply ourselves diligently to the work of our own sanctification. The sin we need to be most concerned with is the sin in our own lives. Only as the church becomes holy can it begin to have a true, powerful effect on the outside world.

How will you apply yourself diligently to the work of your sanctification?

The Vanishing Conscience, 12–13

God Controls but Does Not Cause Sin

Let no one say when he is tempted, "I am tempted by God"; for God cannot be tempted by evil, nor does He Himself tempt anyone.

James 1:13

The whole course of all events and circumstances is ordained in the divine decree, from the most profound milestone of the divine plan to the most trivial detail. God even determines the number of hairs on our heads (Matt. 10:30).

Ultimately, we must concede that sin is something God *meant* to happen. He planned for it, ordained it. Sin is not something that sneaked in and took Him by surprise, caught Him off guard, or spoiled His plans. The reality of sin figured into His changeless purposes from eternity past. Thus evil and all its consequences were included in God's eternal decree before the foundation of the world.

Yet by the same token God cannot be considered the author, or originator, of sin. "God cannot be tempted by evil, nor does He Himself tempt anyone" (James 1:13). "God is light and in Him is no darkness at all" (1 John 1:5).

God in no sense *causes* sin, *incites* it, *condones* it, *authorizes* it, *approves* it, or otherwise *consents to* it. God is never the cause or the agent of sin. He only *permits* evil agents to do their deeds, then overrules the evil for His own wise and holy ends. God's purposes in permitting evil are always good. That is why Joseph could say to his brothers, who had sold him into slavery, "You meant evil against me, but God meant it for good in order to bring about this present result, to preserve many people alive" (Gen. 50:20 NASB).

How would you respond to the question of why God permits evil in the world?

The Vanishing Conscience, 113–114

True Spiritual Warfare

For we do not wrestle against flesh and blood, but against principalities, against powers, against the rulers of the darkness of this age, against spiritual hosts of wickedness in the heavenly places.

EPHESIANS 6:12

What, actually, was Paul attacking in 2 Corinthians 10:4? He gave the answer very clearly in verse 5: "Casting down arguments and every high thing that exalts itself against the knowledge of God." The New American Standard Bible speaks of "destroying speculations." The King James Version says, "Casting down imaginations." The Greek word is *logismos*, which signifies opinions, calculations, or reasonings. The only other place the word is found in the New Testament is in Romans 2:15, where it is translated "thoughts" and describes the process of rationalizing in order to make an excuse.

In other words, the fortresses Paul was describing are corrupt belief systems, sinister philosophies, false doctrines, evil worldviews, and every massive system of falsehood. Obviously, if we are in a battle for truth, the fortresses we need to demolish are the bastions of *lies*—wrong thoughts, wicked ideas, untrue opinions, immoral theories, and false religions. These are *ideological* forts—philosophical forts, religious forts—spiritual strongholds made of thoughts, ideas, concepts, opinions. In such ideological citadels, sinful people try to hide and fortify themselves against God and against the gospel of Christ.

Spiritual warfare as Paul described it is therefore ideological rather than mystical. Our enemies are demonic, but the warfare against them isn't waged by commanding them, claiming authority over them, or any of the other common tactics some people usually refer to as "spiritual warfare." We attack them by tearing down their fortresses of lies.

When have you experienced spiritual warfare in your life?

Called to Lead, 139–140

The Weapons of Spiritual Warfare

Stand therefore, having girded your waist with truth, having put on the breastplate of righteousness.

Ephesians 6:14

What, precisely, are our weapons? If the fortresses are constructed of "arguments and every high thing that exalts itself against the knowledge of God" (2 Cor. 10:5; thoughts, concepts, opinions, ideologies, philosophies), it seems obvious that the only power that will destroy such things is the power of *truth*. Indeed, when the apostle Paul listed the armor of spiritual warfare in Ephesians 6:13–17, he named only one offensive weapon in the panoply: "the sword of the Spirit, which is the word of God" (v. 17). The power of God for salvation is the power of the gospel alone (Rom. 1:16; cf. 1 Cor. 1:21).

In other words, "the weapons of our warfare" are the instruments of truth. The Word of God. The gospel. Sound doctrine. The truth of Scripture.

The simple fact is that you can't fight spiritual warfare with magic phrases and secret words. You don't overpower demons merely by shouting at them. I don't have anything to say to a demon anyway. I'm not interested in talking to them. Let the Lord do that (cf. Jude 9). Why would I even want to communicate with evil spirits? But I have a lot to say to people who have barricaded themselves in fortresses of demonic lies. I want to do everything I can to tear down those palaces of lies. And the only thing that equips me to do that well is the Word of God.

Spiritual warfare is all about demolishing evil lies with the truth. Use the authority of God's Word and the power of the gospel to give people the truth.

What comforts you most in regard to the weapons given to you for spiritual warfare?

Called to Lead, 141

God's Protection

Your rod and Your staff, they comfort me.

Psalm 23:4

We are] protected by the power of God through faith for a salvation ready to be revealed in the last time" (1 Peter 1:5 NASB). Working our way carefully through this verse, we note this phrase: "you . . . are protected by the power of God through faith." We are *protected* by the power of a supreme, omnipotent, sovereign, omniscient, almighty God. The verb tense speaks of continuous action. Even now we are *being protected*. "Neither death nor life, nor angels nor principalities, nor things present nor things to come, nor height nor depth, nor any other created thing, shall be able to separate us from the love of God which is in Christ Jesus our Lord" (Rom. 8:38–39). "If God be for us, who can be against us?" (Rom. 8:31 KJV).

Furthermore, we are protected *through faith*. Our continued faith in Christ is the instrument of God's sustaining work. God didn't save us apart from faith, and He doesn't keep us apart from faith. Our faith is God's gift, and through His protecting power He preserves it and nurtures it. The maintenance of our faith is as much His work as every other aspect of salvation.

But to say that faith is God's gracious gift, which He maintains, is not to say that faith operates apart from the human will. It is *our* faith. We believe. We remain steadfast. We are not passive in the process. The means by which God maintains our faith involves our full participation. We cannot persevere apart from faith; only *through* faith.

When have you experienced God's protection in the midst of a spiritual battle?

The Gospel According to the Apostles, 185

The Unforgivable Sin

Therefore I say to you, every sin and blasphemy will be forgiven men, but the blasphemy against the Spirit will not be forgiven men.

MATTHEW 12:31

People are often troubled by the notion that there is such a thing as unforgivable sin. Some worry about whether they might have inadvertently committed it.

This concern can be easily answered, if we keep the context of Matthew 12:31–32 in view. These Pharisees were guilty of unpardonable sin because they knowingly—not in ignorance or by accident, but *deliberately*—wrote Jesus' work off as the work of the devil. Moreover, their rejection of Christ was a full, final, settled renunciation of Christ and everything He stood for. Contrast their sin with that of Peter, who later denied knowing Christ and punctuated his denials with swearing and curses. But Peter found forgiveness for his sin. If we think carefully about what was happening here and what Jesus actually said, the notion of unpardonable sin is not really so mysterious.

This passage and its cross-references (Mark 3:28–29; Luke 12:10) are the only places where Scripture mentions unpardonable sin.

Don't miss the fact that Jesus' words about this one unpardonable sin begin with a sweeping promise of forgiveness for "every sin and blasphemy" (Matt. 12:31). Our God is a forgiving God; that is His nature (see Mic. 7:18; Ps. 86:5).

Jesus emphatically states that the *severity* of sin never hinders God's forgiveness. The grossest sin ever committed was the crucifixion of Jesus (Acts 2:23), and yet one of Jesus' last sayings before He died was a prayer for forgiveness for His executioners and the crowd who mocked Him (Luke 23:34). The *number* of sins a person commits does not make his case unpardonable (see James 5:20).

What comfort can you offer to someone who fears he or she has committed the "unforgivable sin"?

The Jesus You Can't Ignore, 174–176

Phony Christians

Beware of false prophets, who come to you in sheep's clothing, but inwardly they are ravenous wolves.

Matthew 7:15

This is the whole point of the parable of the tares: the tares *look* like wheat in every superficial way. Until they bear fruit and it ripens it is virtually impossible to tell wheat from tares. The tares therefore represent people who look and act like Christians—false professors. They blend into the fellowship of the church, give a fine-sounding testimony about their faith in Christ, and otherwise *seem* exactly like authentic believers. But they are not authentic. Their faith is a sham. They are unregenerate hangers-on. We know there are tares in almost every fellowship of believers, because Jesus gave that parable as an illustration of what His kingdom would be like in the church age, and because from time to time one of the tares will abandon the faith completely, embrace some damnable heresy, or sell out to some sin that he or she is unwilling to abandon or repent from. In such cases, we *are* supposed to confront the individual, call them to repentance, and put them out of the church if they steadfastly refuse to repent (Matt. 18:15–18).

Phony Christians and worldly pretenders are permitted by God to fall away for the very purpose of reminding us that not everyone who claims to be a Christian really is. "They went out from us, but they were not of us; for if they had been of us, they would have continued with us; but they went out that they might be made manifest, that none of them were of us" (1 John 2:19).

How would you explain to someone your assurance of faith in Christ?

The Jesus You Can't Ignore, 203–204

The Great Delusion

Many will say to Me in that day, "Lord, Lord, have we not prophesied in Your name, cast out demons in Your name, and done many wonders in Your name?" And then I will declare to them, "I never knew you; depart from Me, you who practice lawlessness!"

MATTHEW 7:22–23

Matthew 7:21 says that only "he who does the will of My Father in heaven" will enter the kingdom. If you do not live a genuinely righteous life, it doesn't matter what you claim. You are deceived. Both of the closing paragraphs to this great sermon, verses 21–23 and 24–27, contrast a right and a wrong response to the invitation of Christ, and they show that the choice we make determines our eternal destiny.

Remember that the Lord wasn't speaking to irreligious people here, but to people who were obsessed with religious activity. They were not apostates, heretics, atheists, or agnostics; they were extremely religious people. But they were damned because they were self-deluded and on the wrong road.

This is an important issue, because I am convinced that the visible church today is jammed full of people who aren't Christians but don't know it. When I hear statistics such as two billion people in the world are Christians and five billion aren't, then I wonder who has established the criteria for being Christian. The Bible says many take the broad road, but few take the narrow way to Christ.

You can be deluded about a lot of things, but to be deceived about whether you're a Christian affects your eternal destiny. We have multitudes of deceived people who are bouncing along on the Jesus bandwagon and thinking everything is good. For them, judgment is going to be one big surprise.

What are you willing to do to help those who might be deluded about Christ?

Hard to Believe, 95–96

Spotting Deceived People

Now this I say lest anyone should deceive you with persuasive words.

Colossians 2:4

How does a deceived person know he's deceived? And how can we spot such a person? Here are some keys, although not everybody doing these things will be deceived.

First, look for someone who's seeking feelings, blessings, experiences, healings, angels, and miracles. He is more interested in the by-products of the faith than the faith itself. He is more interested in what he can get than the glory God can get; more interested in himself than in the exaltation of Christ.

Second, look for people who are more committed to the denomination, the church, or the tradition than to the Word of God. Their kind of Christianity may be purely social. They're more committed to the organization than they are to the Lord and His Word.

Third, look for people who are involved in theology as an academic interest. You'll find them all over the colleges and seminaries of our land: people who study theology, write books on theology, and are absolutely void of any real righteousness. Theology, for them, is intellectual activity.

Fourth are people who always seem stuck on one overemphasized point of theology, like those who never teach on anything but the second coming of Christ in relation to current events. This is the person who bangs the drum constantly for his own little issue, point, or crazy quirk. He would like you to think that he is so close to God, he has a great divine insight no one else has, but the fact is, he is seeking a platform for feeding his ego.

How will you help someone who is deceived but does not yet know that he or she is deceived?

Hard to Believe, 99

NOVEMBER

MONEY, GIVING, DISCIPLINE, AND SELF-CONTROL

How We Should See the Apostles

And with great power the apostles gave witness to the resurrection of the Lord Jesus. And great grace was upon them all.

ACTS 4:33

The apostles properly hold an exalted place in redemptive history, of course. They are certainly worthy of being regarded as heroes of the faith. The book of Revelation describes how their names will adorn the twelve gates of the heavenly city, the New Jerusalem. So heaven itself features an eternal tribute to them. But that doesn't diminish the truth that they were as ordinary as you and I. We need to remember them not from their stained-glass images, but from the down-to-earth way the Bible presents them to us. We need to lift them out of their otherworldly obscurity and get to know them as real people. We need to think of them as actual men, and not as some kind of exalted figures from the pantheon of religious ritualism.

Let's not, however, underestimate the importance of their office. Upon their selection, the twelve apostles in effect became the true spiritual leaders of Israel. The religious elite of *apostate* Israel were symbolically set aside when Jesus chose them. The apostles became the first preachers of the new covenant. They were the ones to whom the Christian gospel was first entrusted. They represented the true Israel of God—a genuinely repentant and believing Israel. They also became the foundation stones of the church, with Jesus Himself as the chief cornerstone (Eph. 2:20). Those truths are heightened, not diminished, by the fact that these men were so ordinary.

They *became* great spiritual leaders and great preachers under the power of the Holy Spirit, but it was not because of any innate oratorical skill, leadership abilities, or academic qualifications these men had. Their influence is owing to one thing and one thing only: the power of the message they preached.

What do you find inspiring about the lives of the apostles?

Twelve Ordinary Men, 12–13

A Growing Lie

And He said to them, "Go into all the world and preach the gospel to every creature."

MARK 16:15

There's a frightening new belief growing in the evangelical world: the theory that it isn't necessary to take the gospel to the ends of the earth, because people are being saved without it.

This view has several labels that we can examine by veering off into a little theology class for a minute. One name for it is *natural theology*, the notion that somebody can get to heaven without the gospel. It holds that mankind can ascend naturally to a knowledge of God and a relationship with Him by virtue of his reason and innate desire to obey God's will. This is a natural, as opposed to supernatural, approach.

Supernatural theology says God has to come down and save man. Natural theology says man can climb up to God, thanks to a natural reasoning process, and that the Scripture is unnecessary. Advocates of this view say mankind may discover the basic existence, attributes, and nature of God by human reason, apart from scriptural revelation, and attain to a saving knowledge of God.

People who advocate natural theology have a flawed view of man's depravity. Their point of view is that man can make it to heaven without the Bible, so what's all the missionary fuss about? You don't need repentance toward God and faith in Jesus Christ, as Paul said he had to preach in Acts 20:21. This view holds that the lost don't need to hear the gospel. They don't need to have Bibles. Apparently, we don't need all these people such as Robert Morrison and Henry Martyn sacrificing their lives in remote areas with isolated populations.

What is your part in the Great Commission?

Hard to Believe, 188–189

OK to Lie?

So the king of Jericho sent to Rahab, saying, "Bring out the men who have come to you." . . . Then the woman took the two men and hid them. So she said, "Yes, the men came to me, but I did not know where they were from."

JOSHUA 2:3–4

Rahab's actions in protecting the spies involved the telling of a lie. Was that justified? By commending her for her faith, is Scripture also condoning her methods? Good men have argued over that question. Let's face it. It is not an easy question. Scripture says, "Lying lips are an abomination to the LORD, but those who deal truthfully are His delight" (Prov. 12:22). God Himself cannot lie (Titus 1:2; Num. 23:19; 1 Sam. 15:29), and therefore He cannot condone or sanction a lie. Some have tried to argue that because of the circumstances, this was not, technically, a "lie," but a military feint, a legitimate stratagem designed to trick or outwit the enemy in warfare. Others argue that even lying is acceptable if the motive is a greater good. Such a situational approach to ethics is fraught with very serious problems.

I see no need to try to justify Rahab's lie. Shadrach, Meshach, and Abednego might have escaped punishment by lying too. And they might have argued convincingly that it was for a "greater good." But there is no greater good than the truth, and the cause of truth can never be served by lying. Shadrach and friends told the truth—in fact, they seized the opportunity to glorify God's name—and God was still able to save them from the furnace. He certainly could have saved Rahab and the spies without a lie.

There's no need for clever rationalization to try to justify her lie. Scripture never commends the lie. Rahab isn't applauded for her ethics. Rahab is a positive example of faith.

When, if ever, have you been tempted to rationalize a lie for a "greater good"?

Twelve Extraordinary Women, 59

The Best Efforts of Humans Are Still Bad

Knowing that a man is not justified by the works of the law but by faith in Jesus Christ, even we have believed in Christ Jesus, that we might be justified by faith in Christ and not by the works of the law; for by the works of the law no flesh shall be justified.

Galatians 2:16

Romans 3:10 is the universal indictment of humanity: "There is none righteous, no, not one." Man's religions are "bad good." They may be good on the human level through emphasizing kindness or being charitable. But they are "bad good," because the motive is not to glorify God, and anything less than that is a wrong motive. People don't do good in the sense of righteous good that pleases God. In fact, they're wretched on the inside; their throats are like open graves. They open their mouths and out comes the stench of death.

Paul says of the law that "it stops every mouth" (see Rom. 3:19). Don't open your mouth and try to defend yourself. Don't say, "But . . . God . . . I tried. I'm a pretty good person, and You know I'm certainly better than the people over there." All that natural revelation does for you is make you accountable to God, and inexcusable. It shuts your mouth, and you have nothing to say, because in verse 20, your deeds, your works of the law—meaning your good deeds, your religious deeds—will never be justified in God's sight. You can't be good enough to get there on your own.

If you can be saved without the gospel, then salvation is by works. The only way of salvation comes in Romans 3:23–24: "All have sinned and fall short of the glory of God, being justified freely by His grace through the redemption that is in Christ Jesus." The only way to be saved is by faith in Jesus Christ.

How would you explain to someone the basis for your justification?

Hard to Believe, 210–211

The Necessity of Preaching Repentance

Truly, these times of ignorance God overlooked, but now commands all men everywhere to repent.

ACTS 17:30

Repentance was always at the heart of Paul's evangelistic preaching (Acts 17:30; 20:20–21; 26:19–20).

From the beginning of the book of Acts to the end, repentance was the central appeal of the apostolic message. The repentance they preached was not merely a change of mind about who Jesus was. It was a turning from sin (3:26; 8:22) and a turning toward the Lord Jesus Christ (20:21). It was the kind of repentance that results in behavioral change (26:20).

I am deeply concerned as I watch what is happening in the church today. Biblical Christianity has lost its voice. The church is preaching a gospel designed to soothe rather than confront sinful individuals. Churches have turned to amusement and show business to try to win the world. Those methods may seem to draw crowds for a season. But they're not *God's* methods, and therefore they are destined to fail. In the meantime, the church is being infiltrated and corrupted by professing believers who have never repented, never turned from sin, and therefore, never really embraced Christ as Lord *or* Savior.

We must return to the message God has called us to preach. We need to confront sin and call sinners to repentance—to a radical break from the love of sin and a seeking of the Lord's mercy. We must hold up Christ as Savior *and* Lord, the one who frees His people from the penalty *and* power of sin. That is, after all, the gospel He has called us to proclaim.

How would you convince someone of his or her need to repent?

The Gospel According to the Apostles, 84–85

Confronting Sin in Fellow Christians

But now I have written to you not to keep company with anyone named a brother, who is sexually immoral, or covetous, or an idolater, or a reviler, or a drunkard, or an extortioner—not even to eat with such a person.

1 CORINTHIANS 5:11

One reason discernment is so rare today and apostasy is such a serious problem is the almost universal failure of churches to follow Jesus' instructions in Matthew 18:15–17 on how to deal with sinning church members. Sadly, few Christians obey Christ in this crucial area of confronting sin in one another's lives.

If you see a brother in sin, go to him. Confront him. Try to lift him up, build him up, strengthen him. Urge him to repent. If he refuses to repent, he must ultimately be put out of the church. Paul said to not even eat with such a person (1 Cor. 5:11). This is not to suggest you should treat him like an enemy, but rather that you love him enough to seek his repentance by whatever means possible. Paul even instructed the Corinthians to "deliver such a one to Satan for the destruction of the flesh, that his spirit may be saved in the day of the Lord Jesus" (v. 5).

The church must hold up a high and holy standard. A very clear line must be drawn between the world and the church. Known and open sin cannot be tolerated. As soon as the church stops dealing with sin seriously, the world mingles with the church and the difference is obliterated. That is why Christians are not supposed to be able to go on sinning unchallenged by one another.

The church that tolerates sin destroys its own holiness and subverts the discernment of its own members. There can be no true church at all without clear boundaries.

When have you had to challenge someone about sin?

The Truth War, 207–210

The World Rejects Righteous Lives

If you were of the world, the world would love its own. Yet because you are not of the world, but I chose you out of the world, therefore the world hates you.

John 15:19

Persecution is inevitable for the righteous. Paul warned Timothy, "Yes, and all who desire to live godly in Christ Jesus will suffer persecution" (2 Tim. 3:12). The true believer stands apart from the world because he has been made holy through identification with Jesus Christ. He lives righteously and does not belong to the system. Because a genuine Christian represents God and Christ, Satan uses the world's system to attack him. That is why Jesus prayed for the Father's protection of His followers: "I do not pray that You should take them out of the world, but that You should keep them from the evil one" (John 17:15).

Our lives are to be a rebuke to the sinful world. Ephesians 5:11 says, "And have no fellowship with the unfruitful works of darkness, but rather expose them." If you are not experiencing much rejection from the world, your life may not be a rebuke to the world. To have an impact for Christ on this hostile and perverted world, you must avoid sin and "become blameless and harmless, children of God without fault in the midst of a crooked and perverse generation, among whom you shine as lights in the world" (Phil. 2:15).

You stand out from the world because Jesus has chosen you for that. In John 15:19 He says, "I chose you out of the world." Jesus is literally saying, "I chose you for Myself." He has chosen you to be different. So be the living rebuke to the rest of the world that Christ called you to be.

How do your actions reflect your chosen status?

Welcome to the Family, 71–72

The Cost of Following Jesus

He who loves his life will lose it, and he who hates his life in this world will keep it for eternal life.

John 12:25

In Luke 14:26, a great multitude was following Jesus, and He turned and spoke to them: "If anyone comes to Me"—meaning those who wanted to be His true followers—"and does not hate his father and mother, wife and children, brothers and sisters, yes, and his own life also, he cannot be My disciple." Self-hate? What a powerful truth! This is not salvation by good works but the very opposite: salvation by rejecting all hope of pleasing God on our own.

Following Jesus is not about you and me. Being a Christian is not about us; it's not about our self-esteem. It's about our being sick of our sin and our desperation for forgiveness. It is about seeing Christ as the priceless Savior from sin and death and hell, so that we willingly give up as much as it takes, even if it costs us our families, our marriages, and whatever else we cherish and possess.

It might even cost us our lives, as Jesus said in Luke 9:24 and reaffirmed in 14:27: "And whoever does not bear his cross"—that is, be willing to die and give his life—"and come after Me cannot be My disciple."

It can't be any clearer than that. If you try to hold on to you, your plan, your agenda, your success, your self-esteem, you lose forgiveness and heaven.

The path that Jesus was going down was the path to persecution and death (see John 12:24–25).

So you want to follow Jesus, do you? It'll cost you absolutely everything.

How would you answer the question in the last paragraph? Why?

Hard to Believe, 10–11

The Need for Discipline

And everyone who competes for the prize is temperate in all things. Now they do it to obtain a perishable crown, but we for an imperishable crown.

1 CORINTHIANS 9:25

Athletes in Paul's day trained hard just to be able to compete in the competition. In order to enter the Isthmian games, athletes had to give proof of ten months' full-time training. For thirty days before the event, the athletes trained together daily, in public view. Then, as now, it was a serious commitment to be a world-class athlete.

That was precisely how Paul portrayed the discipline he followed as a leader of God's people. This was no mere game to him. He was more serious than any track-and-field athlete. He wanted to win a race that had far more significance than any arena sport. Therefore it required even more diligence and discipline.

"Everyone who competes for the prize is temperate [moderate, self-restrained, not given to excess] in all things," he said in 1 Corinthians 9:25. You can't break the training regimen and win. That is true not only in athletics. It is true in everything. It is *especially* true in leadership.

Genuine success always comes at a high price. Every athlete knows this.

Discipline has to become a passion. It isn't merely a question of doing whatever is mandatory and avoiding whatever is prohibited. It involves voluntary self-denial.

Why is discipline important? Discipline teaches us to operate by principle rather than desire. Saying no to our impulses (even the ones that are not inherently sinful) puts us in control of our appetites rather than vice versa. It deposes our lust and permits truth, virtue, and integrity to rule our minds instead.

When have you experienced God's discipline? What happened as a result?

Called to Lead, 152–153

Learning Self-Control

But also for this very reason, giving all diligence, add to your faith virtue, to virtue knowledge, to knowledge self-control, to self-control perseverance, to perseverance godliness.

2 PETER 1:5–6

"Therefore I run thus: not with uncertainty. Thus I fight: not as one who beats the air" (1 Cor. 9:26). Notice Paul was not shadow-boxing, and he was not sparring. He was in a serious fight. *While* he was running, he was also fighting. He had an opponent he had to keep punching out, because the opponent would otherwise get him off track.

This opponent, remember, was his own flesh—meaning the sinful tendencies that are so often associated with bodily appetites and carnal lusts. He was running to win and boxing to keep from losing. In positive terms, he was cultivating the discipline of mental toughness to keep his eyes on the prize and his feet moving the right direction. In negative terms, he was cultivating the discipline of self-control in order to keep his own flesh from costing him the race.

Every athlete knows what this struggle is like. Every good athlete must keep his body under control. He can't be overweight, and he can't be unhealthy. He nourishes his body, exercises it to stay fit, and works it to build muscle. He stays in control of his body.

Most people, by contrast, are controlled by their bodies. Their bodies tell their minds what to do. That is why the sin principle is called "the flesh" throughout the Pauline epistles. It is not that the body itself is inherently evil. But evil desires are often associated with the body. So Paul said we need to "put to death the deeds of the body" (Rom. 8:13) and "[crucify] the flesh with its passions and desires" (Gal. 5:24).

What have you found most challenging about the development of the fruit of self-control?

Called to Lead, 158–159

Get Serious

Therefore let us not sleep, as others do, but let us watch and be sober.

1 THESSALONIANS 5:6

Let your laughter be turned to mourning and your joy to gloom" (James 4:9). James is not calling for an outlook on life that is always and only gloomy. He is not condemning laughter and joy in every context. In fact, Christians are supposed to be joyful (Phil. 1:25; 2:17–18).

But in this context, James is describing an attitude of repentance. He is teaching that when we contemplate our own sin, it ought to make us sorrowful, sober, and serious-minded.

We live in a society that rarely takes anything seriously, especially the reality of sin and personal guilt. James's point is that those who desire the blessing of God ought to view their own sin with the utmost sorrow and sobriety. Life in a sinful world cannot and should not always be filled with laughter and mirth. Sin is serious, and it ought to be contemplated seriously. Those who realize their sin and mourn will be comforted (Matt. 5:4), but the mourning is the necessary prelude to the blessing of divine comfort. We have no legitimate right to ask for divine blessing until we have contemplated our sin in all seriousness.

When Jeremiah thought about the sin of his people, he wrote, "The joy of our heart has ceased; our dance has turned into mourning. The crown has fallen from our head. Woe to us, for we have sinned!" (Lam. 5:15). Such an attitude is one of the necessary conditions for God's blessing on any people.

What do you find "sobering" these days?

Can God Bless America? 21–23

True Lamentation

Draw near to God and He will draw near to you. Cleanse your hands, you sinners; and purify your hearts, you double-minded. Lament and mourn and weep! Let your laughter be turned to mourning and your joy to gloom.

JAMES 4:8–9

Lament and mourn and weep!" (James 4:9). James is calling for misery and sorrow and tears over our sin.

It describes the heartache we should feel when we realize our own wretchedness as sinners. Perhaps the best New Testament example of this is the tax collector Jesus described in a parable—the publican who went to the temple to pray. But sensing his own sinful unworthiness, he did not even dare enter the temple itself, but "standing afar off, would not so much as raise his eyes to heaven, but beat his breast, saying, 'God, be merciful to me a sinner!'" (Luke 18:13).

The kind of misery that makes us lament our own sinfulness is a necessary condition for true blessing. Jesus contrasted him with a self-righteous Pharisee whose prayer expressed how good and superior he was compared to others. The Pharisee forfeited blessing because of his smugness and pride. The tax collector, by contrast, found blessing while in the throes of his own misery.

The misery James calls for is not the typical kind of depression people feel when they are dissatisfied with their lot in life. It has nothing to do with the despondency of self-pity or the lack of contentment felt by those who think life has been unfair to them. It is a misery that stems from a true sense of one's own guilt and a recognition that, because we are sinners, we don't deserve divine blessing. It is the cry of the heart that knows it has offended the righteousness of God and has no hope apart from God's mercy.

When was the last time you felt a sense of mourning over sin?

Can God Bless America? 17–18

All Riches Come from God

"The silver is Mine, and the gold is Mine," says the LORD of hosts.

HAGGAI 2:8

The Old Testament prophets set forth the truth that all wealth comes from God: "'The silver is Mine, and the gold is Mine,' says the LORD of hosts" (Hag. 2:8; cf. Job 28; Ps. 104:24). Because God, as creator of the earth, owns everything anyway, He certainly doesn't forbid mankind from using money. God granted man the wisdom and privilege to turn the earth's rich resources into valuable commodities and his own talents into marketable services. A natural result was the use of various metals from the earth to make coins, and the use of trees to make paper for currency. He wants us to wisely take advantage of the earth's natural resources for those and other economic purposes.

In Deuteronomy 8:18 (NASB), God moves a step further: "But you shall remember the LORD your God, for it is He who is giving you power to make wealth." He has not only created the raw materials for wealth, but has also given us the mental and physical ability to gain wealth and to use it.

God wants you to understand that money by itself is morally neutral and that He, as the ultimate source of it and all material goods, has distributed all wealth as a stewardship. We all manage God's wealth. Money and possessions then become tests of morality and pose these personal questions: What are you going to do with the wealth you have? Will you pass this crucial, ongoing test of your moral and spiritual life?

Knowing that everything belongs to God, how does this affect your view of giving?

Whose Money Is It Anyway? 5–6

True Vision

If therefore the light that is in you is darkness, how great is that darkness!

MATTHEW 6:23

The lamp of the body is the eye. If therefore your eye is good, your whole body will be full of light. But if your eye is bad, your whole body will be full of darkness. If therefore the light that is in you is darkness, how great is that darkness!" (Matt. 6:22–23). The eye is the body's only channel of light, and therefore the only means of vision. Likewise, the heart (mind) is the soul's only channel through which spiritual realities shine. Through it we receive God's truth, love, peace, and every other kind of spiritual blessing. Therefore it is essential that you keep your heart, or spiritual eye, clear and properly focused.

The King James translation renders the Greek for "clear" as "single," referring to a heart that has singleness of purpose and is devoted to what's right—regarding resources as well as every other aspect of the Christian life.

A "bad eye," one that is damaged because of disease or injury, stands in contrast to that clarity and singleness of purpose. It does not allow light to enter and leaves the whole body full of darkness. If our hearts become weighed down and preoccupied with material concerns, they become blind and insensitive to spiritual concerns—"full of darkness." According to Jesus' illustration, a "bad eye" equals a selfish and indulgent heart. Such a heart is self-deceived and cannot recognize true light. What it thinks is light is actually darkness, and Jesus emphasized how tragic that condition is when He exclaimed "how great is that darkness!"

How would you help someone who is deceived about sin?

Whose Money Is It Anyway? 59–60

The Truth About Money

No one can serve two masters; for either he will hate the one and love the other, or else he will be loyal to the one and despise the other. You cannot serve God and mammon.

MATTHEW 6:24

Our Lord taught more about such stewardship (one out of every ten verses in the Gospels) than about heaven and hell combined. The entire Bible contains more than two thousand references to wealth and property, twice as many as the total references to faith and prayer. What we do with the *things* God has given us is very important to Him. Money in itself is neither righteous nor evil—it is morally neutral. However, money is an accurate measure of one's morality. A look over your checkbook ledger or credit card statement will easily reveal where your money goes. And where you spend your money determines where your heart is and what your life's priorities are (Matt. 6:20–21). Someone who sees the pattern of your spending can fairly well discern the moral direction of your life.

Contrary to the fact that money is amoral, conventional wisdom for centuries has believed money necessarily corrupts. But that assessment goes against normal experience and good logic. There are certainly corrupt wealthy people who manifest their corruption through the misuse of their wealth, but there are also the righteous wealthy who demonstrate their righteousness by the godly way they invest their wealth. Similarly, among the ranks of the poor there have always been those who are corrupt and those who are righteous. So, money doesn't necessarily corrupt. But the use of it does reveal the inherent internal corruption of people. Money is not the essential problem; it is simply an indicator of the real problem, which is a sinful heart.

How do your actions reveal your choice between God and money?

Whose Money Is It Anyway? 3–4

Riches and Salvation

Then Zacchaeus stood and said to the Lord, "Look, Lord, I give half of my goods to the poor; and if I have taken anything from anyone by false accusation, I restore fourfold." And Jesus said to him, "Today salvation has come to this house."

Luke 19:8–9

Zaccheus's salvation immediately affected the financial area of his life (Luke 19:1–10). The initial evidence of his transformed life was his completely changed attitude toward his money. As a tax collector in the Roman Empire, he had been totally focused on accumulating as much wealth as possible, even if it meant defrauding taxpayers and withholding contributions to people in need.

Zaccheus's transformation was so genuine and dramatic that Jesus made this clear-cut declaration: "Today salvation has come to this house" (Luke 19:9).

Not all such encounters with Jesus had a positive outcome. The Synoptic Gospels (Matt. 19; Mark 10; Luke 18) each contain the story of the rich young ruler.

The Lord picked a command that would reveal whether he really was repentant concerning salvation. Jesus said to him, "One thing you lack: go and sell all you possess and give to the poor, and you will have treasure in heaven; and come, follow Me" (Mark 10:21 NASB).

Sadly, the young man—unwilling to obey Christ if it meant parting with his wealth—left, averse to following Jesus' instructions.

Those two significant occasions in which Jesus closely related one's attitude toward money with one's status before God stand in sharp contrast to each other. In the story of Zaccheus, the fact that his attitude toward wealth changed was solid evidence that his repentance and seeking after God were genuine. In the story of the rich young ruler, his stubborn refusal to let go of his wealth was evidence of his worship of self.

How is your view of money connected to your status before God?

Whose Money Is It Anyway? 21–22

God Owns Everything

The earth is the LORD's, and all its fullness, the world and those who dwell therein.

PSALM 24:1

God is the sole proprietor of everything you have—your clothes, your house, your car, your children, your computer, your iPod, your investments, your sports equipment, your lawn and garden—and everything else imaginable. King David affirmed that truth several times: "For all that is in heaven and in earth is Yours. . . . Both riches and honor come from You, and You reign over all" (1 Chron. 29:11, 12); "The earth is the LORD's, and all it contains, the world, and those who dwell in it" (Ps. 24:1 NASB).

Since God owns everything, you can never really acquire anything new because it is already His. Embracing this fact is crucial in attaining a biblical attitude of contentment.

Either from your own perspective or God's, you have to deal with your possessions. As long as they belong to Him, you should stop worrying and let Him take care of them. That's the way John Wesley reacted one day when he received the news that fire had destroyed his house. He simply said, "The Lord's house burned down. One less responsibility for me."

Wesley's approach was the right one, but it is not how the world teaches us to respond. The self-centered accumulation of property is the world's legacy to us, but we need to change that perspective. *We do not own anything*. Therefore, if you ever lose something, you don't really lose it, because you never owned it. If someone needs some of what you have, he may be as entitled to it as you are, because you don't own it—God does.

How have you shown that you embrace the biblical attitude of contentment?

Whose Money Is It Anyway? 10

The True Provider

Now godliness with contentment is great gain. For we brought nothing into this world, and it is certain we can carry nothing out.

1 TIMOTHY 6:6–7

One of the most lovely Hebrew names for God is *Jehovah-jireh*, "the Lord who provides" (see Gen. 22:14). God's provision for those who trust in Him is so characteristic of His nature that it is one of His names. You may never doubt most of God's attributes (for example, His holiness, love, goodness, power, justice, and glory), but you may at times wonder whether or not He will provide your needs. However, that is exactly what Jesus cautioned His followers against in Matthew 6:25–34 when He said they should not worry about what to eat, drink, or wear.

The world worries and scrambles and works—often to the point of exhaustion—to make sure it has enough wealth. But that is so unnecessary because our heavenly Father knows our needs and promises to provide for us every day.

If you know God owns everything in the world, controls all its assets, and can provide for you as His child, then there is no need for you to trust in luxury, be enticed by materialism, or stockpile for the future. Your daily life as a Christian need not revolve around those concerns, but in being content with what you have (1 Tim. 6:6–8; Heb. 13:5). You don't have to own everything or be in control of every circumstance to have enough money for your basic needs. Instead, you can set aside all worry and anxiety about your needs and gladly receive whatever God gives you to invest in His kingdom (Matt. 6:31–34).

How can you attest to the fact that God can and does provide?

Whose Money Is It Anyway? 12–13

Robbing God

Will a man rob God? Yet you have robbed Me! But you say, "In what way have we robbed You?" In tithes and offerings.

Malachi 3:8

The love of money, which is idolatry, will invariably cause you to steal from God. That means in your stewardship of money and possessions you will not do what is right; you will not render to God what is His. The people of Malachi's time were guilty of stealing from God: "Will a man rob God? Yet you have robbed Me! But you say, 'In what way have we robbed You?' In tithes and offerings" (Mal. 3:8).

As absurd as the question of robbing God sounded, the prophet had to ask it. And he answered his own question with a resounding yes. When the people, who obviously loved their money too much, asked how they were stealing from God, Malachi simply answered, "In tithes and offerings." In other words, they hadn't given God all that was rightfully His.

There was a very clear remedy for that sinful situation. "'Bring the whole tithe into the storehouse, so that there may be food in My house, and test Me now in this,' says the Lord of hosts, 'if I will not open for you the windows of heaven and pour out for you a blessing until it overflows'" (Mal. 3:10 NASB).

If you are a slave to the love of money, you need to have the same kind of response Malachi commanded for his listeners. You may think you are not stealing from God and that you never will, but if you are not placing a generous portion of your resources into God's kingdom, you are robbing Him.

Where do you invest your resources?

Whose Money Is It Anyway? 28

Jesus' True Economic Condition

"For you have the poor with you always, but Me you do not have always."

Matthew 26:11

The assertion that Jesus grew up with the poor and was homeless is simply not true. A brief overview of Israel's socioeconomic structure at the time of His incarnation may help us better understand His actual status. At the lowest level was a rather large segment of poor people.

Then, as in most countries, Israel had a small but influential upper class of wealthy people. They were the landowners and religious leaders, those who wielded power and authority under the direction of the occupying Romans.

At the time of Christ, in the center of Jewish society was a significant middle class composed of craftsmen and tradesmen. This segment included farmers, toolmakers, pottery makers, builders, and other artisans. Jesus was born into such a middle-class family. His earthly father, Joseph, had his own construction business.

It's likely that Joseph was a good carpenter who took advantage of the many construction opportunities around Nazareth and, with Jesus' help, built a thriving business.

It's therefore wrong to conclude that Jesus entered the world as a poor and homeless individual who led a poverty-stricken life.

Instead of assuming that Jesus was poor and somehow encouraged His followers to live likewise, I believe we ought to recognize His middle-class birth and upbringing and seriously consider God's purpose behind it. The Father very likely sent the Son to a middle-class working environment where He could thoughtfully and wisely speak to the wealthy and also comfort and understand the poor. Jesus would have been able to identify fairly well with each of the other classes.

How do you show your acceptance of people no matter what their social class?

Whose Money Is It Anyway? 34–35

Giving Thanks for the World

Then God saw everything that He had made,
and indeed it was very good.

GENESIS 1:31

God through Scripture and general revelation provides an unmistakable affirmation of the goodness of this disposable planet. When you combine the richness of the earth with mankind's God-given ability to cultivate (raising livestock and grains), enjoy limitless tastes and smells, and extract that richness (retrieving valuable metals, gems, minerals, and fuels), you have the fulfillment of God's purpose for men and women to enjoy life.

As with everything else, however, the earth's goodness and our enjoyment and use of it have been seriously marred by sin. God originally gave Adam and Eve the freedom to manage everything in the Garden of Eden. God still allows mankind freedom to use the earth's resources, but sadly people abuse those good things and turn them into products of destruction (weapons that maim and kill, narcotics and poisons that destroy people's lives). Or they turn these resources into material gods and in effect worship those instead of the true God.

But even with mankind's sinful excesses in handling the world's goods, God does not command us to stop using and enjoying them. The sin is not in enjoying the earth's bounty. The sin is overindulgence and waste—flaunting your wealth and engaging in a self-centered, compassionless consumption.

The scriptural, godly approach is to have the right heart attitude in partaking of God's many material blessings. If you enjoy them, give Him thanks, and become willing to share generously with others. Then you have made righteous use of the wealth God has entrusted to you.

How do you show your stewardship of the resources God gave you?

Whose Money Is It Anyway? 38–39

True Giving Is Regular Giving

As it is written: "He has dispersed abroad, He has given to the poor; His righteousness endures forever."

2 CORINTHIANS 9:9

On the first day of the week let each one of you lay something aside, storing up as he may prosper, that there be no collections when I come" (1 Cor. 16:2). Paul says the most fitting time for Christian giving is weekly, during the public worship. Paul's reference to the first day of the week indicates that the early worship services included a regular offering. It is also a strong indicator that our giving should be consistent and systematic, not spasmodic and subjective ("as the Spirit leads"), or whenever we happen to remember it. Obviously, the Holy Spirit can sometimes prompt us to give in response to special appeals for urgent needs. However, as in every other major aspect of the Christian life, the Spirit uses scriptural instructions like Paul's to guide our giving.

The apostle's guidelines are not rigid, requiring that people divide their offering money so they always have something to put into the plate or basket each Sunday. It may work better for them to give just once a month, if they are paid monthly, or less frequently than that, if they are paid periodically as a commissioned salesperson or freelance worker. The point is simply this: you should be consistently aware of and responsive to the needs of your church (which includes budgeting ahead of everything else how much you will give to the Lord), even when you don't have anything to give on a particular Sunday. The offering is a required part of weekly worship and fellowship, one of your Christian responsibilities in lifting up "spiritual sacrifices" to God (1 Peter 2:5).

What are some needs in your community to which you can give?

Whose Money Is It Anyway? 75

How Much Should I Give?

On the first day of the week let each one of you lay something aside, storing up as he may prosper, that there be no collections when I come.

1 CORINTHIANS 16:2

The biblical model does not mandate a certain amount or proportion of what we ought to give. Instead, the apostle Paul says believers have complete discretion to give as God prospers them. That disproves the claim among some Christians that says believers should give at least 10 percent of their income to the Lord's work, just as the ancient Israelites had to.

In some ways your giving corresponds only generally to the Old Testament pattern. You give tax payments to support the government (Rom. 13:6), just as the Jews gave tithes to support their leadership (Lev. 27:30; Num. 18:21; Deut. 14:28–29; cf. Matt. 17:24–27; 22:15–21). In attitude, however, there is a direct parallel. You are to decide with joy what to give (2 Cor. 9:7), just as the Israelites gave from the heart (Ex. 25:1–2; 36:5–6; cf. 2 Sam. 24:24). God is always pleased when His people follow those basic guidelines of proportional and sacrificial giving.

If you are affluent, you can afford to give much before it even touches your lifestyle—and you should give sacrificially, so that it does limit your self-indulgence, unlike the rich donors who preceded the widow at the temple treasury (Mark 12:41–44). Though it is not easy to give much when you have a low income, that should not be an excuse for giving nothing. If you start out by being generous when you have modest resources, you will much more likely be generous when you have greater wealth (cf. Luke 16:10).

Where do you sense the Lord's leading in regard to giving?

Whose Money Is It Anyway? 77–78, 76

Giving in Difficulties

For I bear witness that according to their ability, yes, and beyond their ability, they were freely willing.

2 CORINTHIANS 8:3

True biblical giving will also transcend the most difficult of circumstances. Such circumstances had no negative impact on the Macedonians' giving. "That in a great ordeal of affliction their abundance of joy and their deep poverty overflowed in the wealth of their liberality" (2 Cor. 8:2).

The believers in Macedonia easily could have excused themselves from any giving by making one or more statements like: "Well, we can't give right now because we're in extremely difficult times and we don't know what our economic future holds." "We'd better hang on to what little we have because we're being persecuted mercilessly and we don't know if we'll have enough for tomorrow." "We don't think we can get involved in any offering at this time because we have to deal with a lot of hostility from the Jews since we identified with Christ."

Acts 17:1–15 records that the Macedonians really were in some very difficult situations, and Paul's letters corroborate the reality of suffering, affliction, persecution, and tribulation for those churches (Phil. 1:29; 1 Thess. 1:6; 2:14–15; 3:3–10; 2 Thess. 1:4). Yet in the face of those overwhelming, relentless hardships, the Macedonians displayed no "poor me" mentality. They offered no excuses. Instead they gave, even though they were enduring intense, prolonged suffering and deprivation. That's the way devout Christians react. By God's grace we can always find a way to give, because even the worst circumstances should never hinder our devotion to Jesus Christ and our desire to obey His commands on giving.

When is it most challenging for you to give?

Whose Money Is It Anyway? 85

Giving Leads to Blessings

It is more blessed to give than to receive.

ACTS 20:35

"Give, and it will be given to you. They will pour into your lap a good measure—pressed down, shaken together, and running over. For by your standard of measure it will be measured to you in return" (Luke 6:38 NASB). The underlying truth is simply this: generosity in giving results in a greater reward from God.

Paul, in his farewell exhortation to the Ephesian elders, further reinforces the New Covenant validity of the principle by quoting another statement from Jesus: "Remember the words of the Lord Jesus, that He Himself said, 'It is more blessed to give than to receive'" (Acts 20:35). Out of Jesus' many unrecorded words (cf. John 21:25), the Holy Spirit chose to include only that short statement about the blessings of giving.

Those two monumental promises from Jesus should be all we need to make us welcome with joy every giving opportunity. They ought to motivate you and me—whether it's through the weekly offering at church or meeting someone's individual need—always to give as generously, unselfishly, and sacrificially as possible.

In Luke 6:38, the Greek for "give" is in the imperative, which makes it a command from Jesus that must be obeyed. Giving is therefore an issue of believing His command and following through in faithful obedience. If you do, you demonstrate your trust in His promises. If you don't, you sin against Christ in the sense that you have no faith in what He promised about the blessings of giving.

What motivates you to give?

Whose Money Is It Anyway? 66–68

The Answer to Spiritual Hunger

And Jesus said to them, "I am the bread of life. He who comes to Me shall never hunger, and he who believes in Me shall never thirst."

JOHN 6:35

Salvation is giving up your life and embracing His. It is taking in Christ by faith, acknowledging the reality of who He is and what He did. This is an invitation to receive Christ, and only the hungry eat; only the thirsty drink. The spiritual traitor is not hungry for real salvation. He's not starving in sin and ravenous for righteousness. He's full of the world, and more than that, full of himself, satisfied, fed with the prevailing food of the world that perishes. When someone comes to Christ, he comes out of a driving spiritual hunger. As Jesus said in the Sermon on the Mount, "Blessed are those who hunger and thirst for righteousness, for they shall be filled" (Matt. 5:6).

The image of eating illustrates graphically the personal appropriation of these realities. I can look at Christ and like what I see, but it's no good unless I take it in. When a sinner loves his sin, is stuffed with the world and happy with all the husks that he shares with the pigs, he won't seek true salvation. To him, the thought of the bread of Christ is ridiculous, repulsive, and nauseating, and he disdains it in his self-satisfied bloatedness. He pushes Christ away.

But once a person is broken over sin, awakened to his lost condition and his purposelessness; once he senses the void and the gnawing hunger of his soul for God, then he cries out to be fed, takes Christ, and confesses Him as Lord and Savior. He says, "He's my life, He's my bread!"

How do you satisfy your spiritual hunger?

Hard to Believe, 178–179

What Faith Does

Now faith is the substance of things hoped for, the evidence of things not seen. For by it the elders obtained a good testimony.

HEBREWS 11:1–2

Faith obeys. That, in two words, is the key lesson of Hebrews 11. Here we see people of faith worshipping God (v. 4); walking with God (v. 5); working for God (v. 7); obeying God (vv. 8–10); overcoming barrenness (v. 11); and overpowering death (v. 12).

Faith enabled these people to persevere to death (vv. 13–16); trust God with their dearest possessions (vv. 17–19); believe God for the future (vv. 20–23); turn away from earthly treasure for heavenly reward (vv. 24–26); see Him who is unseen (v. 27); receive miracles from the hand of God (vv. 28–30); have courage in the face of great danger (vv. 31–33); conquer kingdoms, perform acts of righteousness, obtain promises, shut the mouths of lions, quench the power of fire, escape the edge of the sword, from weakness be made strong, become mighty in war, and put foreign armies to flight (vv. 33–34). This faith has overcome death, endured torture, outlasted chains and imprisonment, withstood temptation, undergone martyrdom, and survived all manner of hardship (vv. 35–38).

And faith endures. If anything is true about Hebrews 11 faith, it is that it cannot be killed. It perseveres. It endures no matter what—holding to God with love and assurance no matter what kind of assaults the world or the forces of evil might bring against it.

Make no mistake—real faith will always produce righteous works. Faith is the root; works are the fruit. Because God Himself is the vinedresser, fruit is guaranteed. That's why whenever Scripture gives examples of faith, faith inevitably is seen as obedient, working, and active.

What are some words or statements you would use to describe your faith?

The Gospel According to the Apostles, 48–50

Gray Areas

One person esteems one day above another; another esteems every day alike. Let each be fully convinced in his own mind.

Romans 14:5

Not every issue is cast in black and white. There are many questions to which Scripture does not explicitly speak. For example, there is no list of holidays and holy days for Christians to observe or avoid celebrating. The issue is explicitly left in the realm of indifferent matters by the apostle Paul: "One person esteems one day above another; another esteems every days alike. Let each be fully convinced in his own mind" (Rom. 14:5). Paul says something similar about foods and dietary restrictions.

But many of the issues being compromised within the evangelical movement today are not questionable. Scripture speaks very clearly against homosexuality, for example. The Christian position on adultery is not at all vague. The question of whether a believer ought to marry an unbeliever is spelled out with perfect clarity. Scripture quite plainly forbids any Christian to take another Christian to court. Selfishness and pride are explicitly identified as sins. These are not gray areas. There is no room for compromise here.

Nevertheless, I constantly hear every one of those issues treated as a gray area—on Christian radio, on Christian television, and in Christian literature. People want all such matters to be negotiable. And too many Christian leaders willingly oblige. They hesitate to speak with authority on matters where Scripture is plain. The lines of distinction between truth and error, wisdom and foolishness, church and world are being systematically obliterated by such means.

In truth, far more issues are black and white than most people realize.

What "gray areas" have you faced this week? What does Scripture say about them?

The Truth War, 194–195

Discerning the Truth

I have not written to you because you do not know the truth, but because you know it, and that no lie is of the truth.

1 JOHN 2:21

All truth sets itself against error. Where Scripture speaks, it speaks with authority. It speaks definitively. It speaks decisively. It calls for absolute conviction. It demands that we submit to God and resist the devil (James 4:7). It urges us to discern between the spirit of truth and the spirit of error (1 John 4:6). It commands us to turn away from evil and do good (1 Peter 3:11). It bids us reject the broad way that seems right to the human mind (Prov. 14:12; 16:25) and follow the narrow way prescribed by God (Matt. 7:13–14). It tells us that our ways are not God's ways nor our thoughts His thoughts (Isa. 55:8). It orders us to protect the truth and reject lies (Rom. 1:25). It declares that no lie is of the truth (1 John 2:21). It guarantees that the righteous shall be blessed and the wicked perish (Ps. 1:1, 6). And it reminds us that "friendship with the world is enmity with God. Whoever therefore wants to be a friend of the world makes himself an enemy of God" (James 4:4).

Discernment demands that where Scripture speaks with clarity, a hard line must be drawn. Christ is against human philosophy, against empty deception, against human tradition, and against the elementary principles of this world (Col. 2:8). Those things cannot be integrated with true Christian belief; they must be repudiated and steadfastly resisted. Scripture demands that we make a definitive choice: "How long will you falter between two opinions? If the LORD is God, follow Him; but if Baal, follow him" (1 Kings 18:21).

How has Scripture helped you discern the truth recently?

The Truth War, 196–197

The Truth of a Familiar Story

The LORD your God in your midst, the Mighty One, will save; He will rejoice over you with gladness, He will quiet you with His love, He will rejoice over you with singing.

ZEPHANIAH 3:17

Most people today are somewhat familiar with the parable of the prodigal son, found in Luke 15:11–32. Even those who know next to nothing else about the Bible know something about this tale. But what does it mean?

The prodigal represents a typical sinner who comes to repentance. The father's patience, love, generosity, and delight over the son's return are clear and perfect emblems of divine grace. The prodigal's heart change is a picture of what true repentance should look like. And the elder brother's cold indifference—the real focal point of the story, as it turns out—is a vivid representation of the same evil hypocrisy Jesus was confronting in the hearts of the hostile scribes and Pharisees to whom He told the parable in the first place (Luke 15:2). They bitterly resented the sinners and tax collectors who drew near to Jesus (v. 1), and they tried to paper over their fleshly indignation with religious pretense. But their attitudes betrayed their unbelief and self-centeredness. Jesus' parable ripped the mask off their hypocrisy.

This, then, is the central and culminating lesson of the parable: Jesus is pointing out the stark contrast between God's own delight in the redemption of sinners and the Pharisees' inflexible hostility toward those same sinners. Keeping that lesson fixed firmly in view, we can legitimately draw from the larger story (as Jesus unfolds it) several profound lessons about grace, forgiveness, repentance, and the heart of God toward sinners. Those elements are all so conspicuous in the parable that almost everyone should be able to recognize them.

Knowing of God's delight in you, how does that encourage you to come to Him when you've done wrong?

A Tale of Two Sons, xi, xvi

December

JESUS' BIRTH AND LIFE

What Is Grace?

Therefore, having been justified by faith, we have peace with God through our Lord Jesus Christ, through whom also we have access by faith into this grace in which we stand, and rejoice in hope of the glory of God.

Romans 5:1–2

Grace is a terribly misunderstood word. Defining it succinctly is notoriously difficult. Some of the most detailed theology textbooks do not offer any concise definition of the term. Someone has proposed an acronym: GRACE is God's Riches At Christ's Expense. That's not a bad way to characterize grace, but it is not a sufficient theological definition.

At the heart of the term *grace* is the idea of divine favor. Intrinsic to its meaning are the ideas of favor, goodness, and goodwill.

Grace is all that and more. Grace is not merely unmerited favor; it is favor bestowed on sinners who deserve wrath. Showing kindness to a stranger is "unmerited favor"; doing good to one's enemies is more the spirit of grace (Luke 6:27–36).

Grace is not a dormant or abstract quality, but a dynamic, active, working principle: "The grace of God has appeared, bringing salvation . . . and instructing us" (Titus 2:11–12 NASB). It is not some kind of ethereal blessing that lies idle until we appropriate it. Grace is God's sovereign initiative to sinners (Eph. 1:5–6). Grace is not a onetime event in the Christian experience. We stand in grace (Rom. 5:2). The entire Christian life is driven and empowered by grace: "It is good for the heart to be strengthened by grace, not by foods" (Heb. 13:9 NASB). Peter said we should "grow in the grace and knowledge of our Lord and Savior Jesus Christ" (2 Peter 3:18).

Thus we could properly define grace as *the free and benevolent influence of a holy God operating sovereignly in the lives of undeserving sinners*.

When did the concept of grace really hit home to you?

The Gospel According to the Apostles, 57–58

The Gift of Grace

I do not set aside the grace of God; for if righteousness comes through the law, then Christ died in vain.

Galatians 2:21

Grace is a gift. God "gives a greater grace. . . . [He] gives grace to the humble" (James 4:6 NASB). Christians are said to be "stewards of the manifold grace of God" (1 Peter 4:10). But that does not mean that God's grace is placed at our disposal. We do not possess God's grace or control its operation. We are subject to grace, never vice versa. Paul frequently contrasted grace with law (Rom. 4:16; 5:20; 6:14–15; Gal. 2:21; 5:4). He was careful to state, however, that grace does not nullify the moral demands of God's law. Rather, it fulfills the righteousness of the law (Rom. 6:14–15). In a sense, grace is to law what miracles are to nature. It rises above and accomplishes what law cannot (cf. Rom. 8:3). Yet it does not annul the righteous demands of the law; it confirms and validates them (Rom. 3:31). Grace has its own law, a higher, liberating law: "The law of the Spirit of life in Christ Jesus has made me free from the law of sin and death" (Rom. 8:2; cf. James 1:25). Note that this new law emancipates us from *sin* as well as *death*. Paul was explicit about this: "What shall we say then? Are we to continue in sin that grace might increase? May it never be! How shall we who died to sin still live in it?" (Rom. 6:1–2 NASB). Grace reigns through *righteousness* (Rom. 5:21).

There are two extremes to be avoided in the matter of grace. We must take care not to nullify grace through legalism (Gal. 2:21) or corrupt it through licentiousness (Jude v. 4).

How does your life reflect your view of the gift of grace?

The Gospel According to the Apostles, 59

Two Types of Grace

And of His fullness we have all received, and grace for grace.

JOHN 1:16

Theologians speak of *common grace* and *special grace*. Common grace is bestowed to mankind in general. It is the grace that restrains the full expression of sin and mitigates sin's destructive effects in human society. Common grace imposes moral constraints on people's behavior, maintains a semblance of order in human affairs, enforces a sense of right and wrong through conscience and civil government, enables men and women to appreciate beauty and goodness, and imparts blessings of all kinds to all peoples. God "causes His sun to rise on the evil and the good, and sends rain on the righteous and the unrighteous" (Matt. 5:45 NASB). That is common grace.

Common grace is not redemptive. It does not pardon sin or purify sinners. It does not renew the heart, stimulate faith, or enable salvation. It can convict of sin and enlighten the soul to the truth of God. But common grace alone does not lead to eternal salvation, because the hearts of sinners are so firmly set against God (Rom. 3:10–18).

Special grace, better called *saving grace*, is the irresistible work of God that frees men and women from the penalty and power of sin, renewing the inner person and sanctifying the sinner through the operation of the Holy Spirit.

Every stage of the process of salvation is governed by sovereign grace. In fact, the term *grace* in the New Testament is often used as a synonym for the whole of the saving process, particularly in the Pauline epistles (cf. 1 Cor. 1:4; 2 Cor. 6:1; Gal. 2:21). Grace oversees all of salvation, beginning to end.

How has God's grace enabled you to be gracious toward others recently?

The Gospel According to the Apostles, 59–60

True and False Gospels

Now the Spirit expressly says that in latter times some will depart from the faith, giving heed to deceiving spirits and doctrines of demons.

1 TIMOTHY 4:1

You may have noticed quite a lot of publicity lately about early pseudo-Christian documents such as *The Gospel of Thomas* and *The Gospel of Judas*. Actually, the "gospels" of Thomas and Judas are both well-documented gnostic works. They are pure fiction masquerading as history—full of demonstrably false claims and fanciful mythology. Scholars of every kind (Christian and secular scholars alike) all agree that although these works are authentic relics of early gnostic teaching they cannot possibly be what the gnostics claimed that they were. Like virtually all other gnostic writings, they are anonymous frauds, full of gnostic lies.

Furthermore, these books do not contain any newly uncovered or long-forgotten truths. The existence of these works and many others like them have always been well-known to scholars. *The Gospel of Judas*, for example, was first mentioned at the end of the second century by Irenaeus, who connected it with an especially evil cult of gnostics who made heroes of Cain, Esau, the men of Sodom, Korah, and all the other villains of Scripture. They produced *The Gospel of Judas* in order to portray Judas as a hero. The work turns the biblical account of Jesus' life and ministry on its head, borrowing truth from Scripture here and there—but poisoning it with out-and-out lies. That is the kind of satanic truth twisting that gnostics have always been best known for.

What do you do to combat those who claim to speak the "truth" without the backing of Scripture?

The Truth War, 93–94

The Deadliest Sin

You therefore, beloved, since you know this beforehand, beware lest you also fall from your own steadfastness, being led away with the error of the wicked.

2 PETER 3:17

If you have ever questioned what God's own view of false religion and apostasy is, look to the book of Jude. A theme that runs throughout the whole book is this: *false teaching is the deadliest and most abhorrent of evils*, because it is always an expression of unbelief, which is the distillation of pure evil.

The *deadliest? Most abhorrent?* What about pornography, abortion, sexual perversion, marital unfaithfulness? Those are all gross sins, of course, and they are eating away at the fabric of our society. It is certainly right for us to be morally repulsed and outraged at such monstrous evils. But heresy that undermines the gospel is a far more serious sin because it places souls in eternal peril under the darkness of the kind of lies that keep people in permanent bondage to their sin.

That is why there is no more serious abomination than heresy. It is the worst and most loathsome kind of spiritual filth. Therefore, Jude says, we should no more risk being defiled by apostasy than we would want to clasp someone's filthy, stained underwear close to ourselves. Scripture employs this same shocking imagery in other places too. Isaiah 64:6, lamenting the apostasy of Israel, says, "But we are all like an unclean thing, and all our righteousnesses [i.e., self-righteousness and false religion] are like filthy rags." In that text, Isaiah uses a Hebrew expression that speaks of soiled menstrual cloths. In Revelation 3:4, Christ says to the church at Sardis, "You have a few names even in Sardis who have not defiled their garments." That has a similar meaning, for He is referring to the defilement of heresy and apostasy.

What is your plan for immersing yourself in God's truth this week?

The Truth War, 181–182

Abandoning the Truth

But the ones on the rock are those who, when they hear, receive the word with joy; and these have no root, who believe for a while and in time of temptation fall away.

Luke 8:13

Apostasy is the technical name for serious, soul-destroying error that arises from within the church. It comes from the Greek word *apostasia*, which is translated "falling away." The word is closely related to the Greek word for "divorce." It speaks of abandonment, a separation, a defection—the abdication of truth altogether.

Can a genuine Christian fall away from the faith and become an apostate? No. Scripture is quite clear about that. Those who do depart from the faith, like Judas, simply demonstrate that they never had true faith to begin with. "They went out from us, but they were not of us; for if they had been of us, *they would have continued with us*; but they went out that they might be made manifest, that none of them were of us" (1 John 2:19, emphasis added). Jesus said of His true sheep, "I give them eternal life, and they shall never perish; neither shall anyone snatch them out of My hand. My Father, who has given them to Me, is greater than all; and no one is able to snatch them out of My Father's hand" (John 10:28–29).

Nonetheless, there are lots of apostate people. Ever since the time of Judas, there have been people who profess faith in Christ and identify themselves as disciples but who never genuinely embrace the truth. They may *understand* the truth. They may even seem to follow it enthusiastically for a while. They might identify with a church and therefore become active and integral parts of the earthly Christian community. Sometimes they even become leaders in a church. But they never really *believe* the truth with an undivided heart.

What will you do to reach out to someone who has abandoned faith in God?

The Truth War, 43

The Power and Motive of False Religion

For when they speak great swelling words of emptiness, they allure through the lusts of the flesh, through lewdness, the ones who have actually escaped from those who live in error.

2 PETER 2:18

Apostate religion is dynamic in the same way gospel truth is—but it produces exactly the opposite results. It intensifies sin's bondage, multiplies sin's pollutions, and magnifies sin's consequences. In every way imaginable, false religion makes the calamity of sin worse than ever.

Heresy always breeds more evil, and the closer any lie comes to the heart of the gospel, the more diabolical is the fruit it bears.

The evil borne by false doctrine is no incidental or unintentional side effect. The actual goal—and the inevitable result—of all false doctrine is to "turn the grace of our God into lewdness" (Jude v. 4). That is also the true aim and ambition of every apostate. According to Jude, in the mix of the evil motives behind every heresy, you will always discover an appetite for evil things.

The driving passion of all false teachers is their lust (vv. 18–19). It may be a craving for carnal pleasure (v. 7), greed for money and material things (v. 11), or a rebellious hankering after power (v. 11). Many times it is all of the above. Look closely at any false teacher and you will see corruption caused by lust—manifest not only in the love of money and power but also in an inability to control the flesh.

Peter said exactly the same thing. Scoffers are driven by "their own lusts" (2 Peter 3:3). In fact, Peter says that one of the primary objectives of every apostate teacher is to lure people back into the bondage of immorality after they have been exposed to the liberating truth of the gospel (see 2 Peter 2:18–19).

When, if ever, has someone tried to convert you using false doctrine?

The Truth War, 120–121

The Need for Careful Study of Scripture

Be diligent to present yourself approved to God, a worker who does not need to be ashamed, rightly dividing the word of truth.

2 Timothy 2:15

The person who is not a diligent student cannot be an accurate interpreter of God's Word. Scripture indicates that such a person is not approved by God and should be ashamed of himself (2 Tim. 2:15).

People do not usually buy into false doctrine purposely. They err because of laziness, ineptness, carelessness, or foolishness in handling Scripture. In 2 Timothy 2:17–18, Paul describes the destructive impact of false teachers this way: "Their message will spread like cancer. Hymenaeus and Philetus are of this sort, who have strayed concerning the truth, saying that the resurrection is already past; and they overthrow the faith of some."

The Greek verb translated "strayed" is *astochï*, which literally means "to miss the mark." It suggests that Hymenaeus and Philetus weren't actually trying to devise error, but being careless and unskilled in handling the truth, they turned to "profane and idle babblings" (v. 16), which led them to conclude that the resurrection had already taken place. And their error, absurd as it was, had already upset the faith of others. That is precisely why in verse 15 Paul urged Timothy to be a diligent student of the Word of truth.

What Paul was calling for is exactly the opposite of the shoot-from-the-hip ad-libbing that takes place in many contemporary pulpits. That is a dangerous, deadly approach. It invariably perverts the truth, and it subverts people's ability to differentiate between sound doctrine and error. We can't establish sound biblical principles for discernment until we understand what Scripture means.

What Scriptures helped expose false doctrine you've heard?

The Truth War, 205–206

Commitment to Unchanging Truth

For the message of the cross is foolishness to those who are perishing, but to us who are being saved it is the power of God.

1 Corinthians 1:18

In practical terms, the movement to accommodate the world has diminished Christians' confidence in divinely revealed truth. If we can't trust the preaching of God's Word to convert the lost and build the church, how can we trust the Bible at all—even as a guide for our daily living? People are being misled by the example of some of their church leaders. They are buying into the delusion that faithfulness to the Word of God is optional.

Christians ought to have learned by now that we cannot avoid being an offense to the world and still remain faithful to the gospel. The gospel is inherently offensive. Christ Himself is offensive to unbelievers. He is an offense to all in error. He is an offense to all who reject the truth. He is "'a stone of stumbling and a rock of offense.' They stumble, being disobedient to the word, to which they also were appointed" (1 Peter 2:8). The message of the cross is also a stumbling block (Gal. 5:11).

Authentic Christianity has always recognized that truth is unchanging. The Word of God is settled forever in heaven (Ps. 119:89). Jesus Christ is the same yesterday, today, and forever (Heb. 13:8). God Himself does not change (Mal. 3:6). How could we ever view truth as transient, pliable, or adaptable?

When the church loses its commitment to the inflexibility of truth, it loses its will to discern. It forfeits precise theology, precise morals, and precise conduct.

Right thinking and right living therefore demand careful discipline and an unyielding commitment to the truth.

How do you show your commitment to the truth?

The Truth War, 201–202

Remain in the Truth

Set your mind on things above, not on things on the earth.

COLOSSIANS 3:2

We need to build one another up in the faith and maintain our spiritual stability. Above all, stay committed to the truth. Don't waver.

Jude includes four aspects of this principle. First, he says we must seek to remain faithful by "building yourselves up on your most holy faith." He is urging us to edify one another by the Word of God. The phrase "your most holy faith" is a reference to sound doctrine—a right understanding of the truth as it is revealed in Scripture. This is a call to the spiritual discipline of studying the Word.

Second, maintain your spiritual stability and equilibrium by "praying in the Holy Spirit." The faithful life is kept steady through means of the spiritual disciplines of study and prayer.

Third, Jude says, "Keep yourselves in the love of God" (v. 21). That is a way of reminding us to be obedient. Jude verse 21 is simply echoing the words of Jesus in John 14:21; 15:9–10. It is a call for obedience.

Finally, Jude says, keep "looking for the mercy of our Lord Jesus Christ unto eternal life." That speaks of an eager expectation of Christ's second coming.

All of those are ways of reminding us to set our minds on heavenly things, not on the things of this world (Col. 3:2). That is the only way to survive in a time of apostasy. Ultimately, only what is eternal really matters—and that means the truth matters infinitely more than any of the merely earthly things that tend to capture our attention and energies.

How will you build up someone in the faith this week?

The Truth War, 175–176

The Reality of Stealth: False Teachers

They told you that there would be mockers in the last time who would walk according to their own ungodly lusts. These are sensual persons, who cause divisions, not having the Spirit.

JUDE VV. 18–19

There is never any kind of armistice in the Truth War. Our generation is certainly no exception. Some of the greatest threats to truth today come from within the visible church. Apostates seem to be everywhere in the evangelical culture today, making merchandise of the gospel.

But false teachers aren't necessarily that obvious. They usually try hard not to stand out as enemies of truth. They pretend devotion to Christ and demand tolerance from Christ's followers. They are often extremely likable, persuasive, and articulate. That is what makes apostasy such an urgent matter of concern for the church. It produces people who can infiltrate the church by "[creeping] in *unnoticed*" (Jude v. 4, emphasis added).

Paradoxically, people sometimes imagine today that there are no such things as false teachers and apostates, since Christianity has become so broad and all-embracing. There is no need to engage in a battle for the truth—since truth itself is infinitely pliable and thus capable of making room for everyone's views. The problem of apostasy, then, is especially acute in the radically tolerant climate of today's postmodern drift.

But conflict is not always avoidable. To remain faithful to the truth, sometimes it is even necessary to wage "civil war" within the church—especially when enemies of truth posing as brethren and believers are smuggling dangerous heresy in by stealth.

What steps are you taking to remain faithful to the truth?

The Truth War, 72–73

False Teachers Not a Threat to God's Sovereignty

For if, after they have escaped the pollutions of the world through the knowledge of the Lord and Savior Jesus Christ, they are again entangled in them and overcome, the latter end is worse for them than the beginning.

2 PETER 2:20

God is absolutely sovereign, even over false teachers. That is the main truth Jude wants to emphasize when he declares that the damnation of false teachers has been planned and prepared by God already (Jude v. 4).

God's ultimate judgment against the false teachers is unavoidable. Their apostasy marks them as men who are past any hope of redemption (Phil. 3:18–19; Heb. 6:4–6; 10:26–27; 2 Peter 2:20; cf. Matt. 12:31–32; 1 John 5:16). Thus he takes a very hard line against them. There is no point in trying to persuade them, appeal to them, or rescue them from their own heresy. We *do* seek to rescue their victims from a similar fate, of course (Jude vv. 22–23), but the false teachers themselves are people who have already seen the truth and rejected it.

The text also plainly means that God Himself decreed their destruction as part of His original plan. The verdict concerning these apostates is not something God decided just recently. It was decreed before time began, in eternity past. It is still in effect even now—with full, infallible, divine authority.

This, of course, is an unqualified affirmation of the absolute sovereignty of God. Every tiny detail of His eternal plan will be fulfilled to absolute perfection. His grand design has always included both the false teachers and their inevitable destruction. So their evil work never disrupts any component of His plan or derails even one aspect of His good intentions.

What is your belief about the sovereignty of God in regard to plans you've made for your life?

The Truth War, 123–124

Dealing with False Teaching

Thus you also have those who hold the doctrine of the Nicolaitans, which thing I hate.

REVELATION 2:15

A prominent theme in practically all Jesus' messages to the seven churches in Revelation 2 is the issue of how they responded to false teachers and rank heretics in their midst. Ephesus was strongly commended *twice* because they refused to tolerate false teachers. Before He admonished them about leaving their first love, Jesus praised them for their steadfast resistance to false apostles (vv. 2, 6).

The epistle to Pergamos was basically the flip side. Christ commended the saints at Pergamos for holding fast to His name and not denying the faith, even though they dwelt where Satan's throne was. In other words, they had successfully persevered in the faith despite *external* threats of persecution. Nevertheless, Christ had a list of rebukes for them, and these were all related to their tolerance of false doctrine in their own midst. It was as if they were utterly insensible to *internal* dangers that came with a tolerant attitude toward deviant doctrines (vv. 14–15).

Likewise to Thyatira (see v. 20). The churches at Sardis and Laodicea had clearly already lost their will to oppose false doctrine and purge sin from their midst. They had not been sufficiently wary of false teaching, and therefore they had not remained devoted to Christ alone.

It is clear from those letters to the churches in Revelation that battling heresy is a duty Christ expects every Christian to be devoted to. His style of ministry ought to be the model for ours, and His zeal against false religion ought to fill our hearts and minds as well.

What will you do to battle heresy this week?

The Jesus You Can't Ignore, 207–208

Jesus' Childhood

Jesus increased in wisdom and stature, and in favor with God and men.

Luke 2:52

Then He went down with them and came to Nazareth, and was subject to them, but His mother kept all these things in her heart. And Jesus increased in wisdom and stature, and in favor with God and men" (Luke 2:51–52). That is the end of Luke 2, and it is a perfect summary of Jesus' boyhood.

At first glance, it's not easy to understand how Jesus, as God incarnate, with all the attributes of deity, could possibly increase in wisdom or gain favor with God. But this is a statement about Jesus' *humanity*. As God, He is of course perfect in every way and therefore eternally unchanging (Heb. 13:8). Divine omniscience by definition does not allow for any increase in wisdom. But this text is saying that in the conscious awareness of His human mind, Jesus did not always avail Himself of the infinite knowledge He possessed as God (cf. Mark 13:32). He did not lose His omniscience or cease being God, but He voluntarily suspended the use of that quality—so that as a boy, He learned things the same way every human child learns. Furthermore, in his growth from boyhood to manhood, He gained the admiration of others and the approval of God for the way He lived as a human subject to God's law (Gal. 4:4).

Luke 2:52 is therefore not a denial of Jesus' deity; it is an affirmation of His true humanity. The stress is on the normalcy of His development. In His progress from childhood to manhood He endured everything any other child would experience—except for the guilt of sin.

How are you helping your children increase in wisdom? If you don't have children, in what ways were you aided in that goal as you grew to maturity?

The Jesus You Can't Ignore, 32

The Remarkable Nature of Jesus' Miracles

And He said to him, "Go, wash in the pool of Siloam" (which is translated, Sent). So he went and washed, and came back seeing.

John 9:7

Only God can perform the kind of regenerative miracle necessary to restore the atrophied muscles and brittle bones of a quadriplegic to perfect wholeness in a split second—so that he could literally rise up and walk on command.

Even with the best methods of modern medicine, if someone happens to recover the ability to move after suffering a catastrophic injury of the sort that causes severe paralysis, it usually takes months of therapy for the brain to rediscover how to send accurate signals through the injured nerve paths to the disabled limbs. Regardless of how long this man had been paralyzed, we might expect at the very least that he would need some time to learn how to walk again. But Jesus' healings always bypassed all such therapy. People born blind were given not only their sight but also the instant ability to make sense of what they saw (John 9:1–38; Mark 8:24–25). When Jesus healed a deaf person, He also immediately healed the resultant speech impediment—no therapy required (Mark 7:32–35). Whenever He healed lame people, He gave them not only regenerated muscle tissue, but also the strength and dexterity to take up their beds and walk (Matt. 9:6; Mark 2:12). It strikes me as ironic that when modern faith healers and charismatic charlatans nowadays claim to heal people, the patient usually falls over immobile, or in uncontrollable convulsions. Jesus' healings had exactly the opposite effect. Even a man infirm and bedridden for thirty-eight years could immediately pick up his pallet and walk away (John 5:6–9).

Which of Jesus' miracles really resonates with you? Why?

The Jesus You Can't Ignore, 90–91

Jesus' Hard Teaching of the Truth

The Jews then complained about Him, because He said, "I am the bread which came down from heaven."

JOHN 6:41

"From that time many of His disciples went back and walked with Him no more" (John 6:66). What a tragedy! They had heard Jesus preach in person. They had seen Him do miracles. But they turned away without ever really knowing what it was to have a true disciple's heart; without coming to authentic faith in Him; without understanding even the basics of His message.

Jesus did not run after them with an explanation of what He really meant. He let the multitudes leave, then turned to the Twelve and said, "Do you also want to go away?" Peter, speaking as usual for the group, assured Him of their intention to stay on as disciples, and Jesus simply replied, "Did I not choose you, the twelve, and one of you is a devil?" (v. 70).

Jesus was not being pugnacious, though He probably would be accused of that by some of today's sensitive evangelicals who think conflict of any kind is always unspiritual. He was being *truthful*—in a bold, clear way calculated to force them to declare whether or not they likewise loved the truth. He was asking true disciples to declare themselves; He was exposing the enmity of His antagonists; and He was forcing the halfhearted multitudes who were halting between two decisions to choose either one side or the other.

He was not interested in increasing the ranks of halfhearted disciples. His preaching had one aim: to declare truth, not to win accolades from the audience. For those who were not interested in hearing the truth, He did not try to make it easier to receive. What He did instead was make it impossible to ignore.

Which of Jesus' teachings have you struggled with recently?

The Jesus You Can't Ignore, 159–160

Biblical Truth Doesn't Suit Our World

They profess to know God, but in works they deny Him, being abominable, disobedient, and disqualified for every good work.

TITUS 1:16

Neither Paul nor any other New Testament writer ever sanctions violence, physical force, or carnal weaponry in the Truth War. On the contrary, such things are emphatically and repeatedly condemned (Matt. 26:52; 2 Cor. 10:3–4). Titus 1:11 is by no means an exception to that principle. Paul is in no way suggesting that heretics' mouths must be stopped by physical force. He is very clear about how Titus was to silence the "insubordinate . . . idle talkers and deceivers" (v. 10): Titus needed to confront and refute their lies thoroughly with the clear proclamation of the truth. There is a negative aspect to that: "Rebuke them sharply, that they may be sound in the faith" (v. 13). And there is a positive duty as well: "As for you, speak the things which are proper for sound doctrine" (Titus 2:1).

Even though it is clear from the context that Paul is not advocating the use of any kind of brute violence, his statement about stopping the mouths of false teachers has both a tone of authority and a settled certainty to it that make it sound less than politically correct to postmodern ears. This is not a message well suited for our age.

But then again, Scripture has always been contrary to worldly culture. We need to allow Scripture to rebuke and correct the spirit of our age, and never vice versa. Unfortunately, the visible church today is filled with people who have decided that biblical discernment, doctrinal boundaries, and the authority of divinely revealed truth are worn-out relics of a bygone era.

How would you respond to someone who believes that the Bible is no longer relevant for today?

The Truth War, 94–95

The Example of Jesus

Then many false prophets will rise up and deceive many. And because lawlessness will abound, the love of many will grow cold.

MATTHEW 24:11–12

When it comes to the question of dealing with false teachers and false teaching, we can learn a lot from observing how Jesus dealt with false religion and its purveyors. The boldness with which He assaulted error is very much in short supply today, and the church is suffering because of it.

We don't need a return to the brand of fundamentalism whose leaders fought all the time, and fought over practically everything—often attacking one another over obscure and insignificant differences. Much less do we need to persist in the misguided course of so-called neoevangelicalism, where the overriding concern has always been academic respectability and where conflict and strong convictions are automatically regarded as uncouth and uncivil.

In fact, the very *last* thing we can afford to do in these postmodern times, while the enemies of truth are devoted to making everything fuzzy, would be to pledge a moratorium on candor or agree to a cease-fire with people who delight in testing the limits of orthodoxy. Being friendly and affable is sometimes simply the *wrong* thing to do (cf. Neh. 6:2–4). We *must* remember that.

Someone who makes a loud profession of faith but constantly fails to live up to it needs to be exposed for his own soul's sake. More than that, those who set themselves up as teachers representing the Lord and influencing others while corrupting the truth need to be denounced and refuted—for their sake, for the sake of others who are victimized by their errors, and especially for the glory of Christ.

How does this message combat a "live and let live" mentality?

The Jesus You Can't Ignore, 198

Our Savior Was Truly Human

For we do not have a High Priest who cannot sympathize with our weaknesses, but was in all points tempted as we are, yet without sin.

HEBREWS 4:15

Christ was fully human in every sense. He was beset with the same physical limitations that are common to humanity. He, too, felt fatigue (John 4:6; Mark 4:38). He knew what it was to be hungry (Matt. 21:18). He could be stricken with thirst like any normal person (John 4:7; 19:28). He also experienced the full range of human emotions. At times we see Him weeping and mourning (John 11:35; Luke 19:41). On a few occasions, He showed anger (John 2:15–17). Scripture never explicitly records that He laughed or smiled, but it would clearly be a mistake to conclude that He went through life with a gloomy countenance. We know He rejoiced, particularly when sinners were converted (Luke 15:4–32). His reputation among the Pharisees certainly suggests that He was no dour recluse, but a joyful and gregarious "friend of tax collectors and sinners" (Luke 7:34).

He was fully human like us in every regard, except for our sinfulness. If Scripture seems to stress His sorrow and grief more than His joy, it is only because it is such a great comfort to us in our times of grief to know that He has fully experienced the depth of human sorrow—and to a degree that we cannot imagine. During His prayer that night in the garden, every sorrow He had ever known seemed to assault Him at once. That, combined with an obvious sense of dread for the ordeal He faced on the following day, gives us a remarkable insight into "the Man Christ Jesus" and His mediatorial work on our behalf.

Knowing that Jesus was fully human, how does that encourage you to come to Him with any request?

The Murder of Jesus, 64–65

Jesus Is Not Just a Great Man

But Jesus, knowing their thoughts, said, "Why do you think evil in your hearts? For which is easier, to say, 'Your sins are forgiven you,' or to say, 'Arise and walk'?"

MATTHEW 9:4–5

When Jesus said that the paralytic man's sins were forgiven (Matt. 9:1–8), He deliberately put Himself at the center of a scenario that would force every observer to render a verdict about Him. That's true not only of the people who were eyewitnesses in Capernaum that day but also for those who simply read this account in Scripture. And the choice is clear. There are only two possible conclusions we can make with regard to Christ: He is either God incarnate, or He is a blasphemer and a fraud. There is no middle ground, and that is precisely the situation Jesus was aiming for.

There are a lot of people even today who want to patronize Jesus by saying He was a good person, an outstanding religious leader, an important prophet, a profound ethicist, a paragon of integrity, kindness, and decency—a *great* man, but still merely a man—not God incarnate. But this one episode in His public ministry is sufficient to erase that choice from the list of possibilities. He is either God or the ultimate blasphemer. He purposely erased every possible middle-way alternative.

Jesus did not scold the Pharisees for thinking that only God can forgive sin. They weren't wrong about that. Nor did He write their concern off as a misunderstanding of His intention. That's what He would have done if He were indeed a good man not claiming to be God incarnate, and not really claiming any special authority to forgive sin or justify sinners.

What beliefs have you confronted concerning Jesus' deity and humanity?

The Jesus You Can't Ignore, 88–89

Jesus' Checkered Genealogy

Christ has redeemed us from the curse of the law, having become a curse for us (for it is written, "Cursed is everyone who hangs on a tree").

GALATIANS 3:13

It is highly unusual for women to be named in Hebrew genealogies. Yet Matthew mentions five women. At least three of them were Gentiles. Three of them were disgraced because of their own sin. In fact, all of them, for various reasons, knew what it was to be an outcast—to have some infamy or stigma attached to their reputations:

- Tamar posed as a prostitute and seduced her own father-in-law, Judah, in order to bear a child (Gen. 38:13–30).
- Rahab was a prostitute.
- Ruth was from the Moabite nation, a people generally despised in Israel (Ruth 1:3).
- Bathsheba (whom Matthew refers to simply as "the wife of Uriah") committed adultery with King David (2 Sam. 11).
- Mary, of course, bore the disgrace of an out-of-wedlock pregnancy.

Collectively, they illustrate how God is able to work all things together for good. From a human perspective, the whole genealogy is checkered with outcasts and examples of failure. The women, in particular, underscore how scandal colored so much of the messianic line. It was filled with foreigners, outcasts, and those who were pariahs for various reasons. Still, they nevertheless all found a place in the plan of God to bring His Son into the world.

The scandal motif in Christ's lineage was no accident. The gospel message, too, is a public scandal—mere foolishness and shame as far as those who perish are concerned.

Why do you think Jesus' family line included people with bad reputations?

Twelve Extraordinary Women, 65–66

The Truth About Mary

My soul magnifies the Lord, and my spirit has rejoiced in God my Savior. For He has regarded the lowly state of His maidservant.

Luke 1:46–48

While acknowledging that Mary was the most extraordinary of women, it is appropriate to inject a word of caution against the common tendency to elevate her *too much*. The point of her "blessedness" is certainly not that we should think of her as someone to whom we can appeal for blessing; but rather that she herself was supremely blessed by God. She is never portrayed in Scripture as a source or dispenser of grace, but is herself the recipient of God's blessing. Her Son, not Mary herself, is the fountain of grace (Ps. 72:17).

Mary herself was a humble soul who maintained a consistently low profile in the gospel accounts of Jesus' life. Scripture expressly debunks some of the main legends about her. The idea that she remained a perpetual virgin, for example, is impossible to reconcile with the fact that Jesus had half brothers who are named in Scripture alongside both Joseph and Mary as their parents (see Matt. 13:55). Matthew 1:25 furthermore says that Joseph abstained from sexual relations with Mary only "till she had brought forth her firstborn Son." On any natural reading of the plain sense of Scripture, it is impossible to support the idea of Mary's perpetual virginity.

Mary's immaculate conception and her supposed sinlessness are likewise without any scriptural foundation whatsoever. The opening stanza of Mary's Magnificat speaks of God as her "Savior," thus giving implicit testimony from Mary's own lips that she needed redemption.

In such a biblical context, that could refer only to salvation from sin. Mary was in effect confessing her own sinfulness.

What does Mary's praise of God inspire within you?

Twelve Extraordinary Women, 107–110

The Announcement to Mary

For with God nothing will be impossible.

Luke 1:37

When we first meet Mary in Luke's gospel, it is on the occasion when an archangel appeared to her suddenly and without fanfare to disclose to her God's wonderful plan. Scripture says, simply, "The angel Gabriel was sent by God to a city of Galilee named Nazareth, to a virgin betrothed to a man whose name was Joseph, of the house of David. The virgin's name was Mary" (Luke 1:26–27).

At the time of the Annunciation, Mary was probably still a teenager. It was customary for girls in that culture to be betrothed while they were still as young as thirteen years of age. Marriages were ordinarily arranged by the bridegroom or his parents through the girl's father. Mary was betrothed to Joseph, about whom we know next to nothing—except that he was a carpenter (Mark 6:3) and a righteous man (Matt. 1:19).

Scripture is very clear in teaching that Mary was still a virgin when Jesus was miraculously conceived in her womb. Luke 1:27 twice calls her a virgin, using a Greek term that allows for no subtle nuance of meaning. The clear claim of Scripture, and Mary's own testimony, is that she had never been physically intimate with any man. Her betrothal to Joseph was a legal engagement known as *kiddushin*, which in that culture typically lasted a full year. *Kiddushin* was legally as binding as marriage itself. The couple were deemed husband and wife, and only a legal divorce could dissolve the marriage contract (Matt. 1:19). But during this time, the couple lived separately from each other and had no physical relations whatsoever.

What do you believe about the virgin birth of Christ?

Twelve Extraordinary Women, 111–112

What Jesus Fulfills

"Because I said to you, 'I saw you under the fig tree,' do you believe?" . . . And He said to him, "Most assuredly, I say to you, hereafter you shall see heaven open, and the angels of God ascending and descending upon the Son of Man."

John 1:50–51

One striking fact about Nathanael is obvious from how Philip announced to him that he had found the Messiah: "Philip found Nathanael and said to him, 'We have found Him of whom Moses in the law, and also the prophets, wrote'" (John 1:45). Obviously, the truth of Scripture was something that mattered to Nathanael. Philip knew Nathanael, so he knew Nathanael would be intrigued by the news that Jesus was the One prophesied by Moses and the prophets in Scripture. Therefore, when Philip told Nathanael about the Messiah whom he had found, he did so from the standpoint of Old Testament prophecy. The fact that Philip introduced Jesus this way suggests that Nathanael *knew* the Old Testament prophecies.

This probably indicates that Nathanael and Philip were students of the Old Testament together. In all likelihood, they had come to the wilderness to hear John the Baptist together. They had a shared interest in the fulfillment of Old Testament prophecy.

Notice that Philip didn't say to him, "I found a man who has a wonderful plan for your life." He didn't say, "I found a man who will fix your marriage and your personal problems and give your life meaning." He didn't appeal to Nathanael on the basis of how Jesus might make *Nathanael's* life better. Philip spoke of Jesus as the fulfillment of Old Testament prophecies, because he knew that would pique Nathanael's interest. Nathanael, as an eager student of the Old Testament, was already a seeker after divine truth.

How do you show that you are an eager student of the Old Testament and a seeker after divine truth?

Twelve Ordinary Men, 137

The Unexpected Savior

And when they had come into the house, they saw the young Child with Mary His mother, and fell down and worshiped Him. And when they had opened their treasures, they presented gifts to Him: gold, frankincense, and myrrh.

MATTHEW 2:11

Scripture records that when John the Baptist began his ministry, "The people were in expectation, and all reasoned in their hearts about John, whether he was the Christ or not" (Luke 3:15). As a matter of fact, several of the disciples first encountered Christ for the very reason that they were watching expectantly for Him to appear.

The fact is, virtually all faithful believers in Israel were already expectantly awaiting the Messiah and looking diligently for Him at the exact time Jesus was born. The irony is that so very few recognized Him, because He met none of their expectations. They were looking for a mighty political and military leader who would become a conquering king; He was born into a peasant family. They probably anticipated that He would arrive with great fanfare and pageantry; He was born in a stable, almost in secret.

The only people in Israel who *did* recognize Christ at His birth were humble, unremarkable people. The Magi of Matthew 2:1–12, of course, were foreigners and Gentiles, and they were very rich, powerful, and influential men in their own culture. But the only *Israelites* who understood that Jesus was the Messiah at His birth were Mary and Joseph, the shepherds, Simeon, and Anna. All of them were basically nobodies. All of them recognized Him because they were told who He was by angels, or by some other form of special revelation. Luke recounts all their stories in succession, as if he is calling multiple witnesses, one at a time, to establish the matter.

If you were put on the witness stand, what testimony would you offer about Jesus?

Twelve Extraordinary Women, 130

Simeon's True Prophecy

Lord, now You are letting Your servant depart in peace, according to Your word; for my eyes have seen Your salvation which You have prepared before the face of all peoples, a light to bring revelation to the Gentiles, and the glory of Your people Israel.

LUKE 2:29–32

It is almost certain that in the process of writing his gospel, Luke sought details about Jesus' birth and life from Mary. Luke 1:1–4 indicates that he had access to the testimony of many eyewitness reports. Since he included several details that only Mary could have known, we can be fairly sure that Mary herself was one of Luke's primary sources. Luke's inclusion of several facts from Jesus' early life (2:19, 48, 51) suggests that this was the case. Mary's own eyewitness testimony must also have been Luke's source for the account of Simeon's prophecy, for who but she could have known and recalled that incident? Apparently, the old man's cryptic prophecy had never left her mind.

Years later, as Mary stood watching a soldier thrust a sword into Jesus' side, she must have truly felt as if a sword had pierced her own soul also. At that very moment, she might well have recalled Simeon's prophecy, and suddenly its true meaning came home to her with full force.

While Mary quietly watched her Son die, others were screaming wicked taunts and insults at Him. Her sense of the injustice being done to Him must have been profound. After all, no one understood Jesus' absolute, sinless perfection better than Mary did. She had nurtured Him as an infant and brought Him up through childhood. No one could have loved Him more than she did. All those facts merely compounded the acute grief any mother would feel at such a horrible sight. The pain of Mary's anguish is almost unimaginable.

What truths about Jesus have you seen confirmed recently?

Twelve Extraordinary Women, 124–125

The Truth Is Clear

But concerning the dead, that they rise, have you not read in the book of Moses, in the burning bush passage, how God spoke to him, saying, "I am the God of Abraham, the God of Isaac, and the God of Jacob"?

MARK 12:26

Christ has spoken in the Bible, and He holds us responsible to understand, interpret, obey, and teach what He said.

Jesus held not only the Pharisees but also the common people responsible for knowing and understanding the Scriptures. "Have you not read . . . ?" was a common rebuke to those who challenged His teaching but did not know or understand the Scriptures as they should have (Matt. 12:3, 5; 19:4; 22:31; Mark 12:26). The problem lay not in any lack of clarity on Scripture's part but in their own sluggish faith.

The apostle Paul wrote virtually all his epistles for the common man, not for scholars and intellectuals. Those addressed to churches were written to predominantly *Gentile* churches, whose understanding of the Old Testament was limited. He nevertheless expected them to understand what he wrote (Eph. 3:3–5), and he held them responsible for heeding his instruction (1 Tim. 3:14–15).

Paul and Christ both consistently made the case that it is every Christian's duty to study and interpret Scripture rightly (2 Tim. 2:15). "He who has ears to hear, let him hear!" (Matt. 11:15; 13:9, 16; Mark 4:9).

Protestant Christianity has always affirmed the *perspicuity* of Scripture. That means we believe God has spoken distinctly in His Word. Not everything in the Bible is equally clear, of course (2 Peter 3:16). But God's Word is plain enough for the average reader to know and understand everything necessary for a saving knowledge of Christ. Scripture is also sufficiently clear to enable us to obey the Great Commission, which expressly requires us to teach others "all things" that Christ has commanded (Matt. 28:18–20).

How have the Scriptures helped you make decisions recently?

The Truth War, 156–157

The Gospel, Not Gimmicks

I have not shunned to declare to you the whole counsel of God.

ACTS 20:27

The church today is quite possibly *more* susceptible to false teachers, doctrinal saboteurs, and spiritual terrorism than any other generation in church history. Biblical ignorance within the church may well be deeper and more widespread than at any other time since the Protestant Reformation. If you doubt that, compare the typical sermon of today with a randomly chosen published sermon from any leading evangelical preacher prior to 1850. Also compare today's Christian literature with almost anything published by evangelical publishing houses a hundred years or more ago.

Bible teaching, even in the best of venues today, has been deliberately dumbed down, made as broad and as shallow as possible, oversimplified, adapted to the lowest common denominator—and then tailored to appeal to people with short attention spans. Sermons are almost always brief, simplistic, overlaid with as many references to pop culture as possible, and laden with anecdotes and illustrations. (Jokes and funny stories drawn from personal experience are favored over cross-references and analogies borrowed from Scripture itself.) Typical sermon topics are heavily weighted in favor of man-centered issues (such as personal relationships, successful living, self-esteem, how-to lists, and so on)—to the exclusion of the many Christ-exalting doctrinal themes of Scripture.

In other words, what most contemporary preachers do is virtually the opposite of what Paul was describing when he said he sought "to declare . . . the whole counsel of God" (Acts 20:27). He did not adopt methods to suit the tastes of a worldly culture.

Paul had not thought of catering to a particular generation's preferences, and he used no gimmicks as attention-getters.

When have you seen evidence of the dumbing down of Bible teaching?

The Truth War, 166–167

Scripture, Not Our Sensibilities, Determines Truth

All we like sheep have gone astray; we have turned, every one, to his own way; and the LORD has laid on Him the iniquity of us all.

ISAIAH 53:6

We are right back in the same situation the church was in a hundred years ago, when modernists were busily reinventing the Christian faith. Far from being a strong voice and a powerful force for the cause of truth, the evangelical movement itself has become the main battleground.

Postmodernists who are beginning to dominate the evangelical movement are employing exactly the same strategies, pleading for precisely the same kinds of doctrinal modifications, and even using some of the very same arguments modernists used when they took over the mainline denominations a century ago.

For example, the principle of substitutionary atonement has recently been under heavy assault again at the hands of those who insist that evangelicals need to adapt their message to accommodate *post*modern sensibilities. Scripture is clear: Christ suffered on the cross as a substitute for sinners (Isa. 53:4–10), taking the full brunt of the punishment we deserved (2 Cor. 5:21; Heb. 9:27–28; 1 Peter 3:18). His death was a *propitiation*, or a satisfaction of divine wrath against sin on believers' behalf (Rom. 3:25; Heb. 2:17; 1 John 2:2; 4:10). But that view has been forcefully attacked in recent years by people who advocate the elimination of the offense of the cross because it is too uncouth for their tastes. One influential author referred to the principle of substitutionary atonement as "twisted," "morally dubious," and "a form of cosmic child abuse." Clearly, such claims undermine the majestic glory of Christ's perfect sacrifice.

What is your belief about Jesus' atonement for sin?

The Truth War, 168–169

Heed the Warning

Knowing this first: that scoffers will come in the last days, walking according to their own lusts.

2 PETER 3:3

The apostles said false teachers would come. The influx of false teachers into the church doesn't mean the plan of God has gone awry. God is not surprised by this development; it is what His Word prophesied. Even in the worst of times, we can be certain that nothing is happening that wasn't already foreknown by God. He even *told* us we should expect an influx of apostasy. We were warned about it, and here it is.

Our duty, then, is to respond rightly. Not only should we not be surprised when false teachers appear in the church; we ought to have anticipated and prepared for the reality of it. It is a wake-up call. When an absolutely reliable source tells us terrorists are coming, it then behooves us to find out who they are and expose them before they do their damage.

Today's evangelicals have no excuse for not being vigilant. We have been warned—repeatedly. Jesus commanded us to be on guard against false christs and false prophets. The apostolic era was filled with examples of wolves in sheep's clothing. Church history is strewn with more examples, one after another. Only sinful and willful unbelief can account for the refusal of so many in the church today to heed those warnings.

How will you encourage someone to heed the warning of Scriptures concerning false prophets?

The Truth War, 175

What, After All, Is Truth?

"For My thoughts are not your thoughts, nor are your ways My ways," says the LORD.

ISAIAH 55:8

Truth is not any individual's opinion or imagination. *Truth is what God decrees*. And He has given us an infallible source of saving truth in His revealed Word.

For the true Christian, this should not be a complex issue. God's Word is what all pastors and church leaders are commanded to proclaim, in season and out of season—when it is well received and even when it is not (2 Tim. 4:2). It is what every Christian is commanded to read, study, meditate on, and divide rightly. It is what we are called and commissioned by Christ to teach and proclaim to the uttermost parts of the earth.

Is there mystery even in the truth God has revealed? In 1 Corinthians 2:16, Paul paraphrased Isaiah 40:13–14: "Who has known the mind of the LORD that he may instruct Him?"

But then Paul immediately added this: "We have the mind of Christ." Christ has graciously given us enough truth and enough understanding to equip us for every good deed—including the work of earnestly contending for the faith against deceivers who try to twist the truth of the gospel. Although we cannot know the mind of God *exhaustively*, we certainly can know it *sufficiently* to be warriors for the cause of truth against the lies of the kingdom of darkness.

And we are *commanded* to participate in that battle. Earthly life for the faithful Christian can never be a perpetual state of ease and peace. That's why the New Testament includes so many descriptions of the Christian life as nonstop warfare: Ephesians 6:11–18; 2 Timothy 2:1–4; 4:7; 2 Corinthians 6:7; 10:3–5; 1 Thessalonians 5:8.

How have you been a warrior for the truth recently?

The Truth War, 183–184

About the Author

Widely known for his thorough, candid approach to teaching God's Word, John MacArthur is a popular author and conference speaker and has served as pastor-teacher of Grace Community Church in Sun Valley, California, since 1969. John and his wife, Patricia, have four grown children and fifteen grandchildren.

John's pulpit ministry has been extended around the globe through his media ministry, Grace to You, and its satellite offices in seven countries. In addition to producing daily radio programs for nearly 2,000 English and Spanish radio outlets worldwide, Grace to You distributes books, software, audiotapes, and CDs by John MacArthur.

John is president of The Master's College and Seminary and has written hundreds of books and study guides, each one biblical and practical. Best-selling titles include *The Gospel According to Jesus*, *The Truth War*, *The Murder of Jesus*, *Twelve Ordinary Men*, *Twelve Extraordinary Women*, and *The MacArthur Study Bible*, a 1998 ECPA Gold Medallion recipient.

For more details about John MacArthur and his Bible-teaching resources, contact Grace to You at 800-55-GRACE or www.gty.org.

ALSO AVAILABLE FROM

JOHN MACARTHUR

What does it mean to be a Christian the way Jesus defined it? It all boils down to one word:

ISBN 978-1-4002-0207-2

THOMAS NELSON
Since 1798

Coming this spring from John MacArthur:

THE TRUTH ABOUT SERIES (FIRST INSTALLMENT)

THE TRUTH ABOUT . . . Grace

THE TRUTH ABOUT . . . The Lordship of Christ

THE TRUTH ABOUT . . . Forgiveness

Available spring 2012 wherever books and ebooks are sold.